JOHN LE CARRÉ'S POST-COLD WAR FICTION

JOHN LE CARRÉ'S POST-COLD WAR FICTION

Robert Lance Snyder

UNIVERSITY OF MISSOURI PRESS
Columbia

ISBN: 978-0-8262-2099-8
Library of Congress Catalog Number: 2016945535

∞™ This paper meets the requirements of the
American National Standard for Permanence of Paper
for Printed Library Materials, Z39.48, 1984.

Typeface: Minion

For my grandsons, Colton and Elliot,
who restore my faith in what yet may be

CONTENTS

PREFACE

THIS BOOK IS an extension of a previous one. While writing *The Art of Indirection in British Espionage Fiction*, which sought to chart that subgenre's evolution from Eric Ambler onward, I found myself returning often to John le Carré's post–Cold War novels in order to grasp more fully how they responded to the momentous change in geopolitics that began during the early 1990s. Despite this quantum shift in world affairs, le Carré recognized that the literary mode with which his name is synonymous was not in jeopardy of obsolescence. On November 19, 1989, ten days after the start of the Berlin Wall's demolition, he commented in the *Washington Post* that "if an era is dead, the [spy] genre faces a long and boisterous renaissance." His piece titled "Will Spy Novels Come In from the Cold?" elaborated on this prediction as follows:

> The real excitement will come where it always came from: from the interaction of reality and self-delusion which is at the heart of so many secret lives. From the edgy dither between the ingenious and the idiotic. From the blind trust which politicians, through despair or impatience, invest in supposedly unaccountable intelligence services with disastrous results. From our common capacity, whatever nation we belong to, to torture the truth until it tells us what we want to hear. From the way the spy story can take us to the center of any conflict, even if the conflict turns out to be within ourselves. From the infinite variety of motive for loyalty and betrayal; and from the way the motive of the traitor comes to mirror the morality of our times.

Because all of these points are explored in le Carré's fiction of the last few decades, they collectively are pivotal to my argument in this book. For that reason it seems only proper to acknowledge their centrality in this study.

I should point out, too, that my dyadic organization of chapters discussing chronologically sequential pairs of novels does not imply that le Carré wrote with such a schema in mind. It is simply a convenient framework for tracing the larger arc of his narratology, which sometimes expands on fugitive threads of earlier novels but at other times veers off in new directions. Such unpredictability, buttressed by the background of his "classic" Cold War fiction, makes him an intriguing author for those interested in fathoming the cross-currents of our imperiled time.

Here and there I have taken the liberty of incorporating some material from my previous book, albeit sparingly and with refinements that derive from the opportunity for further reflection on le Carré's post–Cold War novels in the context of transnationalism. While in this confessional vein, I wish to thank the editor of *South Carolina Review* for permitting me to include parts of my earlier article on *Our Kind of Traitor* in this work's fifth chapter.

To Gary Kass, the acquisitions editor at the University of Missouri Press, I owe a special debt of gratitude for his faith in this project after reading its introduction and first four chapters. At every stage of our interaction, both he and his colleagues have been exemplary models of courtesy, encouragement, and professionalism.

Once my full manuscript had been accepted for publication, I researched images of le Carré that could be used for the book's front cover. Among the many possibilities, none seemed to capture so well le Carré's projected presence in his recent fiction as Stephen Alcorn's 2007 relief-block portrait of the novelist. When I contacted Mr. Alcorn for his permission to reproduce the print, he graciously agreed and even waived his standard fee. I was delighted then to learn not only that the image had graced no other book but also that le Carré had commissioned the portrait. A credit line on the jacket flap acknowledges Stephen's contribution, but I wish here to express my personal indebtedness for his generosity.

Every effort has been made to obtain permission to quote from le Carré's post–Cold War novels. I gratefully acknowledge the following permissions.

Reprinted with the permission of Scribner, a Division of Simon & Schuster, Inc., from *Single & Single* by John le Carré, copyright © 1999 by David Cornwell; *The Constant Gardener* by John le Carré, copyright © 2000 by David Cornwell; and *A Most Wanted Man* by John le Carré, copyright © 2008 by David Cornwell. All rights reserved.

A note regarding this book's coverage: On the last page of his well-received biography of le Carré, which came out a few months after my completed manuscript was already in the hands of its publisher, Adam Sisman indicates that in 2015 le Carré abandoned a twenty-fourth novel on which he had been working since finishing *A Delicate Truth*. Meanwhile, the author's website reveals that in September 2016, one month before his eighty-fifth birthday, Penguin Random House will release le Carré's *The Pigeon Tunnel: Stories from My Life*. According to Sisman, le Carré contemplated using this memoir title for three of his earlier novels; this suggests that life and art may be reaching a grand culmination for this writer.

Finally, with the kind of consuming hope that is inspired by the birth of grandchildren, I have dedicated this study to them. May they inherit a safer and saner world than the one so powerfully depicted by le Carré.

ABBREVIATIONS

(*AF*)   *Absolute Friends*

(*CD*)   *Call for the Dead*

(*CG*)   *The Constant Gardener*

(*DT*)   *A Delicate Truth*

(*MS*)   *The Mission Song*

(*MW*)   *A Most Wanted Man*

(*NM*)   *The Night Manager*

(*OG*)   *Our Game*

(*OK*)   *Our Kind of Traitor*

(*SP*)   *The Secret Pilgrim*

(*SS*)   *Single & Single*

(*SW*)   *The Spy Who Came In from the Cold*

(*TP*)   *The Tailor of Panama*

JOHN LE CARRÉ'S POST-COLD WAR FICTION

INTRODUCTION

John le Carré's Post–Cold War Journey

At age eighty-one, as of this writing, David John Moore Cornwell, better known to the public at large as John le Carré, has just published his twenty-third novel. Viking's release of *A Delicate Truth* (2013) coincided with Penguin's issuing a fiftieth-anniversary edition of *The Spy Who Came In from the Cold* (1963), the author's hugely successful third book, which one scholar in 1988 proclaimed "the best spy story ever written" and which *Time* magazine included in its 2005 roster of one hundred preeminent novels since the periodical's founding.[1] These events merged in the April 2013 issue of *Harper's*, where promotional excerpts from le Carré's most recent work were followed by the author's reflections on the text that first conferred his celebrity as a writer:

> The merit of *The Spy Who Came In from the Cold*, then—or its offense, depending [on] where you stood—was not that it was authentic but that it was credible. The bad dream turned out to be one that a lot of people in the world were sharing, since it asked the same old question that we are asking ourselves fifty years later: How far can we go in the rightful defense of our Western values without abandoning them along the way?[2]

I begin with this quotation because it encapsulates two motifs interwoven throughout le Carré's prolific career. The first is the distinction between veridical authenticity and fictional credibility, which he has insisted on repeatedly and hinted at as far back as 1965, when he told interviewer Véra Volmane that "the material that I have chosen *extrapolates* the theme of espionage."[3] The second motif is the still unresolved question, "How far can we go in the rightful defense of our Western values without abandoning them along the way?"

3

This issue surfaces so frequently in his oeuvre that it would be fatuous here to document its recurrence. The present study's overarching thesis includes the argument that the author of *A Delicate Truth*, as well as nine other novels since the Cold War's end in late 1991, no longer can be pigeonholed as simply an adroit craftsman of genre fiction.

Elsewhere I have discussed how Jacques Barzun prepared the ground for such marginalization in his essay "Meditations on the Literature of Spying."[4] After Ian Fleming's death a year earlier, Barzun referred with manifest sarcasm to *The Spy Who Came In from the Cold* as "a really real realistic tale of modern spying," thereby caricaturing its author as a demythologizing proponent of "authenticity."[5] The irony of this representation is that even so estimable a critic apparently could not see beyond the veil of verisimilitude that le Carré had fashioned. Subsequent commentators recognized the novelist's antipathy toward the "James Bond kind of hero."[6] They were so beguiled by the plausibility of his invented tradecraft jargon of "moles," "lamplighters," "scalphunters," "pavement artists," "listeners," "cutouts," and the like that they too regarded him more often than not as primarily a writer of quasi-documentary fiction.[7] Almost by default, then, the literary establishment of the time categorized him as a "spy novelist," a designation that has long been code for an author of second-rate fare. The corollary assumption voiced in many quarters was that once the global standoff between the two superpowers became a thing of the past, le Carré's artistic creativity would wither away as well.

Clearly that did not happen. When asked in 1997 whether he had difficulty finding adversarial situations for his protagonists after the Cold War, le Carré replied no and added, "I'm not saying that I made the transition easily. I think I stumbled a couple of times." He then remarked, "All of a sudden everything was up for grabs. It was extremely comic that the uninformed were saying that spying is over, hence le Carré is over. The one thing you can bet is that spying is never over."[8] The comment is important not only because it confirms le Carré's awareness that he initially "stumbled" in reorienting himself as a novelist but also because it adumbrates his working premise that espionage serves as a prism for refracting the obliquities of truth and deception, loyalty and betrayal, and integrity and dissemblance. Then too we should take seriously his declaration in 1969 that "I am really not a person of conviction. If I were, I wouldn't write."[9]

More recently, of course, the expression of political concerns within le Carré's fiction has acquired a sharper edge. Just a few months before his fifty-fifth birthday he admitted to *World Press Review*, "I see in what I write a constant progress toward individual values and an anger that is growing more intense toward injustice."[10] Some detractors have complained that the tone of his work, particularly after the World Trade Center and Pentagon attacks of September 11, 2001, has become too stridently polemical, too Swiftian in its indignation, but such a judgment depends on how we appraise le Carré's liberal humanism, which demonstrates a strong affinity to that of George Orwell, Aldous Huxley, and Graham Greene.

As projected in his novels of the 1960s through the 1980s, this stance led one critic to allege that le Carré is "a writer with ambivalent politics" who shies away from taking sides.[11] According to the same widespread construction, le Carré exposes the venality of the bureaucratized "secret world," whether sponsored by the East or by the West, in its systemic subversion of human autonomy and moral honesty.[12] Dissenting from this opinion, Stewart Crehan draws attention to textual strategies of assimilation in le Carré's early corpus whereby, leveraging "a political economy of information based on the principle of *scarcity* and *ownership*," he juggles perspectives through indirect narration to "co-opt the reader into a fictional world that is, in the strictest sense, constituted by ideological closure."[13] Guided by insights drawn from theorists Wolfgang Iser, Tzvetan Todorov, and Gérard Genette, Crehan counters the claim that le Carré's characteristic method is "open-ended."[14] Instead, Crehan postulates, the acclaimed author alternates between divulging and withholding information essential to the solving of a complex puzzle, as in a detective mystery.[15] I single out Crehan's 1988 analysis because it illuminates a key dimension of le Carré's narratology in both his Cold War fiction and his subsequent fiction.

Two problems with which this novelist has struggled, however, should be acknowledged here. The first paradoxically involves one of his main strengths as a stylist—namely, an extraordinary capacity for ventriloquism in rendering his characters' defining idiolects. Harold Bloom suggests that such virtuosity "may also be his greatest flaw, since his own voice remains imitative."[16] My opening chapter refers to this diegetic (narrative) element as echolalia, which can be found to a greater or lesser degree in all ten of le Carré's novels since 1993 but which, beginning with *The Constant Gardener* (2001), is modulated by the requirements of plot structure.

The second problem, points out James M. Buzard, is that of "maintaining the illusion of a coherent Western (liberal humanist) subject in the face of considerable evidence of that subject's dispersal, corruption, or loss."[17] Le Carré's protagonists typically cling to the concept of independent agency even when they are besieged by all the forces that call its efficacy into question. His most recent fiction often goes beyond the earlier corpus by intimating that the individual can resist, if not always evade altogether, the snares of compromise that lead, for example, to Magnus Pym's suicide at the end of *A Perfect Spy* (1986). These narratives often close with their ideologically unaligned protagonists poised on the brink of a moral precipice, a stratagem that compels readers to wrestle with the issues at hand and project a plausible coda.

My decision to trace this author's post–Cold War journey arises from a forensic shift I detect in his career as a widely popular novelist and from my interest in how a literary subgenre traditionally dependent on binary oppositions, the spy story, morphs in response to the geopolitical phenomenon of transnationalism. The course that le Carré pursues is neither straight nor unerring. Even so, we can recognize a major distinction between the texts that he published immediately after *The Secret Pilgrim* (1990)—*The Night Manager* (1993), *Our Game* (1995), *The Tailor of Panama* (1996), and *Single & Single* (1999)—and those that succeeded *The Constant Gardener: Absolute Friends* (2003), *The Mission Song* (2006), *A Most Wanted Man* (2008), *Our Kind of Traitor* (2010), and *A Delicate Truth* (2013).

The dividing line, of course, is 9/11 and the subsequently declared War on Terror. His novels of the 1990s, it is said, "reveal le Carré's emerging assessment of the Cold War's ambiguous legacy," which encompasses the enduring allure of clandestinity for those who would evade their pasts, "and the state of Western society in its moment of premature triumphalism."[18] If so, then his novels after that watershed event, especially the three most recent ones, build on *The Constant Gardener* by dissecting—brilliantly, I would contend—"the transnationalization of crime, terrorism, and policing."[19]

In the process le Carré significantly reshapes the traditional espionage genre. David Seed notes that the "spy novel is a close but distinct variant on the tale of detection with the difference that there is no discreet crime but rather a covert action."[20] What we find in *A Most Wanted Man*, *Our Kind of Traitor*, and *A Delicate Truth*, however, is a taxonomic hybrid that "bring[s] the genre closer to the *noir* existentialism of transgressor-centered crime fiction."[21] It thus is disappointing, remarks Andrew Pepper, that scholarly studies such as Ann Keniston and Jeanne Follansbee Quinn's edited collection *Literature after 9/11* as well as Kristiaan Versluys's *Out of the Blue: September 11 and the Novel* dismiss such contributions to understanding the cataclysm's aftermath on the basis of narrow assumptions about their being supposedly formulaic and, as a result, incapable of nuanced insight in bearing witness to human tragedy.[22]

The bias against texts that blur a preconceived but specious boundary between "popular" and "serious" genres was reinforced in 1977 by Bruce Merry's *Anatomy of the Spy Thriller*. Offering a structuralist analysis of "this plebeian art form," he catalogued its many marketable conventions before reflecting on espionage fiction's "literariness," by which he means style of writing. Le Carré, decided Merry, is incongruous when compared to Len Deighton, author of *The Ipcress File* (1962) and several other spy narratives, because he "operates self-consciously on the high-brow side" in aspiring to the "Great Novel."[23]

Seven years later John Atkins dispensed with such quibbling over genre by asserting that le Carré's "best spy novels are also mainstream novels, not patchwork affairs."[24] His judgment was consonant with le Carré's statement to interviewer Michael Dean in 1974: "There is this endless debate about the difference between a thriller and a novel, and it really is a very feeble one."[25] Since then eleven books devoted to le Carré's early corpus have been published, although none explore the overall trajectory of his post–Cold War fiction as a compelling refinement of his antecedent texts.

Eight of these academic studies appeared in a flurry between 1985 and 1988, a fact that perhaps suggests this novelist's galvanic challenge to the literary canon's gatekeepers. Besides Harold Bloom's and Alan Bold's anthologies of critical essays, the tally includes monographs by Peter Lewis, Tony Barley, Eric Homberger, Peter Wolfe, and David Monaghan. The 1990s, in turn, saw the publication of three updated overviews by LynnDianne Beene, John L. Cobbs, and Myron J. Aronoff, which were followed in 2004 by Matthew J. Bruccoli and Judith S. Baughman's useful compilation of scattered le Carré interviews. In addition, books by LeRoy L. Panek, Lars Ole Sauerberg, John G. Cawelti and Bruce A. Rosenberg, and myself contain chapters on le Carré, although only one deals with some of his most recent work. A particularly interesting statistic derives from an online search of the *MLA International Bibliography*: by mid-2013 two PhD dissertations exclusively on le Carré had been completed, compared to thirty-five on the late John Fowles, a British novelist to whom le Carré has been likened but who wrote more identifiably postmodernist metafiction.[26]

What the preceding summary of secondary sources indicates is a fairly remarkable dearth of scholarship on le Carré's post–Cold War narratives. Both John Cobbs and Myron Aronoff extended coverage through *The Tailor of Panama* in 1996, but little sustained attention has been paid to the novels released between 1999 and 2013. The situation is no better with journal articles. Exactly one essay apiece has been devoted to *The Constant Gardener*, *Absolute Friends*, and *Our Kind of Traitor*, though another essay published in 2014 discusses *Absolute Friends* and *A Most Wanted Man* in tandem.[27] Le Carré, moreover, goes almost completely unnoticed in seven book-length surveys that, shortly after the century's turn, took stock of contemporary British fiction. Four of these synoptic examinations did not mention the author at all, two cited him in passing, and one spared three pages for his work.[28]

The present study's purpose is to give le Carré his due by expanding analysis of the novels that succeeded his "classic" explorations of Cold War duplicity. Tony Barley posited that up to the mid-1980s le Carré's spy fiction showed no development but merely a pattern of "serialized repetition," not least because it revolved so often around the figure of George Smiley. Although Barley claimed not to be using that phrase in a depreciatory sense, he linked it to liberalism's alleged "instability" when its adherents "confront the issue of taking sides." To his credit, however, this early critic ended by observing, "John le Carré refuses to foreclose on each and every issue he engages with. For that reason, reading him—if he is to be read as he deserves—must continue to be an unfinished business."[29] The last point is well-taken, yet the time has come when we can assess le Carré's cumulative, nonlinear development as a novelist after the Cold War.

Writing about him in 1986, the same year as Barley, Eric Homberger concluded that the author of *The Spy Who Came In from the Cold* and *Tinker, Tailor, Soldier, Spy* presents us with "an ethics of the way we live now."[30] That is even truer today after the seismic events of 9/11 "triggered a . . . redefinition of the enemy" and a wave of Islamophobia in high places.[31] Moreover, the key to the ethics of which Homberger spoke is the maintenance of a "skeptical balance," as Aronoff persuasively argued, in understanding the contemporary complexities of international politics.[32]

The paucity of scholarship on le Carré's most recent fiction is matched by his having been overlooked, at least until 2011, as a candidate for the prestigious Man Booker Prize. Given its selection committee's notoriously fractious and politically charged deliberations, this neglect is unsurprising, but even a partial list of the novelists chosen for the honor since the 1970s reveals the company from which le Carré has been excluded: Nadine Gordimer, Iris Murdoch, William Golding, Salman Rushdie, J. M. Coetzee, Kingsley Amis, Peter Carey, Kazuo Ishiguro, A. S. Byatt, Graham Swift, Ian McEwan, Margaret Atwood, John Banville, and Julian Barnes. It is therefore noteworthy that McEwan, a 1998 recipient seventeen years younger than le Carré and the author of more than a dozen novels, including his espionage-centered *The Innocent* (1990) and *Sweet Tooth* (2012),[33] has said the following about his deservedly celebrated precursor:

I think [le Carré] has easily burst out of being a genre writer and will be remembered as perhaps the most significant novelist of the second half of the [twentieth] century in Britain. He will have charted our decline and recorded the nature of our bureaucracies like no one else has. But that's just been his route into some profound anxiety in the national narrative. Most writers I know think le Carré is no longer a spy writer. He should have won the Booker a long time ago. It's time he won it, and it's time he accepted it. He's in the first rank.[34]

The other side of this commendation is that le Carré, who undoubtedly realizes that his criticism of postimperial Britain has not endeared him to the Man Booker Prize's arbiters, reportedly refuses to allow his books to be entered in competitions. Quite sensibly he expresses a healthy skepticism about the significance of such laurels. On the day of his first appearance at the Hay Festival in May 2013, a wry le Carré thus confided to Jake Kerridge of the *Telegraph* that "I get very confused when people wonder whether I should be promoted to the Sixth Form of literature. . . . Generally, as far as I've observed, prizes, the big literary prizes, tend to go to the people with the fewest enemies in the room."[35]

Before I set the stage for the ensuing chapters with a consideration of *The Secret Pilgrim*, written while the Berlin Wall, le Carré's backdrop for *The Spy Who Came In from the Cold*, was being demolished by jubilant German citizens, it will be useful to stipulate how I am deploying the term *transnationalism*. In a collaborative article published in 2008, Laura Briggs, Gladys McCormick, and J. T. Way demonstrated how slippery though indispensable is the valence of transnationalism as a category of analysis in the social sciences.[36] This is no less true in the humanities, where the rubric, or its cognate forms, appears in the titles of thousands of contributions to scholarly discourse since the 1990s, most often in relation to such topics as postcolonialism, globalization, and ethnographic diasporas. Transnationalism, as I am invoking the concept, signifies *both* an irreversible development in geopolitics today—namely, a precipitous decline in the nation-state's perceived or real autonomy—*and* a correspondingly heightened consciousness of the interconnectivity among populations, cultures, and countries linked to the quest for a universal, or supranational, ethics of justice and human rights. The last point, as we already have seen from Pierre Assouline's interview of le Carré, has been at the forefront of the novelist's attention since at least 1986, and over the ensuing years it has only become more deeply ingrained in his narratives. Le Carré's post–Cold War texts thus chart his deepening engagement with contemporary events as they dramatize the elusiveness of a transcendent code of ethical accountability in a transnational world.

By means of its structure and prevailing mood, *The Secret Pilgrim* anticipates this development. Jost Hindersmann regards le Carré's thirteenth novel
as a montage of tales more or less thematically continuous with its author's
earlier work, but his brief comments fail to take into account the retrospective's intricately layered design, which presents a revealing postmortem on
Cold War espionage and limns what might follow in its wake.[37] Let us then
sift that collection of vignettes for what it discloses about le Carré's redirected
course as a novelist.

∗ ∗ ∗ ∗ ∗

The Secret Pilgrim, commented reviewer Paul Gray in *Time* magazine, reads
like a "series of outtakes from a story that has already been told."[38] The description is accurate as far as it goes. Departing from his usual reliance on a
third-person point of view, le Carré begins with the framing device of his protagonist, Ned (never identified by a surname), autobiographically recounting
an invitation he extended to retired spymaster George Smiley to address the
graduating class at Sarratt Nursery (*SP*, 12), the training school for fledgling
Cambridge Circus, or MI6, agents that he oversees after his reassignment (i.e.,
demotion) as defector Barley Blair's handler in *The Russia House* (1989). Over
the course of the legendary Smiley's after-dinner speech, his remarks give rise
to several embedded narratives that involve, as Jonathan Goodwin puts it,
Ned's "remembering something that Smiley said that made Ned remember
something."[39] For readers these recursive recollections trace the protagonist's
postings in Hamburg, Munich, Beirut, and elsewhere that were major hubs of
covert activity by British intelligence from the early 1960s onward. For Ned,
however, the same reveries highlight personal failures that resulted from his
conformity to the expectations of the secret world he so obediently served. The
focal episodes that compose le Carré's novel, therefore, constitute a summative
dossier on the damage done to individuals by the manifold deceptions of Cold
War espionage during the mythicized, even millenarian, conflict between hegemonic Good and hegemonic Evil.[40]

Le Carré's opening paragraphs establish immediately that Ned, conditioned by a lifetime of secrecy, is unaccustomed to openness with either
himself or others. Had he not "on the spur of the moment" contacted former
mentor Smiley about the speaking engagement at Sarratt, "I would not be
making so free to you with my heart" but instead would be "offering you the
sort of laundered reminiscence with which, if I am honest, I was a bit too inclined to regale my students" (*SP*, 1). We also learn that the animus for a self-
reckoning has been gathering within Ned for some time. "I suspect," admits

this furtive pilgrim, "that my impulse to write to Smiley had been brewing in me longer than I realised" (*SP*, 2).[41] Sagacious George Smiley seems to intuit that Ned has arrived at a pivotal crossroads of self-examination. Later, for instance, addressing Sarratt's director as much as its cadre of "tomorrow's spies," the doyen of Cambridge Circus replies to a query about interrogation by saying, "Oh, there's *some* art to faulting the liar, of course. . . . But the real art lies in recognising the truth, which is a great deal harder" (*SP*, 7, 73). The same precept applies to Ned's coming to terms with tableaux from his past as an undercover agent.

Smiley's introductory reflections on espionage, reports his host, are those of an "iconoclastic prophet of the future" who "scoffed at the idea that spying was a dying profession now that the Cold War had ended" because "with each new alignment, each rediscovery of old identities and passions, with each erosion of the old status quo, the spies would be working around the clock" (*SP*, 8). That conviction, as we shall see, is amply substantiated in le Carré's subsequent fiction. Smiley is then allowed to express a caution in his own voice, a few sentences of which (italicized below) bear directly on Ned's impasse while wrapping up his Cambridge Circus career on the sidelines:

> "*By being all things to all spies, one does rather run the risk of becoming nothing to oneself,*" he confessed sadly. "Please don't ever imagine you'll be unscathed by the methods you use. The end may justify the means—if it wasn't supposed to, I dare say you wouldn't be here. *But there's a price to pay, and the price does tend to be oneself.* Easy to sell one's soul at your age. Harder later."
> (*SP*, 9; emphasis added)

Given George Smiley's role of clear-eyed discernment in seven previous novels and le Carré's comments in a *Washington Post* article written while he was drafting *The Secret Pilgrim*, it is safe to assume that Smiley functions as a spokesman for the author's own views.[42] Just as significant, however, is the impact of the above remarks on Ned. Smiley, he avers, "was speaking straight into my heretical heart," awakening "the secret questioner" or "less obedient person who is also inside me and whom, if I am honest, I had refused to acknowledge since I had embarked on this final lap of my career" (*SP*, 6).[43] Taking this description a step further, Ned adds, "He got rid of the acceptance in me and revived the slumbering rebel that my exile to Sarratt had silenced" (*SP*, 9; see also 273).

At the level of architectonics, then, what is meant to tie together the novel's interpolated tales are some provisional answers to issues that Smiley's admonition about the price of espionage raises: "'Did it do any good?' And 'What did it do to me?' And 'What will become of us now?'" (*SP*, 9). Whether this narratological strategy succeeds can be debated. Thriller author Stephen Hunter found that a "general feeling of dispiritedness" or "postwar exhaustion" permeates *The Secret Pilgrim*, the pieces of which "refuse to assemble themselves into a whole."[44] Two other reviewers, responding to the aptness of the text's broodingly ruminative quality and less concerned with its lack of a traditional plotline leading to closure ("Ned never reaches an epiphany," opined Hunter), hazarded a different verdict. Gail Caldwell observed that *The Secret Pilgrim* is "a quieter book than most le Carré novels, its leaps less dramatic and its payoff far more subtle." The work's latent "voice," she claimed, "is its finest strength."[45] Concurring with the last point, William Boyd extolled the novel's "valedictory tone" and declared that "*The Secret Pilgrim* is, technically, Mr. le Carré's most magisterial accomplishment."[46] Everything hinges, I think, on our agility as readers in inferring the dynamic behind Ned's recollections.

Our Game, another first-person narrative, also gives us the memories of a former case officer for the Secret Intelligence Service (SIS), but it filters them through his highly selective consciousness rather than presenting them as the raw and unconnected reveries of an auditor listening to George Smiley expatiate on the West's dubious Cold War victory. *The Secret Pilgrim*, in other words, demands more of us in forging intratextual links between past and present than does *Our Game*. Ned himself imposes this responsibility when he ends chapter 1 by saying, "George's visit to Sarratt gave back the dangerous edge to my memory. And now that I have the leisure to remember, that's what I mean to do for you, so that you can share my voyage and ask yourself the same questions" (*SP*, 10).[47] The pervasive mood of *The Secret Pilgrim* noted by Hunter— its "general feeling of dispiritedness" or "postwar exhaustion"—is indicative, therefore, of what Brian Crim describes as "le Carré's emerging assessment of the Cold War's ambiguous legacy."[48] So viewed, the novel is a bellwether of the narratives still to come.

Structurally the various episodes that form the outline of Ned's career also project a history of his deepening disenchantment. The vignettes range from the farcical to the tragic as the protagonist discovers within himself a "growing hunger" for human "connection" while he is employed in a vocation that mandates duplicity (*SP*, 209). Pointedly glancing at Ned for the first of many times, Smiley keynotes the work as a whole by assessing his own efforts on behalf of England in the Cold War: "'If I regret anything at all, it's the way we wasted our time and skills. All the false alleys, and bogus friends, the misapplication of our energies. All the delusions we had about who we were'" (*SP*, 11). The confession causes le Carré's narrator to recall his apprentice years when Cambridge Circus "was still basking in its [World War II] glory" and when, as Ned admits, "I was ready to save the world if I had to spy on it from end to end" (*SP*, 12). His début assignment to "Operation Fat Boy," the mission of which is to protect a wealthy Arab sheik who is purchasing ordnance in London, therefore proves comically disillusioning when Ned, eager to rescue the prince's wife from a supposed assassination attempt in an upscale department store, discovers that the kleptomaniacal "Panda" is threatened by nothing more serious than public embarrassment for pilfering costume jewelry.

The next couple of reminiscences are more sobering tales of self-deception. When Smiley tells his audience that "the most difficult agent you will ever have to run is yourself" (*SP*, 30), Ned thinks of his close friend Ben Arno Cavendish, who, after graduating with him from Oxford University and Sarratt Nursery, was rewarded with a coveted job in Berlin supervising a network of counterespionage assets inside East Germany. When Ben inadvertently exposes all his cell members to arrest, he disappears, but not before leaving in a desk drawer a letter of "homosexual longing" for Ned as his "secret twin" (*SP*, 44, 47). Confused and guilt-stricken by this revelation, Ned travels to a remote Scottish island where Ben has sought sanctuary with a distant cousin named Stefanie, "his paragon and proxy sister," who, after an SIS team takes Ben into custody, pronounces an oracular warning to Ned that "it is very dangerous to play with reality" (*SP*, 56, 70).

The ensuing episode develops this theme further. Shortly after he meets an adventurous Latvian, to whom he refers by the alias of Sea Captain Brandt, former Royal Navy midshipman Ned, now freshly appointed station head in Hamburg, romanticizes him as an unimpeachable rogue and recruits Brandt along with his crew for a nocturnal mission to Estonia. When the meticulously planned operation meets with betrayal, suspicion falls on Bella, the captain's girlfriend, with whom Ned has been having an affair during the captain's absence, but a subsequent inquiry makes him realize that Cambridge Circus "played its games in the safety of sealed rooms, with other people's lives for counters" (*SP*, 114). More than twenty years later Brandt is revealed to have been a double agent who served the interests of le Carré's fictional Moscow Centre as had Bill Haydon, the novelist's equivalent for the infamous Kim Philby, who in the mid-1960s was unmasked as a high-ranking MI6 mole.

At this juncture *The Secret Pilgrim* presents a crucial "heresy" by Smiley as he assesses the West's past susceptibility to its own propaganda:

> In the Cold War, when our enemies lied, they lied to conceal the wretched-ness of their system. Whereas when *we* lied, we concealed our virtues. Even from ourselves. We concealed the very things that made us right. Our respect for the individual, our love of variety and argument, our belief that you can only govern fairly with the consent of the governed, our capacity to see the other fellow's view—most notably in the countries we exploited, almost to death, for our own ends. In our supposed ideological rectitude, we sacrificed our compassion to the great god of indifference. We protected the strong against the weak, and we perfected the art of the public lie. We made enemies of decent reformers and friends of the most disgusting potentates. And we scarcely paused to ask ourselves how much longer we could defend our soci-ety by these means and remain a society worth defending. (*SP*, 127)

I have quoted this passage in full because it anticipates conceptually the nov-el's climactic pair of tales involving an ex-spy in Cambodia and a lonely ci-pher clerk in London's Foreign Office, but before that culmination Ned recalls three case studies of the usual motives that prompt individuals to engage in the high-stakes business of international intrigue. Those motives, none of which escape banality, are money, danger, and ideology.

Exemplifying the "con-man and charlatan in the anti-Communist racket" to whom, Smiley observes, the Anglo-American alliance opened its gates after World War II (*SP*, 128), Professor Teodor, a Hungarian émigré whose "cover job was Radio Free Europe's patrician-at-large" (*SP*, 134), is said to have pro-vided the West with only a trickle of secondhand information for fifteen years. When this well-paid poseur realizes that he is about to be cashiered by his sponsors, he concocts, with the connivance of an actor friend who goes by the pseudonym of Latzi, an assassination plot against him by his native country's secret police. Duped as much by their own cover story, or propaganda, about the supposed Iron Curtain watchdog as by Professor Teodor's ruse itself, Toby Esterhase and other Cambridge Circus bureaucrats arrange besides British passports for the professor and his wife, Helena, the "Teodor-Latzi show"—a lucrative lecture tour of the United States "stage-managed by our American Cousins" after the CIA brokers the publication of a spurious bestseller titled *The Kremlin's Killer* (*SP*, 128).

The second motive dramatized for participation in the Great Game is even more vacuous—indeed, nihilistic. After having Ned brutally beaten during an interrogation session somewhere outside Gdansk, a dispassionate Colonel Jerzy, seemingly bored by his sadism as chief of operations for Polish security, revives his victim and unaccountably offers to become a double agent for England. Years later he volunteers a clue to his decision: "No danger is no life. . . . No danger is dead" (*SP*, 188). At the opposite extreme is a German insurgent named Britta reportedly associated with an Islamic terrorist faction in Lebanon. When the narrator interviews her at a detention compound in Israel, she repeatedly taunts him as "Mr. Nobody" while expounding a fervent Marxist critique of the worldwide "bourgeois-materialist conspiracy" (*SP*, 222, 223). Ned dismisses Britta's ideological rant as nonsense, but he is nonetheless unsettled by her self-possession and commitment.

The existential crisis coming to a head for *The Secret Pilgrim*'s protagonist stems, of course, from his profession's inculcation of duplicity. Just before Ned's meeting with Britta, he admits to a mounting sense of fraudulence and evasion: "I felt a rampant incomprehension of my uselessness; a sense that, for all my striving, I had failed to come to grips with life. . . . At my lowest ebb, I saw myself as ridiculous, a hero in the style not of Buchan but of Quixote" (*SP*, 194–95). For that reason, in a reprise of Joseph Conrad's *Heart of Darkness* (1902), Ned sets out to seek the "lapsed spy Hansen," who "in his Cambodian jungle was my Kurtz" (*SP*, 194). Half Dutch like Ned, Hansen, a former Jesuit priest, gravitated to Southeast Asia, where he readily acquired fluency in several indigenous languages before renouncing the Church and offering his services to Cambridge Circus instead. "At a time when the British abroad were being seen by everyone except themselves as Americans without the clout" (*SP*, 234), Hansen had guided US bombers to their targets in Vietnam, but after he is spotted a few years later working in a Bangkok brothel, Ned tracks him down and becomes the man's confessor.

The harrowing tale that Hansen tells—based, as le Carré acknowledges, on the actual ordeal of ethnologist François Bizot—involves his prolonged torture by the Khmer Rouge despite which, even though Hansen's indoctrinated half-Cambodian daughter betrays him, he remains fiercely protective of the girl in her occupation as a prostitute.[49] For Ned, who has been floundering from one relationship to another, the story proves that "there is no reward for love except the experience of loving, and nothing to be learned by it except humility." Of his figurative Kurtz he adds, "I had found what I was looking for—a man like myself, but one who in his search for meaning had discovered a worthwhile object for his life" (*SP*, 273).

Significantly, however, in Ned's final recollection we witness scant evidence of any abiding or deep-seated change within the narrator. Midway through the novel, peering into a mirror, Ned had been shocked to see "the face of a spy branded by his own deception" (*SP*, 196). That image carries over to his interaction with Cyril Arthur Frewin, of whom Ned is reminded when Smiley remarks that "some interrogations" are "communions between damaged souls" (*SP*, 289). Assigned by Leonard Burr, the head office's new executive, to investigate Frewin after the receipt of an anonymous letter accusing the clerk of being a security leak, the compliant protagonist has his mark's house bugged. Then, over the span of forty-five pages, Ned relentlessly manipulates the emotionally starved bachelor—who, like Hansen, defines love as sacrificial commitment (see *SP*, 317)—into making a full confession of his perfidy.

The pathos of this culminating episode is that Frewin's motive for relaying classified information to Sergei Modrian, the Moscow Centre's first secretary at the Soviet embassy in London, is not money, danger, or ideology but simply a yearning for reciprocal acceptance. If Cyril figures as a damaged soul, so does Ned. As the interrogation presses to a close, Ned declares, "It was sickening me that a trickster like Modrian had contrived to turn Frewin's loneliness to treachery. I felt threatened by the notion of love as the antithesis of duty" (*SP*, 345). The last statement reveals the sad truth about Ned after all his opportunities to embrace personal freedom. Thus, although he recognizes that he "was on the brink of destroying a man for love" (*SP*, 353), he forges ahead anyway and for his success receives a promotion to head of secretariat.

Earlier in *The Secret Pilgrim*, presiding guru Smiley had assured his audience of Sarratt neophytes that "spying is eternal," ending his peroration by vouching for the reliability of the following maxim: "For as long as nations compete, and politicians deceive, and tyrants launch conquests, and consumers need resources, and the homeless look for land, and the hungry for food, and the rich for excess, your chosen profession is perfectly secure" (*SP*, 193). As though to bear out this prognosis, the novel's coda introduces Sir Anthony Joyston Bradshaw, "self-styled merchant venturer" and "one of England's natural shits" (*SP*, 365, 364). On the eve of his retirement Ned is assigned to visit Bradshaw in the hope of persuading him to cease his international trafficking in contraband, including munitions, as a formerly protected Cambridge Circus crony. Ned's polite overtures and appeal to the dictates of conscience, however, are crudely rebuffed by a man whose only god is Mammon. In a passage that sounds a requiem for an entire generation of secret agents, the narrator reflects as follows:

> All my life I had battled against an institutionalised evil. It had had a name, and most often a country as well. . . . But the evil that stood before me now was a wrecking infant in our own midst, and I became an infant in return,

disarmed, speechless and betrayed. For a moment, it was as if my whole life had been fought against the wrong enemy. . . . I remembered Smiley's aphorism about the right people losing the Cold War and the wrong people winning it. . . . I thought of telling him that now we had defeated Communism, we were going to have to set about defeating capitalism, but that wasn't really my point: the evil was not in the system, but in the man. (*SP*, 373–74)

The last sentence distills a major preoccupation of le Carré's subsequent fiction when a "cryptojournalist" Sarratt intern named Maggs baits the evening's illustrious speaker by trying to draw him out on the amoral nature of espionage. "It's true that we are obliged to sup with the Devil," responds Smiley, "and not always with a very long spoon. . . . All the same, our obsession with virtue won't go away. Self-interest is so *limiting*. So is expediency" (*SP*, 274). Nevertheless, if that conviction represents an article of faith for Smiley, he also advises the trainees that it is time to bring down the curtain on "yesterday's cold warrior," for "the worst thing you can do is imitate us" (*SP*, 358).

Ultimately, the questions that at the novel's outset Ned says he has been asking himself for most of his career—"'Did it do any good?' And 'What did it do to me?' And 'What will become of us now?'"—are answered for us as attentive readers, albeit not explicitly for the memoirist, whose summing up is plaintive, resigned, and epitaphic:

You see your face. It's no one you remember. You wonder where you put your love, what you found, what you were after. You want to say: "I slew the dragon, I left the world a safer place." You can't really, not these days. Perhaps you never could. (*SP*, 374)

Ned's inability to discern a pattern in the mosaic of his "fragmented recollections," mute "remnants of a life withheld" (*SP*, 197), constitutes *The Secret Pilgrim*'s metatextual story, which requires much of us as hermeneutists, and it also paves the way for le Carré's later explorations of what ensued in the Cold War's wake. The rest of this book follows him on that journey.

* * * * *

At age thirty-four, in one of his earliest interviews, le Carré distinguished between a "literature of escapism" and a "literature of involvement."[50] In the first category, to no surprise, he placed Ian Fleming, whose "consumer-goods hero" James Bond typifies "some of the worst things" of an affluent and materialistic Western society, such as a "hard-nosed cynicism towards any sense of moral obligation."[51] Conversely, although le Carré did not define it in so many words, a literature of involvement actively engages "the dilemma of our time," which during the Cold War was that we were "sacrificing the individual in our battle against the collective."[52] An author in this second category therefore exposes the blind spots of his or her culture in its blithe assumptions of ideological rectitude and does not hesitate to announce that the emperor has no clothes. Le Carré's larger concern then as now is that the West was producing a society unaware of its hypocrisies and riddled with anomie. For that reason, I would submit, he figures as one of the most significant ethicists and Socratic gadflies in contemporary fiction. Fifty years after *The Spy Who Came In from the Cold*, its author still is posing the nagging question echoed in *The Secret Pilgrim* of "How far can we go in the rightful defense of our Western values without abandoning them along the way?" However we may blunder our way toward an answer in today's world of transnationalism, which is infinitely more complex than the Cold War's polarity between a monolithic East and West, le Carré continues to map the challenges that confront us.

Construing this novelist as writing a "literature of involvement" may suggest to some readers the thinking of Jean-Paul Sartre. Although I do not systematically invoke this philosopher's ideas as a theoretical framework, they linger tacitly in the background because the general orientation of le Carré's novels dovetails well with Sartre's brand of existential humanism. Moreover, the French polymath's concept of literary creation as an "appeal" and "act of confidence in the freedom of men" comports with the characteristic lack of decisive closure in le Carré's fiction, which except in *The Night Manager* invites readers to arrive at their own conclusions about his protagonists in light of the choices they make.[53] Then too le Carré consistently urges the case for a "moral order beyond ideology" while championing individuals' human rights when they conflict with institutions' vested interests.[54]

Marxist critics such as Fredric Jameson posit that any distinction between a "moral order" and "ideology" is untenable since the first is purportedly an offshoot of the second, both being products of a certain historical moment and sociocultural context. These critics' deontological orientation, moreover, suggests that one cannot speak of the "individual," which is an essentialist Judeo-Christian construct, but only of a "subject" molded by the contingencies of deterministic circumstance. As long as the two terms are not taken to signify a hypostatic entity, they can be yoked, as Jameson somewhat conveniently does in the following passage:

To imagine that, sheltered from the omnipresence of history and the implacable influence of the social, there already exists a realm of freedom . . . is only to strengthen the grip of Necessity over all such blind zones in which the individual subject seeks refuge, in pursuit of a purely individual, a merely psychological, project of salvation. The only effective liberation from such constraint begins with the recognition that there is nothing that is not social and historical—indeed, that everything is "in the last analysis" political.[55]

This theorist's privileging of a Marxist hermeneutic based on its methodology of an ongoing dialectic ultimately derives, however, from a set of a priori assumptions that le Carré's texts simply do not share. The moral order he envisions is intrinsically opposed to *any* form of collectivist ideology, as usually understood, that infringes on or abrogates the principles of an independent conscience. These forces of institutional indoctrination can run the gamut from Britta's cliché-choked diatribe against a global "bourgeois-materialist conspiracy" in *The Secret Pilgrim* to the corporate rhetoric of "vulture capitalism" in *The Constant Gardener* to CIA agent Newton's rabid defense of "extraordinary rendition" in *A Most Wanted Man*.

The present study, I should acknowledge finally, makes no attempt to read le Carré's fiction of the last twenty years through the lens of a single or univocal literary theory. That fact does not imply an antipathy toward theory per se. Terry Eagleton is surely right in observing that "hostility to theory usually means an opposition to other people's theories and an oblivion of one's own."[56] While discussing I. A. Richards, he also notes that "there is . . . no such thing as a 'pure' literary critical judgement or interpretation."[57] Rather than imposing a grid of "totalizing" abstractions on le Carré's post–Cold War corpus, I instead try to take my analytical cues from elements emphasized within the novels themselves. At various points, therefore, I will introduce pertinent insights from Mikhail Bakhtin, Jean Baudrillard, Luc Boltanski, Michel Foucault, Martin Heidegger, Frank Kermode, and others. Nor does this way of proceeding constitute a lazy eclecticism. Its practical benefit accrues, in my estimation, from Jameson's recognition of the "uneasy struggle" in contemporary criticism "between theoretical speculation and textual analysis, in which the former seeks to transform the latter into so many mere examples, adduced to support its abstract propositions, while the latter continues insistently to imply that the theory itself was just so much methodological scaffolding."[58] These caveats duly noted, it is time to assess le Carré's engagement with the transnational geosphere that succeeded the Cold War's binary.

1

THE NIGHT MANAGER AND *OUR GAME*

"We Have Met the Enemy, and He Is Us"

The forms of materialism that we justified for ourselves during the anti-Communist crusades are now . . . accusing us. . . . There has to be some grander answer to Communism than gross materialism. When we talk about the new enemy, to some extent, it's ourselves.

—John le Carré[1]

The self-determination of oppressed nations was a cornerstone of our anti-Communism. For half a century we preached from the rooftops that on the day democracy replaced tyranny, the victim would be raised above the bully and small nations would be free to choose their fate.

Fat chance.

It is our careless modern assumption that as trade borders fall and systems of communication advance, the countries of the world will be brought closer together. Nothing could be further from the truth. The end of the Cold War has seen such a loosening of bonds and allegiances, and such a dying of forbearance on the part of the oppressed, that the old and new worlds are fragmenting as never before.

—John le Carré[2]

THE STATEMENTS ABOVE were made by le Carré, respectively, shortly after the publication of *The Night Manager* in mid-1993 and nearly ten weeks before *Our Game*'s release about twenty months later. Together they attest to his keen awareness of the advent of transnationalism ("the old and new worlds are fragmenting as never before") put into motion by "a loosening of bonds and allegiances" that coincided with the Cold War triumph of "gross materialism." Lost in this epochal change, as le Carré views it, is the once trumpeted right of subjugated countries to decide their own destinies as the barriers to global trade and communication were rapidly dissolving. The novelist's prescience in this regard is impressive. Even though, as already noted in the introduction, le Carré admitted to having "stumbled a couple of times" artistically when "all of a sudden everything was up for grabs," both *The Night Manager* and *Our Game* dramatize his conviction that the most inescapable "enemy" is "ourselves." It yet remains to be seen how that claim is fleshed out in his initial post–Cold War fictional narratives.

Appearing three years after *The Secret Pilgrim*, *The Night Manager*, le Carré's fourteenth novel, elicited a widespread chorus of favorable reviews, more than a few of which registered almost audible relief that the celebrated spy-fiction author had not lost his touch after the Soviet Union's disintegration. In the *Los Angeles Times*, for example, Jonathan Franzen proclaimed that "few spirits seem to have been more liberated than [le Carré's] by the Cold War's thawing. The torrent of voices . . . and sheer inspired prose-writing in the new novel suggests a river which, having silted up a familiar delta, is suddenly routing out new channels."[3] *The Night Manager*, concluded Franzen fulsomely, "may be le Carré's best . . . book yet," although few close readers of the antecedent corpus, I think, would agree. Three weeks later A. S. Ross commented that the latest effort was "almost operatic in its intensity, . . . introduc[ing] us to a scary new world order where . . . superpower intrigue has been replaced by drugs, gunrunners, venal and power-mad intelligence officials, and a morally bankrupt Britain."[4]

Guardian reviewer Polly Toynbee, however, had a different view. She questioned whether the novelist's "secret world [was] in turmoil," given the end of a four-decades-long struggle between two ideological archrivals. "Alas," she continued, "could le Carré be writing about himself, a coded message that he knows this thin potboiler scarcely attempts to scale the heights of his great past works? Like his secret services, he seems to be lost. He has the tradecraft, and the joes, but where's . . . the cause?"[5]

The "cause," it goes without saying, had rather suddenly evaporated: Western capitalism had outspent the former Soviet Union on thermonuclear armaments while subscribing to a geopolitical doctrine of mutual deterrence.[6] If there no longer loomed the specter of an Evil Empire, which validated its adversary's sense of national mission, the vacuum had been filled, according to le Carré, by a motley array of global opportunists devoted to nothing more than post–Cold War profiteering. In *The Night Manager* he describes their ranks in terms of regular guests at Sir Richard ("Dicky") Onslow Roper's opulent estate on his privately owned Caribbean island:

And after the Frequent Fliers came the Royal & Ancients: the sub-county English debutantes escorted by brain-dead offshoots of the royal brat pack and policemen in attendance; Arab smilers in pale suits and snow-white shirts and polished toecaps; minor British politicians and ex-diplomats terminally deformed by self-importance; Malaysian tycoons with their own cooks; Iraqi Jews with Greek palaces and companies in Taiwan; Germans with Eurobellies moaning about Ossies; hayseed lawyers from Wyoming wanting to do the best by *mah* clients and *mah*self. . . .

After the Royal & Ancients came . . . shiny-cheeked merchant bankers from London with eighties striped blue shirts and white collars and double-barreled names and double chins and double-breasted suits, who said "ears" when they meant "yes" and "hice" when they meant "house" and "school" when they meant "Eton." (*NM*, 267–68)

Clearly this cavalcade of transnational and self-styled entrepreneurs, having long ago abandoned any sense of social responsibility, encompasses those who, irrespective of their countries of origin, are driven only by insatiable greed. Such, then, are the craven plutocrats who, according to le Carré, prop up the economic superstructure of the vaunted New World Order in the early 1990s. And whenever this writer's rhetoric cranks up to enumerate the villainous and the reprobate, perorations that fellow novelist Charles Cumming calls the "longueurs" scattered throughout le Carré's fiction, we can be sure that we are hearing the cadences of authorial outrage.[7]

"What I describe in *The Night Manager*," declared le Carré to Valerie Takahama, "is this period of somnambulism . . . after the Cold War. . . . There is no crusade[;] there is a lot of self-interest, a lot of trotters in the trough, and a lot of misery, a terribly bad distribution of wealth and world resources."[8] Le Carré's admission reflects his liberal humanism in arguing for a moral order that transcends egregious self-interest, but his critique of rampant post–Cold War venality may not tell us everything there is to know about *The Night Manager*. Why, we might ask, did Toynbee characterize the novel as a "thin potboiler" and another reviewer, Philip Marchand, call it a "surprisingly melodramatic" work?[9]

We can begin to seek an answer by taking into account le Carré's introductory profile of his protagonist. Here is how he portrays Jonathan Pine in chapter 3:

Orphaned only son of a cancer-ridden German beauty and a British sergeant of infantry killed in one of his country's many postcolonial wars, graduate of a rainy archipelago of orphanages, foster homes, half-mothers, cadet units and

training camps, sometime army wolf-child with a special unit in even raini-
er Northern Ireland, caterer, chef, itinerant hotelier, perpetual escapee from
emotional entanglements, volunteer, collector of other people's languages,
self-exiled creature of the night and sailor without a destination. (*NM*, 33)

Pine, in other words, is one of the world's alienated outsiders indebted to no
one and haunted by ghosts from his past. He thus figures as an ideal candidate for recruitment by those who would draw him into a venture of state-
sponsored clandestinity.[10] Toynbee makes the point more bluntly: "A man
from nowhere, with no past," Pine is a "cipher" or a "gaping hole of a man."[11]
In this regard we should note that le Carré repeatedly refers to his main character as a "watcher" fixed on "close observation" of those around him (*NM*, 13,
55), substantiating Marchand's view of Jonathan Pine as a voyeur who, saddled
with guilt over former lover Sophie's murder in Cairo, experiences nonstop
replays of that scenario in what the novel describes as the "secret theater" of
his imagination (*NM*, 15).

This initial depiction of le Carré's psychologically crippled antihero accords
closely with Allan Hepburn's construct of a "cipher" (note the same word
choice as Toynbee's) or a "marionette" who finds himself abruptly thrust into
a "culture of intrigue. . . . Acting a part," Hepburn continues, "the twentieth-
century fictional spy tells us that authenticity may be irrelevant to commitment or character. Indeed, a spy's identity is often an illusion."[12] Such is the
case with Pine, who at the outset is bereft of any foundational identity and
naively construes himself as "One of Us—Us being Englishmen of self-evident
loyalty and discretion. Us being Good Chaps" (*NM*, 16). When he learns,
then, that his unquestioning divulgence of information to Mark Ogilvey, his
fellow yachtsman and a British security establishment factotum, contributed
circuitously to Sophie's death, the "undercover soldier" is ripe for reenlistment
(*NM*, 34), though not this time by agencies associated with his country's top-
down security apparatus.

Enter Leonard Burr, who figures briefly, as we have seen in, *The Secret Pilgrim*.
An irreverent former intelligence officer for River House (MI6) and a moral
absolutist inveterately skeptical of Whitehall's current mandarins, he mentors
Jonathan Pine for an elaborate undercover operation, code-named Operation
Limpet, against Richard Onslow Roper, whom the text hyperbolically casts as
"the worst man in the world" (*NM*, 6). Intent on bringing down this "personal
Antichrist" (*NM*, 52), Burr meanwhile must reassure his idealistic behind-the-
scenes sponsor Rex Goodhew—the head of the newly formed Joint Steering
Committee in Britain whose task is to bridge the divide between "espiocrats"

(Geoffrey Darker's Pure Intelligence or Procurement Studies Group within MI6) and "enforcers" (case officers such as Burr and Joseph Strelski, Burr's CIA counterpart [*NM*, 59])—that Operation Limpet is proceeding according to plan.[13] Le Carré's names for the principals—Goodhew, Darker, and Burr— in this Manichean contest are less than subtle. Nevertheless, what sustains the reader's interest in the text in its first half, besides the accounts of Pine's search for authenticity, is whether Burr and Goodhew's connivance in deploying their "close observer" against Roper will prevail against institutionalized corruption and double-dealing. Further aligning two of the novel's stalwarts is the fact that each has experienced an epiphany regarding his life or career to date.

This decisive moment comes for Pine, the Hotel Meister Palace's night manager in Zurich, while he is performing his monthly inventory of the wine cellar; he is immured there for sixteen hours, an experience he recalls as "an introductory course in death" (*NM*, 45). Le Carré elaborates Pine's sepulchral rite of passage as follows:

> And gradually it dawned on him, if a dawning can take place in total black-ness, that his life had consisted of a run of rehearsals for a play he had failed to take part in. And that what he needed to do from now on, if there was going to be a now on, was [to] abandon his morbid quest for order and treat himself to a little chaos, on the grounds that while order was demonstrably no substitute for happiness, chaos might open the way to it. (*NM*, 47)

Nearly twice Pine's age, Goodhew comes to Operation Limpet via a far different but comparably epiphanic route, which le Carré presents obliquely through indirect narration:

> The story was that after twenty-five years before the Whitehall mast, some-thing inside Goodhew had discreetly snapped. Perhaps it was the ending of the Cold War that had caused it. Goodhew had the modesty not to know.
>
> The story was that one Monday morning Goodhew woke as usual and de-cided with no premeditation that for far too long, in the misused name of freedom, he had been sacrificing scruple and principle to the great god expe-diency, and that the excuse for doing so was dead.
>
> And that he was suffering from all the bad habits of the Cold War without their justification. He must mend his ways or perish in his soul. Because the threat outside the gates had gone. Decamped. Vanished. (*NM*, 63)

Both men, despite their radically divergent backgrounds, demonstrate integrity in coming to terms with and opting to rectify their histories of compliance with the status quo. For that reason doughty Leonard Burr, descended from Yorkshire hand-loom weavers who "owned their lives instead of being vassals in a corporate endeavor," serves as the perfect intermediary. Having always been at odds with the likes of "odious Sir Anthony Joyston Bradshaw, gentleman and occasional satrap of Darker's so-called Procurement Studies Group" (NM, 52), Burr dreams of finally bringing to justice all those plunderers willing to line their pockets at the world's expense (NM, 84–85).

The stage is thus set for a pitched battle between the forces of light and darkness, but what immeasurably complicates the novel's plot, to borrow from a couple of the reviewers cited earlier, is the "operatic . . . intensity" of its "torrent of voices." Here the relevance of what Mikhail Bakhtin refers to in *The Dialogic Imagination* as "heteroglossia" cannot be overlooked. According to this well-known theorist, the novel's historical emergence coincided with, and was made possible by, sociocultural upheavals that ruptured the monological discourse and aesthetic distance associated with classical epic poetry. Concomitantly there arose "the problem of alterity in language," as Michael Holquist writes.[14] What today we call the novel became, then, the "carnivalesque" literary medium that gave rein to such "polyglossia." In valorizing the primacy of speech (*parole*) or utterance, however, the new genre lent itself to irony, parody, and indeterminacy, making it more difficult to construe a writer's illocutionary presence. Bakhtin seems to suggest that the novel's "dialogization," which is "variform in speech and voice," does not impinge on "authorial individuality in language," but left unresolved is the degree to which the rhetoric of novelistic discourse is subsumed by stylistics.[15] The issue is not clarified when he subsequently makes this remark:

> The language used by characters in the novel, how they speak, is verbally and semantically autonomous; each character's speech possesses its own belief system, since each is the speech of another in another's language; thus it *may* also refract authorial intentions and consequently *may* to a certain degree constitute a second language for the author.[16]

In terms of *The Night Manager*, one can readily concede that the idiolect of a character such as Richard Onslow Roper, who babbles a slangy patois that le Carré dubs "Roperspeak" (NM, 200), is distinctive or "semantically autonomous," but how do we distinguish a controlling voice when the text is flooded by a host of competing and, for the most part, disingenuous idioms? The final clause of Bakhtin's assertion, relying as it does on the subjunctive *may*, is not especially helpful in this regard.

A major challenge for readers, again, is that *The Night Manager*'s teeming multiplicity of voices—its dimension of echolalia—overwhelms the text's thematic structure, which is transparently allegorical. Le Carré has always been renowned for his ability to render the defining inflections of his fictional personas, but in his first post–Cold War novel the deployment of heteroglossia swells exponentially, almost as though its author is intent on exhaustively capturing all the ways in which conditioned habits of speech not only individuate but also betray his entire cast of characters. The narrative thus spills over with many other idioms than Roperspeak.

For example, the ostensible heroine, Jemima W. Marshall (alias "Jeds," per her lover Roper's shorthand parlance), prattles in the breathless jargon of the fashion magazines to which she is addicted. Major Lance Montague Corkoran ("Corks" or "Corky," per his employer Roper's designation for this all-purpose flunky) consistently flaunts his homosexuality in lewd innuendos. And Jonathan Pine (aka Jack Linden, Jacques Beauregard, Thomas Lamont, and Derek Stephen Thomas), despite his several impersonations, discourses in the respectfully polite argot of the hotelier he once was. Nor are these proliferating voices limited to this group. Every bit as much as Roper's hirelings and suborned members of Parliament such as, respectively, Lord Sandy Langbourne and Sir Anthony Joyston Bradshaw, members of le Carré's phalanx of the virtuous have their own encoded dialects for communicating with one another. Readers are thus immersed in a welter of largely artificial ways of speaking, the net effect of which reinforces the idea of linguistic masquerade and dissemblance.

At the same time we know exactly who constitute the wicked and the righteous in this modern morality play. Heading the former tribe, as le Carré's text frequently reminds us, is "the worst man in the world." When Pine asks Burr, "What makes him run?" (*NM*, 86), his handler is at a loss to explain Roper in terms of a formative background: "Father a small-time auctioneer and valuer at the shires. Mother a pillar of the local church. One brother. Private schools the parents couldn't afford." Richard Onslow Roper, concludes Burr, is simply prima facie proof that "evil exists" (*NM*, 87). Burr's ensuing litany of what "Dicky" Roper peddles to any and all comers, in exchange for massive shipments of cocaine to offset the losses of his legitimate but recession-besieged enterprise named Ironbrand Land, Ore & Precious Metals Company of Nassau, depicts him as a latter-day Mephistopheles and the epitome of what le

Carré denounced as "unbridled capitalism" at work in the international marketplace.[17] Burr's litany is as follows:

> We're talking boots, uniforms, poison gas, cluster bombs, chemicals, MREs—
> that's meals ready to eat—inertial navigation systems, fighter airplanes,
> signal pads, pencils, red phosphorus, grenades, torpedoes, custom-built sub-
> marines, motor torpedo boats, fly killer, guidance systems, leg irons, mobile
> kitchens, brass buttons, medals and regimental swords, Metz flashguns and
> spook laboratories got up as chicken batteries, tires, belts, bushings, ammo of
> all calibers, both U.S. and Sov[iet]-compatible, Red Eyes and other shoulder-
> held launchers such as Stingers, and body bags. (NM, 87)

Over the thirty-year span of his trade in high-tech munitions that Roper eu-
phemizes as "toys," his clientele has ranged from Ugandan dictator Idi Amin
to Colombian drug lords, but of steadily increasing importance to this underworld linchpin has been the collusion of political functionaries in England.
Both directly and indirectly, such amoral establishment types as Geoffrey
Darker and his lieutenant Neal Marjoram, the unnamed cabinet-level "master" of Rex Goodhew, double agent Dr. Paul Apostoll, and lily-livered lawyer
Harry Palfrey have become accessories to this global syndicate. The upshot is
that an opposing and fragile coalition of the virtuous is vastly outnumbered
from its campaign's inception.

The Night Manager achieves its strongest effects when le Carré develops
his subplot of internecine duplicity within MI6, given its subservience to the
CIA. His ventriloquistic virtuosity is full-throated in mimicking the espiocrats' doublespeak as they jockey for oversight of Operation Limpet and flout
the "*Lex Goodhew*" that mandates interagency cooperation (NM, 56). When
the minions of both security empires convene in London to discuss the infil-
tration of Roper's worldwide bazaar for proscribed weaponry, we thus recognize the self-interest that lurks behind their rhetorical gambits. For example,
"Darling Katie," officially "Mrs. Katherine Handyside Dulling, Economic
Counselor of the British Embassy in Washington," bombastically dominates
the other attendees in order to preserve CIA control of the mission, although
Geoffrey Darker tries to defend his stake in the game (NM, 116). What emerges from such dialogical sparring over the supervision of Operation Limpet is
heightened insight into a "widespread loss of purpose" within bureaucracy
that "results ultimately in the victory of technique over principle, the with-
ering of individual responsibility, and a pervasive tendency towards human
betrayal."[18]

The same effect surfaces later when le Carré recounts Neal Marjoram's blandishments that, in exchange for a bribe of 750,000 pounds, Rex Goodhew must abandon his crusade to pursue and prosecute Richard Onslow Roper. When an overture is made, in Harry Palfrey's clipped words, to play "the world's game" by "making a few bob on the side" because "everybody else does" (*NM*, 231), Goodhew valiantly adheres to principle, even though later that decision nearly costs him his life. What such exchanges reveal is the espiocrats' collective mendacity, on the basis of which we are led to side with the righteous.

That structural dynamic, however, runs the risk of making the reader feel manipulated in this David-versus-Goliath story, nor is the impression alleviated by le Carré's attributing—à la Ian Fleming and seasoned, perhaps, by a dash of Len Deighton—consummate expertise in sailing, mountain climbing, watercolor painting, tennis, and gourmet cooking to his protagonist. Jonathan Pine consequently comes across as "an energized superspy of awesome skill and attractiveness" who is intent on toppling supreme Philistine "Dicky" Roper.[19] After months of carefully planned misadventures under different aliases in West Cornwall and Canada, all orchestrated by Leonard Burr to provide deep cover for his recruit, the man from "Nowhere Really" finds himself employed as a chef at Mama Low's restaurant in the Caribbean, where, again by his handler's prearrangement, he rescues Roper's eight-year-old son, Daniel, from a pair of larcenous thugs (*NM*, 96).

Through his heroism, which costs him a bludgeoned face and a fractured skull, Pine ingratiates himself to "the worst man in the world," who after thorough background checks grooms his convalescent houseguest to replace the besotted Major Corkoran as his signatory agent and puppet in various money-laundering schemes. Meanwhile a wary affinity grows between these antagonists. Although the "close observer" is "sick of being someone's creature," he still lends himself "with his limitless adaptability" to this new role and, in mimetic rivalry for Roper's mistress, soon manages to usurp him in her affections (*NM*, 251, 256). Whether intended or not, what le Carré gives us is a classic case of doubling between a clandestine spy and his opponent that undercuts, or at least qualifies, his larger allegory of the forces of right in fell battle with the forces of wrong.[20]

So viewed, *The Night Manager* would indeed seem to qualify as an essentially melodramatic potboiler. Lithesome "Jed," another of the author's less than convincing female characters, may avow to Jonathan that "I'm obsessed by you. . . . I don't know who you are, if you're anyone at all" (*NM*, 289), but beyond this declaration of libidinal yearning—which, we might note, is fueled by her attraction to Pine's subversive anonymity—we question which of the two is the more deluded. Both Jonathan Pine and Jemima Marshall are seeking redemption by escaping together into a fantasy of idyllic mutuality balanced by the elusive possibility of regained autonomy. In this regard, unfortunately, the novel's denouement strains credibility. When Roper discovers Pine's true objective, he imprisons Jonathan in the hold of his 250-foot yacht named the *Iron Pasha*, where the protagonist is subjected to repeated beatings before realizing, through a spiritualized "sense of kinship with Sophie," that "his life was in order" and "he was free" (*NM*, 458, 459). After Burr brokers a deal with Roper for the lovers' release, Jonathan and Jed are glimpsed in the novel's final chapter living happily together at Lanyon Head in West Cornwall, where they reportedly plan to "breed horses and paint pictures" (*NM*, 472). The only element missing, it seems, is the cultivation of a garden.

At the same time, we should recognize that this concluding vignette merely constitutes a truncated epilogue to the novel. Noteworthy too is the fact that, less than three full pages in length, chapter 31 is mediated through the rustic voices of brothers Pete and Redfers Hosken as well as village maven Ruth Trethewey, all of whom are familiar with Jonathan Pine only as "Jack Linden" when he once took up temporary residence near their Cornish community a few miles from Land's End.[21] It could be argued, I suppose, that by appending this epilogue le Carré was throwing a sop to the readers of his earlier works who felt uneasy with what the author himself called the "Gothic gloom" of his endings.[22]

If so, he succeeded with at least one reviewer. In a generally disappointing piece in the *New York Times*, Herbert Mitgang averred that *The Night Manager* "leaves us with the possibility of change. After such a rough but remarkably readable journey through the arms and drug culture, Mr. le Carré deserves credit for keeping the flames of romance and idealism glowing."[23] David Remnick is far more reliable in his mildly sarcastic summation: "In the end, Pine is victorious—or at least alive—and the credits roll over his return to the pastoral English shoreline where he lives out his life having found love with fair Jed and a new identity courtesy of the British government."[24] The plot developments whereby the protagonist and his consort are freed from captivity aboard the *Iron Pasha* to pursue shared bliss at Lanyon Head have, ultimately, little to do with the narrative's roseate postscript.

Myron Aronoff astutely observes that the novel's "moral center" is not Jonathan Pine but rather Leonard Burr as "the true hero of the story."[25] The Yorkshire-bred MI6 veteran warrants this distinction because when Operation Limpet is compromised by River House officials' duplicity, he immediately abandons any vestiges of corporate loyalty and, with fierce determination, opts for individual loyalty instead. That theme, as le Carré acknowledged in a 1979 interview, has consistently informed all of his fiction.[26] In *The Night Manager* it comes to the fore when Burr realizes that his idealistic sponsor Rex Goodhew has been outflanked by the Machiavellian maneuvers of Geoffrey Darker. He therefore decides to abandon the mission, even though it has long been his private crusade, for the sake of rescuing an imperiled agent.

Toward that end Burr successfully dupes Sir Anthony Joyston Bradshaw into believing that both he and Richard Onslow Roper are about to be apprehended, all the while understanding that "no two bluffs are the same, but one component is necessary to all of them, and that is the complicity between the deceiver and the deceived, the mystical interlocking of opposing needs" (*NM*, 441). By resorting to this tactical ploy, Burr adopts the methods of his enemy but does so for a noble purpose. When he first enlisted Pine in his "five-star unimpeachable cause, guaranteed to improve the lot of mankind" (*NM*, 84), the grizzled spymaster had promised a safe resettlement afterward, and he is not about to renege on that commitment. What that decision on Burr's part means, however, is that after a temporary setback the scurrilous Roper is free to resume his worldwide trafficking in the instruments of death.

The sobering import of that trade-off involving Pine's release for Roper's escape can be gauged from the kind of sophistry that "the worst man in the world" is fond of spouting. While still intent on luring the novel's protagonist into his netherworld, for example, Roper indulges in the following homily:

World's run by fear, you see. Can't sell pipe dreams, can't rule with charity, no good at all. Not in the real world. . . . If a bunch of chaps want to make war, they're not going to listen to a lot of wet-eared abolitionists. If they don't, [it] doesn't matter whether they've got crossbows or Stingers. Fact of life. Sorry if it bothers you. . . .

Guns go where the power is. . . . Armed power's what keeps the peace. Unarmed power doesn't last five minutes. First rule of stability. (*NM*, 262)

Not long after this self-vindicating speech, Roper expatiates further to le Carré's "close observer":

Today's guerillas are tomorrow's fat cats. Good luck to 'em. Real enemies were the big power governments. Everywhere you looked, big governments were there ahead of you, flogging anything to anybody, breaking their own rules, cutting each other's throats, backing the wrong side, making it up to the right side. Mayhem. Us independent chaps got squeezed into the corner every time. Only thing to do, get in ahead of 'em, beat 'em to the draw. (*NM*, 271)

Although part of this pronouncement—"Everywhere you looked, big governments were . . . backing the wrong side"—undoubtedly echoes the author's long-standing critique of American interventionism, the passage emphasizes how facile Roper's attempt is to portray himself as one of the "independent" entrepreneurs who have been "squeezed into the corner" by state-backed arms deals. As a result, then, of Burr's negotiations to rescue Pine, the scourge represented by his "personal Antichrist" is at liberty once more to dominate a global market for interdicted weapons. And given his already established zones of influence in Panama and Colombia, where he equips paramilitary insurrectionists of all stripes (*NM*, 363–78, 384–90), Roper is well positioned to extend even farther his octopuslike outreach to the world's discontented.

What claims final attention in *The Night Manager*, however, is not plot outcomes per se but rather the Anglo-American security establishment's machinations while scuttling Operation Limpet through a bureaucratic ruse known as Flagship, which succeeds in screening off Burr from up-to-date intelligence. In order to convey how this suppression is orchestrated, le Carré introduces a character named Ed Prescott, the Yale-educated US deputy assistant attorney general, who intones an unctuous admonition to Joe Strelski that he, along with colleagues Pat Flynn, Rob Rooke, and Leonard Burr, should quit their interagency pursuit of Roper and concentrate instead on Pine. According to the artful Prescott, Burr's "undercover soldier" is nothing more than a "psychopathic fantasist" and rogue agent (*NM*, 430). The federal prosecutor's desire to quash the investigation by vilifying Pine, of course, confirms Burr's darkest suspicions of corrupted officials on both sides of the Atlantic who stand to gain from turning a blind eye to Roper's illicit activities.

Ironically, it is Harry Palfrey, the morally derelict lawyer for Geoffrey Darker's Procurement Studies Group given to playing both ends against the middle, whose broken rhetoric provides a credible overview of what drives the novel's underlying conflict. Discoursing in his ejaculatory mode of delivery, reminiscent of Roperspeak, Palfrey explains to Rex Goodhew the syndrome that compels River House's current hierarchy to accommodate the American "Cousins":

Good case officers. Cold heads left over from the Cold War. Scared of being out of a job. . . .

Duplicity trained, naturally. . . . Market economy chaps. Peaked in the eighties. Grab it while you can, everybody does it, never sure where the next war's coming from. All dressed up, nowhere to go. . . . Still got *power*, of course. . . .

Not *bad* chaps, Rex. Mustn't be too critical. Just a bit marooned. No more Thatcher. No more Russian bear to fight, no more Reds under the bed at home. One day they've got the world all carved up for them. . . . Next day they get up in the morning, they're sort of—well, *you* know . . . nobody likes a vacuum, do they? (*NM*, 231)

However spineless and unprincipled, Palfrey understands—perhaps because of those selfsame qualities—that espionage is a market-based enterprise like any other and that what steers it is simple expedience. His analysis obviously makes the dynamic of a post–Cold War spy regime such as MI6 the same as that which informs Richard Onslow Roper's rationale for his criminal activities. In this regard a comment by le Carré in 1977 is apposite. When asked by interviewer Godfrey Hodgson, "Is the secret world for you a model of all human systems and relationships?" the novelist answered, "Yes. For me, it's a microcosm of all institutional behavior, and of the ever-repeated dilemma which overcomes individuals when they submit their talent for institutional exploitation."[27] During an uncertain time when, Palfrey adds, "no one's got the whole picture, so no one knows there isn't one" (*NM*, 232), the collusion between Roper and his network of enablers is thus almost inevitable.

In an imaginary conversation with Jonathan Pine while *The Night Manager*'s climax is unfolding, Leonard Burr pleads, "*Betray me, betray us all. We've betrayed you, haven't we? Then do it back to us and save yourself. The enemy's not out there. He's here among us.*" En route to confront Sir Anthony Joyston Bradshaw, he then remembers Rex Goodhew's stand on behalf of rectitude and reflects, "We are honorable . . . English people with self-irony and a sense of decency . . . and a good heart. What the hell's gone wrong with us?" (*NM*, 434). Whether that question invariably guides le Carré's fourteenth novel I doubt, given its relentless and blistering dissection of British moral decay amid a New World Order, but it is still one that must be asked. Le Carré's next work moves significantly beyond *The Night Manager* as a critique of this emergent global culture by concentrating on the plight of two MI6 agents who are "marooned," in Harry Palfrey's words, by the Cold War's end.

*   *   *   *   *

International jihadist terrorism does not yet appear as a theme in le Carré's fiction, no doubt owing to the fact that it would be another half a dozen years before the horrific attacks of 9/11 galvanized widespread awareness of its real and present threat to the West. Nevertheless, *Our Game*, le Carré's fifteenth novel, offers an intricate psychodrama of two former spies drawn away from their safe havens in the United Kingdom to the crucible of seething ethnic and religious conflict in the North Caucasus region, specifically the predominantly Muslim Republic of Ingushetia, which in mid-1992 separated from neighboring Chechnya under the Russian federation. One commentator finds this geographical focus indicative of le Carré's canny "realization that the Caucasus had the most potential for becoming the Balkans of the post–Cold War world."[28]

Both first-person narrator Timothy D'Abell Cranmer, having been shunted into early retirement by the "Office" because "Cold Warriors of forty-seven don't recycle" well in the "New Era" (*OG*, 20, 51), and Dr. Lawrence Pettifer, whom Cranmer recruited two decades ago to dupe Moscow as a supposed double agent, have been trying to discover a lost sense of purpose ever since their ouster from the Great Game. Cranmer's adjustment to life after MI6 comes more easily than Pettifer's. Heir to an uncle's estate in Somerset and enamored with a beautiful pianist half his age named Emma Manzini, with whom he resides at Honeybrook Manor, "Timbo," as Larry dubs his friend, tries to re-create himself in the guise of a country squire devoted to viniculture and the sponsorship of local charities. Meanwhile, his Byronic protégé Pettifer, only three years Cranmer's junior, yearns for renewed engagement abroad. Having tired of the academic routine of his resettlement at Bath University, where the charismatic firebrand is scheduled to deliver an inaugural lecture titled "The Squandered Victory: Western Foreign Policy since 1988" (*OG*, 44), Pettifer wrestles with which of the world's "Hopeless Causes" (*OG*, 42) he will champion to escape his forced sequestration.[29] When he then interposes himself into his former controller's bucolic life in the Mendips and succeeds in seducing Emma to his side as a political activist on behalf of Ingush freedom, Cranmer's "creation" (*OG*, 33), Pettifer, becomes a figure whom he must vanquish as well as honor by way of belated homage. At the same time it is not at all clear that the novel's principal male characters are separate fictional personas.

John L. Cobbs provides insight into this dimension of what I am calling a psychodrama. "*Our Game* recounts . . . a journey of the soul," he posits, before arguing that le Carré's protagonist, loosely modeled on Elizabethan cleric Sir Thomas Cranmer in the service of King Henry VIII, seeks spiritual redemption for having stolen Pettifer's innocence by inducting him into the duplicity of Cold War intrigue.[30] This interpretation is supported by "Pan child" (*OG*, 32) Larry's own declaration to his overseer early in the novel:

> "Our problem, Timbo, is my purblind, incurable, omnivorous innocence. I can't leave life alone. I love it. Its fictions and its facts. . . ."
>
> "And the corollary to that?"
>
> "And the corollary to that is that you've got to be jolly careful what you ask of me. Because I'll do it. . . . Got to be *sparing*, follow me? Ration yourself. Don't take all of me all the time. . . .
>
> "I mean, it's all right for *you*, selling your soul. You haven't got one. But what about mine?" (*OG*, 34–35)

If Pettifer constitutes Cranmer's schizoid projection of a fantasized alter ego, then le Carré, while continuing to probe the "disease" of secrecy (*OG*, 143), imbues his critique with greater psychological depth than in any earlier narrative except *A Perfect Spy*. Cobbs comments that "le Carré presents the world of espionage as one of divided personalities, in which not only do the ally and the enemy become one, but each spy is [also] aware of his incompleteness and the degree to which he and both his partner and his enemy may become one."[31] This assessment accords with George Smiley's previously noted admonition to a graduating class of MI6 trainees in *The Secret Pilgrim*: "By being all things to all spies, one does rather run the risk of becoming nothing to oneself. . . . The end may justify the means. . . . But there's a price to pay, and the price does tend to be oneself."

The evidence for so construing *Our Game* mounts in its first half through the narrator's frequent, almost obsessively confessional, self-revelations. Besides the comment that Pettifer was his specular "creation," Cranmer records, after returning home by train from a visit to MI6's new headquarters in London, that "I remember little of the journey beyond the reflection riding beside me in the black window, and sometimes the face was Larry's, sometimes mine" (*OG*, 84). Subsequently we are told that he "knew Larry's [face] like the map of my own soul" (*OG*, 108). And when he tries to ascertain Pettifer's current whereabouts by reluctantly conferring with ex-wife Diana, formerly an MI6 colleague whom he divorced seven years ago and who is now a psychotherapist, Timbo explains that "unfortunately, we [Cranmer and Pettifer] are inextricably involved with each other, and I have to find him for my own salvation and probably for his" (*OG*, 146). These and other passages profile Larry as Cranmer's doppelgänger, who, ever since their overlapping stints at Winchester College and later Oxford University, has represented "the risk I would never take" (*OG*, 75). When Tim's career-making asset then denounces his Cold War handler as an "*espiopath*" with "good manners that do duty for a heart" (*OG*, 94), he repudiates once and for all the entire foundation of blinkered conformism on which Cranmer as the novel's protagonist has constructed his life to date. Le Carré makes abundantly clear that the sundering of their relationship, which by extension is a schism within the spymaster's own soul, cannot be disassociated from the regnant imperative of institutionalized espionage.

Ever since he burst onto the literary scene with *The Spy Who Came In from the Cold*, of course, le Carré has been renowned for exposing the deviant pathology of secrecy. In *Our Game*, while Cranmer is contemplating his "years of clandestine incarceration" (*OG*, 139), the point surfaces most explicitly when he asks himself, "What good had it ever done us, this cloak-and-dagger rigmarole? What harm had it done us, this endless wrapping up and hiding of our identities?" (*OG*, 30–31). Nonetheless, he is slow to fathom the implications of an answer to the second question. Even in his retirement Timbo cannot wean himself from long-ingrained tradecraft habits of dissemblance. Thus, when in the opening chapter Special Branch detectives Percy Bryant and Oliver Luck interrogate him about Pettifer's disappearance from England on October 10, 1994, he reverts automatically to tactics of sly evasion. Moreover, after Pettifer criticizes him for "still living the old lie" by telling Emma that he is "a retired Treasury boffin," Cranmer, as her lover, is unable to confide his true background for fear of violating the Official Secrets Act (*OG*, 28, 46). Later, suspected by MI6's Marjorie Pew and Jake Merriman of having been Pettifer's accomplice in bilking Russia of 37 million pounds, Tim retreats to his "priesthole" redoubt in the tower of an early Gothic church on his Somerset estate where he has cached a "personal escape kit" and "reserve identity" documents under the pseudonym of Colin Bairstow (*OG*, 92, 93). Elaborating on his conditioned need for such a sanctuary, le Carré's protagonist states the following:

Nobody who has not lived in secrecy can appreciate its addictive powers. No-body who has renounced the secret world, or been renounced by it, recovers from his deprivation. His longing for the inner life is at times unendurable, whether of the religious or clandestine kind. At any hour he will dream of the secret hush reclaiming him in its embrace. (*OG*, 92)

Dissimulation, subterfuge, and equivocation prove not only expedient but also nearly inescapable for those such as Timothy D'Abell Cranmer who have allowed themselves to be shaped by secrecy's "addictive powers."

A decisive rupture between the two halves of Cranmer's being occurs, how-ever, when the retired agent runner realizes that he can no longer manipulate or suppress Pettifer's long-simmering revolt against a Cold War mentality. Cranmer admits his complicity in cultivating this cathected, and conve-niently deniable, version of himself by asking, "How could Larry be anything except what *we* had made him: a directionless English middle-class revolu-tionary, a permanent dissident, a dabbler, a dreamer, a habitual rejecter; a ruthless, shiftless, philandering, wasted, semicreative failure, too clever not to demolish an argument, too mulish to settle for a flawed one?" (*OG*, 24). Such extenuation is how Timbo simultaneously accepts and deflects personal re-sponsibility for Larry as his avatar. Because Pettifer roundly condemned the West's inertia when faced with the "underground continuum of Russian ex-pansionism" in 1992, followed by the "demonisation of Islam as a substitute for the anti-Communist crusade," the staid Cranmer, who "believed whatever was necessary to the job at the time," has effectively bracketed off the side of himself associated with a principled conscience (*OG*, 15, 56, 57). The upshot is that he has become a man bereft of any meaningful direction or moral commitment.

The manner in which Tim later disburdens himself, given his convention-ality, to an undefined audience discloses something else about his compart-mentalized psyche. With more vehemence than perhaps he intended, the narrative voice proclaims the following:

I cursed the goad of Englishness that had held me back and spurred me for-ward all my life. . . .

And after I had cursed the England that had made me, I cursed the Office for being its secret seminary, and Emma for luring me from my comfortable captivity.

And then I cursed Larry for shining a lamp into the cavernous emptiness of what he called my dull rectangular mind and dragging me beyond the limits of my precious self-mastery.

Above all I cursed myself. (*OG*, 146–47)

The passage can be read in two ways. On the one hand, its parallel clauses and rhetorical brio, atypical for the customarily understated Cranmer, suggest that this amounts to a breakthrough moment. If earlier he arraigned what "*we* had made" Pettifer, he now is indicting "Englishness" and "England" for what *they* have made him.[32] Such an interpretation would indicate that Tim is at last recognizing the pernicious effect of secrecy on his life. On the other hand, the excerpt's second half fulminates against Emma and Larry as those responsible for "luring me from my comfortable captivity" and "dragging me beyond the limits of my precious self-mastery." The mechanism of displacement is clearly at work here. If the protagonist disavows accountability for a scenario of which *he* is the architect, what stock should be placed in his concluding statement, "Above all I cursed myself"?

I would propose that it's less than he might wish, but that determination depends, as we shall see, on what one makes of the novel's final fifty pages, especially its concluding paragraph, and Cranmer's conceivable motive(s) for recounting his tale. Before addressing that issue, however, we need to take into account a pivotal episode that supposedly occurs at Priddy Pool in Somerset on September 18, 1994. I say "supposedly" because both Tim, *Our Game*'s narrator, and le Carré through him obfuscate any distinction between illusion and reality in this hallucinatory (non)event when Cranmer, desperate to end Pettifer's encroachment on his postretirement life with Emma Manzini, thinks that he has murdered his friend. The surrealistic "memory" disorients readers, yet we also recognize that Tim as resurgent "Operational Man" is engaged in "picking through the rubble of [his] past, looking for the fragments of the bomb that had destroyed it" (*OG*, 7, 113).

Whether the incident actually occurred or was merely imagined, the protagonist believes that "I have defeated him at last, Larry, the true version of me, as he calls himself, the Timbo Unbound whose life I never dared to lead until I led it vicariously through him" (*OG*, 95). Shortly thereafter, though, Cranmer confides that "perhaps I only killed myself," whatever "did or didn't happen at Priddy Pool" (*OG*, 98). This uncertainty soon compels him to flee England, where the former spymaster is now under suspicion by MI6. Thinking that he has been the victim of a "honey trap . . . foisted on me by a conspiracy of my enemies," he pursues both Emma and Larry overseas (*OG*, 129).

That compulsion, which radically alters the trajectory of the novel's second half, lends itself in turn to additional angles of interpretation. In terms of the narrative's plot scaffolding, it may arise from Cranmer's need to exonerate himself in light of MI6's suspicion that he abetted Pettifer's grand larceny of 37 million pounds, which actually was coordinated with the latter's former KGB "blackarse" controller named Konstantin Abramovich Checheyev to support the Ingush insurgents' cause.[33] At another level his renewed "spy's odyssey" (*OG*, 183) possibly stems from Tim's obsessive desire to assure himself that he has not been gulled by a former subagent who is notoriously indifferent to his MI6 compensation, or "Judas money," and equally inept in managing his financial affairs (*OG*, 61). Then again, le Carré's protagonist may be hounding Emma and Larry for the sake of personal retaliation. Finally, it may be the case that Cranmer is seeking to resolve his festering spiritual conflict. Whatever impels the cautious Timbo to push beyond the safe parameters of his life in Somerset, he launches on a journey that arguably reawakens an anaesthetized sense of responsibility for others' welfare.

The germinal seed for that transformation is planted when, having figured out Emma's line of retreat from documents in his priesthole, Cranmer deduces that she has sought refuge in Paris with Contessa Ann-Marie von Diderich ("Dee"), a former protector whose "fabulous empty castle" on the Ile St.-Louis seems to be a halfway house for women and children in need (*OG*, 267). First, however, his detectivelike sleuthing in England reveals several facts of which he was previously unaware. One is that Larry and Emma, before her furtive departure from Honeybrook Manor, had established a company in Bristol known as Free Prometheus Ltd. by means of which they have been bankrolling covert arms shipments to Ingush rebels. A grislier discovery comes when Timbo— "the man who believes in nothing, and therefore has space for everything" (*OG*, 199)—finds the grotesquely mangled corpses of Aitken Mustafa May, a middleman for such embargoed trafficking, and two of his business associates in a remote Macclesfield compound. Emma had earlier proclaimed to her fence-straddling lover that "you can't be *no* side, Tim. That's like not existing. We have to have an object of faith. Otherwise we're not defined" (*OG*, 136). In a significant change of outlook, Cranmer declares that "my guilt, so recently shuffled off, returned, and I began to see myself as the . . . negative instigator . . . who by his intolerance brings about the circumstance he most deplores" (*OG*, 207). This insight is a genuine turning point, at least potentially, for the former agent runner. The consequences can be gauged from what ensues after Tim confronts Emma at Dee's residence.

The protagonist's face-to-face conversation with his former lover is actually less important than what Dee says to Cranmer after he arrives at her door. Before ushering him to Emma's upstairs studio, the almost sibylline contessa cross-examines le Carré's protagonist about his intentions in pursuing her asylum-seeking friend. "You were the last of her shells," declares Dee, before adding, "Now she is real. She is defined. She is one person. Or feels she is. If she is not, then at least the different people in her are going in the same direction. Thanks to Larry. Perhaps it is also thanks to you." When Tim demurs that he did not come to Paris to solicit Emma's gratitude or contrition, his interlocutor asserts, "Then for what? For an obligatory scene? I hope not. Perhaps one day you also will be real" (OG, 270). Shortly thereafter, regarding her visitor's pursuit of the fugitive couple, Dee says of Cranmer's relationship to Pettifer, "You know what? I don't think you wish to *find* your friend, only to *become* him" (OG, 271). While rummaging among stacks of documents in his priesthole, Timbo wondered whether he had been "framed, set up, [as] the target of a devilish conspiracy" or was "merely the fool of . . . my own menopausal imaginings" (OG, 188). That issue is laid to rest when, at the end of his brief colloquy with Emma in Paris, Cranmer, who once imagined that he could be her "one-man convent," realizes that he has been an accessory, given "his criminally negligent myopia," to her leaving him for a moral absolutist (OG, 190, 215).

From this juncture onward, according to reviewer Daniel Richler, Our Game devolves into "a shaggy dog story," purportedly demonstrating that its author "seems to know the [espionage] genre is dead."[34] Richler's take on the narrative was anticipated by Charles Gordon's assertion that "once the setting shifts to the North Caucasus, it becomes a mere adventure story, something le Carré has never handled as well as the mind games of the espionage trade."[35] Writing for the Los Angeles Times, Tom Carson was even more acerbic. When le Carré, he pronounced, "closes in on his theme of the Ingush cause, and begins to amplify the symbolic underpinnings of Larry's role as Cranmer's other half, Our Game turns dismayingly diffuse, mawkish, overly earnest, and moony."[36] The resolution to this psychodrama is considerably more complex and intriguing than these criticisms suggest.

Proof for that counterclaim lies in the denouement's ambiguity. To prepare for his expected reunion with Pettifer, Cranmer must first undergo a testing of his spiritual courage much like that of Robert Browning's candidate for knighthood in "'Childe Roland to the Dark Tower Came'" as he makes his way through a phantasmagorical landscape toward his final destination.[37]

Embarked on a "quest for absolutes in a world of botch and falsehood" (*OG*, 186), Tim leaves Paris for Moscow in order to trace "the causality of everything that had happened to me in my life till now" and "fill the pit that for so long had done duty for my soul" (*OG*, 278). What he witnesses, during the initial stage of his journey, in the post-glasnost Russian capital seven years after his last visit there as a "Foreign Office flunkey" is a wasteland whose spectral unreality attests to the incursions of a "dollar economy" (*OG*, 280):

> Tsarist chandeliers lit the vast hall; plaster nymphs cavorted in a rainbow fountain, their shiny torsos reflected to infinity by a carousel of gilt-framed mirrors. A cardboard dancing girl recommended the casino on the third floor[;] imitation air hostesses told me to enjoy my day. They should have told it to the muffled beggarwomen outside on the street corner, or the dead-eyed children hovering purposefully at the traffic lights and in the filthy underpasses, or the twenty-year-old wrecks in doorways, sleeping upright like the dead; or the defeated armies of pedestrians hunting for a morsel of the dollar economy to buy with their evaporating roubles. (*OG*, 279)

Only a page later, finding that "wherever I looked the madness of history answered me," the prodigal espiopath—surrounded now by "the rusting stars of Soviet triumphalism"—discovers that capitalist consumerism has succeeded in supplanting communist socialism. "And everywhere, as evening gathered," writes le Carré, "the beacons of the true conquerors [were] flashing out their gospel: 'Buy us, eat us, drink us, wear us, drive us, smoke us, die of us! We are what you get instead of slavery!'" (*OG*, 280). From this vignette we can infer that his protagonist is glimpsing, in this equivalent of a necropolis, the nullity of an outcome to which he has contributed as a Cold War spy employed by Britain's Secret Intelligence Service.

The next step in Cranmer's dawning sense of his career's vacuity involves a funereal scene in which he meets again with his former Soviet counterpart, Colonel Volodya Zorin. Effectively under house arrest while awaiting trial by the Kremlin as a scapegoat for the theft of 37 million pounds from its coffers, an embittered Zorin hovers solicitously by the deathbed of his mistress, Eugenie, who "should have been" his wife, he declares (*OG*, 282). Although he is still capable of demonizing the Ingush as "a tribe of savages" (*OG*, 284), thanks to his ideological indoctrination, Zorin epitomizes what might have been Tim's fate in England had he not opted to break with his past. Now "a fugitive, homeless and stateless, a small nation of one" (*OG*, 280), Cranmer unshackles himself from all antecedent affiliations in order to seek out the man whom he

believes that he created. Such disconnection from institutional frameworks of
self-definition, implies le Carré, is a necessary prelude to a genuine encounter
with what philosopher Martin Heidegger, in *Sein und Zeit* (1927), famously
called one's *Dasein*, or "being-in-the-world."[38] The reader's expectation at this
point is that "Timbo Unbound" will achieve, ultimately, a liberating openness
to human suffering.

Immediately thereafter, in the third phase of his journey, Timothy D'Abell
Cranmer is subjected to a personal experience of abjection or, in religious
terms, a dark night of the soul. This rite of liminal transition, akin to that
recounted by sixteenth-century Roman Catholic mystic St. John of the Cross,
begins when Cranmer is imprisoned for ten days in a ruinous industrial-park
cell on the outskirts of Moscow, having been brought there by someone named
Issa—ironically, given his name's etymology, a Russian mafioso whose political sympathies lie with the Ingush. After "passing through the looking glass"
during this protracted ordeal (*OG*, 293), le Carré's protagonist learns that "the
greatest freedom in the world [i]s to have no control over one's destiny" (*OG*,
297). Stripped now of any conventional markers of social identity, Tim is on
his own, although he also has "the impression of having joined an underlife"
with his Ingush "hosts" (*OG*, 295).

While in their keeping, Cranmer is taught by a revered elder named Magomed that his protection is the result of a cultural myth. "There is a prophecy,"
explains the savant, "widely believed in Sufist circles since the nineteenth century . . . , that the Russian Empire will one day collapse and the North Caucasus, including Ingushetia and Chechenia, will come under the rule of the
British sovereign" (*OG*, 298). Both men know how unlikely the last part of this
Victorian fable is, but their interaction enables the retired spy to understand
more fully the rebels' abandonment by the West.

That motif is underscored during the culmination of Cranmer's odyssey
when Checheyev tells a sardonic joke about post–Cold War geopolitics: "For
the purposes of peacekeeping in the former Soviet Union[, t]he West supplies
the money [while] Moscow supplies the troops and the ethnic cleansing" (*OG*,
310–11).[39] He then reveals that Bashir Haji, the current leader of the tribal
Ingush mountain men, and as many as two hundred of his followers have
been massacred in a Russian nighttime assault on their mountain stronghold.
Thinking that Pettifer might be among the dead, Cranmer makes a perilous
trek on horseback, escorted by Magomed's small band, to the killing fields near
Vladikavkaz. During their final approach to the devastated village, he reflects
as follows:

In the broken bodies that I saw ahead of me I was witnessing an extinction of my life more absolute than anything that might happen to me on my way to them. . . . But the survival I craved was Larry's, not mine, and the lucid, unencompassable majesty of the mountains drew me upward. (*OG*, 325)

Diluted, frankly, by le Carré's incorporation of what M. H. Abrams famously termed the Romantic sublime's "natural supernaturalism" ("My heart lifted," admits the narrator, "in mystical response" to the alpine scenery), the passage forces us to weigh the import of Cranmer's ensuing thought: "Just let Larry be alive for me when I come over the brow of the last hill, and whatever I have been I will never be again" (*OG*, 325).[40] That unspoken wish or vow makes Tim's commitment to self-transformation contingent on Pettifer's survival, raising issues of his probity in embracing a decisive *metanoia* and of the significance of exactly what Larry represents given the novel's resolution.

Here we need to recall that *Our Game*'s first-person confessor is composing his tale for an indeterminate audience, presumably after his departure from Ingushetia. This fundamental dimension of the memoir's architectonics ought to make us wary of its possible designs on us as readers. I particularly have in mind what Tim Cranmer records after entering the mountaintop village. Met by the "keening of women mourning the dead" and expected to extol a fallen martyr (*OG*, 327), he is called upon to commemorate their former Byronic champion's merits:

I said that Larry was an Englishman who had loved freedom above everything. He had loved the courage of the Ingush and shared their hatred of the bully. And that Larry would live because he had cared, and that it was those who cared too little who died the death. And that since courage went hand in hand with honour, and both with loyalty, it was necessary also to record that, in a world where loyalty was increasingly difficult to define, Larry had contrived to remain a man of honour even if the necessary consequence of this was to go out and find his death like a warrior.

For it occurred to me as I spoke—though I was careful not to say it in so many words—that if Larry had led the wrong life, he had at least found the right death. (*OG*, 331)

Such a grandiloquent peroration, however, leaves one puzzled about both the speaker's and the author's intentions. Is Cranmer, for example, merely

extemporizing a eulogy that will console a stricken population for whom Pettifer was the prefiguration of a nineteenth-century Sufist prophecy's fulfillment?
And, if so, is he not then ratifying the Romantic myth of heroic individualism
that an embattled republic, victimized by the full arsenal of modern warfare,
still venerates? Such questions also have a bearing on le Carré's political vision
in *Our Game*. Through Cranmer's encomium is le Carré presenting Pettifer as
a global adventurer endowed with a conscience, whom others should emulate
in a faithless age of terminal skepticism, or is he instead exposing the velleity
of a sentimental historiography?

We can grope our way toward some provisional answers by recognizing that
if Dr. Lawrence Pettifer is metaphorically a "latter-day Lord Jim" (*OG*, 305), he
is a strangely absent presence in the narrative's second half. Cobbs goes further
by alleging that "Larry literally does not appear in *Our Game*. . . . At no point
in the novel can any of the characters, much less the reader, definitively prove
anything about Larry."[41] As such, Pettifer amounts to a ghost that haunts the
text's margins, flitting in and out as a phantom of collective nostalgia.

The narrative's concluding paragraph brings together all these uncertainties
in the scene's choreography. After lauding his doppelgänger as a champion of
universal freedom, honor, and loyalty, Cranmer, like an agnostic pilgrim in
search of a holy relic, retrieves by way of memento or "connection" a singed
plait of straw that he "slip[s] into his pocket for a future lonely hour" and keeps
"on the off chance that it was a true fragment" of Larry's trademark Winchester
hat (*OG*, 333). While the Ingush survivors are electing Magomed as their new
leader in a ceremony called *tauba*, meaning repentance, Checheyev "turned
his back . . . and, as if sick of my Western uselessness or his own, started down
the hill." Le Carré's stranded protagonist, reduced now to a mere bystander,
shouts "Wait!" but his cry is met by no response. Then comes *Our Game*'s
finale:

> But the chanting was by now too loud, and [Checheyev] couldn't hear me
> even if he wanted to. For a moment longer I stood alone, converted to noth-
> ing, believing in nothing. I had no world to go back to and nobody left to run
> except myself. A Kalashnikov lay beside me. Slinging it across my shoulder, I
> hastened after him down the slope. (*OG*, 337)

Cranmer's predicament, like Checheyev's, is to have lost the grounds for a coherent creed of any kind through his long immersion in espionage's culture of
suspicion. Not even left to him, the text discloses, is the mission of returning to
Paris in order to inform Emma of Larry's death (*OG*, 335). The closing image

of Timbo slinging a Kalashnikov across his shoulder is not, therefore, the image of a warrior arming himself for an impending engagement but instead that of a belated tourist gathering up a battlefield souvenir.

What I have just proposed, of course, is not made explicit in the novel's ending. Le Carré obliges his readers to compose their own epilogue for a man who is now a persona non grata divorced from any context other than what he might possibly invent for himself in the future. Cranmer's valedictory on Pettifer, we nonetheless recognize, bespeaks a plangent longing for an era when one's character was the guarantee of his autonomy, but our parting glimpse of a protagonist who, "believing in nothing," has been "converted to nothing" conveys the impasse of a former Cold Warrior who has stumbled upon what it means to live in "a world where loyalty was increasingly difficult to define." Le Carré thereby recaptures one of his trademark themes—namely, the moral quandary of those who have managed to shake off a reductive mindset only to confront the messy ambiguity of things as they are. For that reason, especially when its final scene is compared to *The Night Manager*'s formulaic coda, *Our Game* signals "an unexpected rebirth of vintage le Carré."[42]

That said, we should not assume that just because the author's fifteenth novel comes to a close by freeze-framing an antihero who has found neither redemption nor salvation, the text concedes the inevitable failure of such aspirations in an age that embraces the ethic of expedience. Timothy D'Abell Cranmer, after all, has taken preliminary steps toward achieving a modicum of personal authenticity. Earlier in the narrative, while intent on tracking down Pettifer, he had sought the assistance of Ockie Hedges, "one of the biggest crooks in [England's] illegal-arms business," who collaborated with an accommodating Tim fifteen years ago in identifying citizens supposedly opposed to the United Kingdom's security interests. Staunchly supporting the reactionary neoconservatism of Prime Minister Margaret Thatcher at that time, Hedges "successively dismissed intellectuals, Jews, blacks, the Yellow Peril, and homosexuals with a benign and universal hatred" (*OG*, 241). Much to his credit, Cranmer has learned to repudiate such inveterate bigotry thinly disguised as patriotism, even though he has not yet managed to commit himself to an alternative cause or endeavor. Without providing a sequel to this protagonist's subsequent career, le Carré charts where his quest leads in the novels to come.

2

THE TAILOR OF PANAMA AND *SINGLE & SINGLE*

Ludic Fabrication, Self-Begotten Sons, and a New World Order

We stand today at a unique and extraordinary moment. The crisis in the Persian Gulf, as grave as it is, also offers a rare opportunity to move toward an historic period of cooperation. Out of these troubled times . . . a new world order . . . can emerge: a new era—free from the threat of terror, stronger in the pursuit of justice, and more secure in the quest for peace. An era in which the nations of the world . . . can prosper and live in harmony. . . . Today that new world is struggling to be born, a world quite different from the one we've known. A world where the rule of law supplants the rule of the jungle. A world in which nations recognize the shared responsibility for freedom and justice. A world where the strong respect the rights of the weak.

—George H. W. Bush to Congress, September 11, 1990

So declared the president of the United States four months before launching Operation Desert Storm against Iraqi leader Saddam Hussein for his invasion of neighboring Kuwait and, by extension, his endangerment of Middle Eastern oil supplies. This grandiloquent part of Bush's speech, often dubbed "Toward a New World Order," is of interest for a couple of reasons. First, he was recycling a key trope from Woodrow Wilson's call for a League of Nations after the devastation of World War I, despite that organization's coming to naught because of its inability to prevent armed aggression by the Axis powers in the 1930s. Second, Bush was echoing Winston Churchill's sentiments shortly before the United Nations was chartered in 1945. Given this thumbnail history of the phrase's usage by Western heads of state, it is noteworthy that eleven years to the day before the cataclysmic events of 9/11 in New York City and Washington, DC, Bush was exalting the defense of "civilized values around the world" while also emphasizing the safeguarding of "our economic strength at home." Although neither *The Tailor of Panama* nor *Single & Single* overtly addresses the postulate of a New World Order, both project a profound skepticism that the construct's laudable ethical vision—"A world where the rule of law supplants the rule of the jungle. A world in which nations recognize the shared responsibility for freedom and justice. A world where the strong respect the rights of the weak"—was anywhere near being realized during the 1990s.

Le Carré's next pair of novels unfolds against a geopolitical background of endemic mistrust, paranoia, and manipulation after the Cold War's presumptive end. Set in the tense interim between the US overthrow of Panamian leader Manuel Noriega in 1989 and the Panama Canal's pending return to its host country on the last day of the twentieth century, per a 1977 treaty signed by General Omar Torrijos and President Jimmy Carter, *The Tailor of Panama* comes to a bloody close with US helicopter gunships strafing the capital city's barrio of El Chorillo in connection with Operation Safe Passage. The framework of *Single & Single* is equally bleak. There the looming threat to "civilized values around the world" is an investment firm in London that launders money for the Russian mafia's flourishing trade in "every dirty product they can lay their hands on, from Afghan heroin for teenagers to Czech Semtex for Irish peace lovers and Russian nuclear triggers for Middle Eastern democrats" (*SS*, 99). Within the context of such rampant venality, both novels revolve around either fatherless or estranged sons who, rejecting their personal pasts, cling to a gift for ludic fabrication when they are plunged into the invariably compromising realm of espionage.

In *The Tailor of Panama*, le Carré's sixteenth novel, exile Harry Pendel has made a career of fictionalized self-invention since he began courting his future wife, Louisa Jenning, thirteen years ago "on an immaculate all-American lawn in the officially abolished Canal Zone with the Stars and Stripes flapping in the smoke of her daddy's barbecue and the band playing hope-and-glory and the black men watching through the wire" (*TP*, 79). The vagaries of Pendel's earlier life explain this almost spontaneous impulse on his part. The illegitimate offspring of a philandering Jewish father and a nubile Irish housemaid, Harry spent his childhood in an orphanage until being rescued by his paternal Uncle Benjamin, who employed the grateful adolescent in his East End clothing factory. Sometime later, after being arrested for torching the warehouse so that his benefactor would collect arson insurance, Harry served a thirty-month prison sentence.

Upon his nephew's release Uncle Benny subsidized Pendel's relocation to Panama where, staked by wealthy family friend Charlie Blüthner—who, says his guardian, "wouldn't be where he is today if Benny hadn't kept *shtum* for him just like you did for me" (*TP*, 87)—Harry launched a haberdashery. To solemnize its founding, and aided by his flair for "Jewish *chutzpah*" coupled with "Irish blarney" (*TP*, 82), Harry concocted a story he called "My Early Struggle" (*TP*, 37). According to this Horatio Alger myth, Harry had been taken under the wing of a purely imaginary patron, Arthur Brathwaite, who upon his death left the apprentice sole proprietorship of "the house of Pendel & Brathwaite [P&B] Co. Limitada, Tailors to Royalty, formerly of Savile Row, London, and presently of the Vía España, Panama City" (*TP*, 3).

Under cover of this fable, Brathwaite's putative heir built a thriving business, married Louisa, and moved to the upscale neighborhood of Bethania with their children, Mark and Hannah. Before the novel opens, however, Harry has unwisely invested his wife's $200,000 inheritance from her father in a failing rice farm and consequently owes corrupt banker Ramón Rudd $150,000, a debt for which he has pledged his shop's assets as collateral. This financial liability renders the cash-strapped tailor susceptible to overtures by Andrew Julian Osnard, an opportunistic twenty-six-year-old field agent for Britain's Secret Intelligence Service, who shows up one rainy Friday morning at P&B to recruit Pendel, under the threat of exposing his fraudulent self-refashioning, as a paid informant on political intrigue in the Central American nation.

Two practiced dissemblers are thus pitted against each other, but their motives for an embroidery of the truth, or "artifactuality," differ vastly.[1] What Uncle Benny describes as his nephew's talent for "fluence" derives from Harry's need to reshape the world according to his "grand vision" of human possibility (*TP*, 13, 201). Le Carré equates this creative ability with the vocational skill that Pendel acquired while in prison: "It was tailoring. It was improving on people. . . . It was running ahead of events and waiting for them to catch up" (*TP*, 52). Earlier the novelist portrayed his protagonist as a "born impersonator" whose job it was "to place himself in the clothes of whomever he [wa]s cutting for, and become that person until the rightful owner claim[ed] them" (*TP*, 15). Harry Pendel's sartorial expertise compensates for the physical shortcomings of others in much the same way that his gift for fabulation readjusts the moral imbalances of everyday reality. In both cases his motivation is charitable generosity.

In diametrical contrast is Andy Osnard, whose sole ambition is to exploit human and institutional weaknesses for his own selfish advantage. The younger son of a family in generational decline, Osnard came of age as a self-tutored expert in "English rot" (*TP*, 164). Concerning this rogue's résumé pursuant to graduation from prep school, le Carré records that after short-lived apprenticeships in journalism, animal charities, and the Anglican Church, he "found his Grail" in the ranks of handsomely budgeted MI6 (*TP*, 165). Henceforth the cynical recruit dedicated himself to bilking that espiocracy of as much money as he could arrange to have deposited into a numbered Cayman Islands account. "Adore a con," says Osnard, in his clipped way of speaking, upon first meeting Pendel. "What life's about" (*TP*, 41). As fictionalists these men are leagues apart, yet both become enmeshed in a rapidly escalating metanarrative that before long neither of them can control or contain.

In light of the geopolitical uncertainty that abounded during the Cold War's immediate aftermath, nothing is too farfetched for Harry Pendel to invent or for Andy Osnard to credit regarding secret developments supposedly afoot in Panama. Drawing on the experiences of his close friends Marta, P&B's accountant, and Mickie Abraxas, both of whom suffered brutalization by Noriega's paramilitary Dignity Battalions after the dictator's seizure by the United States in Operation Just Cause, Harry weaves a spurious tale of the readiness of Dr. Ernesto Delgado, the esteemed head of the Panama Canal Commission and his wife's boss, to engage in clandestine negotiations with the Japanese over the waterway's future while a "Silent Opposition" of dissident students and fishermen slowly gathers strength under Mickie's leadership. Recognizing how this marketable conspiracy will appeal to his gullible supervisor at MI6, Osnard effuses:

> You're God's gift, Harry. Classic, ultimate listening post. Wife with access. Contacts to kill for. Chum in the resistance. Girl in the shop who runs with the mob. Behaviour pattern established over ten years. Natural cover, local language, gift o' the gab, quick on your feet. Never heard anyone pitch the tale better. Be who you are but more of it, and we'll have the whole o' Panama stitched up. Plus you're deniable. You on or not? (*TP*, 66)

Both con artists know that the story is a wild farrago, but they also understand that it can be turned to profit, given the vested interest of temporarily sidelined intelligence agencies in globally actionable "causes." Though wary of each other's overdeveloped capacity for deception, Pendel and Osnard soon set about elaborating a masterplot for MI6's credulous consumption. Their joint efforts are endorsed unhesitatingly at Vauxhall Cross headquarters by the sedulous processors of field intelligence.

From this overview it should be apparent that *The Tailor of Panama* reprises Graham Greene's *Our Man in Havana* (1958), which in 1986 le Carré admitted to having recently reread.[2] How are we to account for this seemingly anomalous work, which pays homage to a literary precursor's satire of the Great Game, as part of his post–Cold War journey? Le Carré is not of much help in answering that question. At the end of his novel's acknowledgments, he says only that "the notion of an intelligence fabricator would not leave me alone" (*TP*, n.p.). If the idea had been percolating in his mind ever since the publication of *A Perfect Spy*, it may have begun to coalesce when le Carré visited Panama in 1989 while conducting research for *The Night Manager*.[3] Then again, after dramatizing ex–Cold Warrior Timothy Cranmer's search for a recovery of existential purpose in *Our Game*, he may have grown tired of following yesteryear's dubious heroes into retirement and been drawn once more, through Greene, to tackling "a very personal book" that explored the creative freedom he took with life material as a source for his fiction.[4]

When asked where he would "fit" *The Tailor of Panama* in relation to his previous novels, le Carré replied, "I think the ones I want to be buried with are *A Perfect Spy* and this one. I have the most affection for the characters in those stories, and somehow . . . they came closest to the bone. By [that] I mean as near as I want to come to my own center."[5] Only two months earlier, however, he had stated, "Artists, in my experience, have very little centre. They fake. They are not the real thing. They are spies. I am no exception."[6] If *The Tailor of Panama* came "as near as [he] want[ed] to come to [his] own center" but "artists . . . have very little centre," le Carré may have welcomed the opportunity to cast off the encrustation of his persona as a "spy novelist," which had been imposed by critics preoccupied with "authenticity," and reveled in composing an oblique exposé of himself as a writer unfettered by the narrow conventions of what some pundits were alleging to be an outmoded genre.[7] So conceived, his sixteenth work constitutes a decisive pivot for an author who by 1996 no longer wished to be typecast in terms of his Cold War corpus.

Much of le Carré's ingenuity in *The Tailor of Panama* consists of endowing Harry Pendel, who by accident of birth is half Jewish, with a double consciousness. An otherwise innocent bystander drawn into the murky world of international intrigue, Pendel is not unlike Richard Hannay in John Buchan's *The Thirty-Nine Steps* (1915), an important text in the evolution of British espionage fiction. As an exile of mixed cultural heritage, however, Pendel, codenamed Buchan, knows what it means to be one of the world's dispossessed. Harry's sense of "the abundance of his good luck" in Panama consequently "instilled in him a keen awareness of its fragility," such that when he is alone at night on his family's Bethania balcony he can hear Uncle Benny's cautionary whisper, "You know this can't last, Harry boy, you know the world can blow up in your face, you've watched it happen from this very spot, and what it's done once it can do again whenever it feels like it, so look out" (*TP*, 71). Despite Pendel's layered and largely suppressed awareness, he still jeopardizes his life of domestic security with Louisa when he agrees, without her knowledge, to cooperate with Andy Osnard in manufacturing a formulaic saga of international betrayal and duplicity.[8]

Harry Pendel's decision to pursue this course of subterfuge prompted reviewer Norman Rush to lament in the *New York Times* that "here we have, however little Mr. le Carré intended it, yet another literary avatar of Judas."[9] Because the charge elicited an angry retort from le Carré and led him a year later to expand on the subject for an article in the *Jewish News*, we need to consider the dispute's cross-currents. Conceding that Pendel was an "arresting creation" and the novel a satirical "tour de force," Rush added in his review, "It's reasonable to make an expatriate British tailor a Jew, but does this Jew, for example, have to defame the only decent, 'saintly' (Pendel's own term) political leader in Panama [Dr. Ernesto Delgado], and then go on to implicate his own wife's utterly innocent Christian study group to boot?"[10]

Rankled by this judgment, and probably also by the stilted reference to Louisa's "utterly innocent Christian study group," the novelist replied a few weeks later, "The whole point of the character, which should be plain to a blind hedgehog, as the Russians say, is that he is an unshaken cocktail of differing, and sometimes conflicting, cultures." On the basis of skewed textual evidence, objected le Carré, "Mr. Rush proceeds to tar me with the anti-Semitic brush," an accusation that his critic flatly denied.[11] Given this squabble, it is revealing that only nine days later le Carré deployed the same metaphor in identifying himself with his fictional projection in *The Tailor of Panama*: "My own background was an unshaken cocktail of influences, exactly as with Harry Pendel. Harry is half a Jew, half a Catholic, a bit of everything else."[12]

Le Carré's sensitivity to Rush's claim that in Pendel he had traced an archetype of Judas Iscariot resurfaced more than thirteen months later in comments he made to Douglas Davis at "an unusual gathering of mostly wealthy, non-Jewish . . . supporters of Israel" at London's Savoy Hotel. Le Carré's invitation to the dinner, we learn, "arrived at a moment when he was 'particularly interested to examine the mystery of my Jewish conscience, to question it quite harshly—its sincerity, its origins, its authenticity—and to puzzle out how it developed . . . in book after book throughout my working life.'" The writer, Davis observes, was "using the language of catharsis" because "what exercises him above all—wounds him—are dark charges of anti-Semitism from the United States." The most recent, le Carré volunteered, was the suggestion by a *New York Times* reviewer of *The Tailor of Panama* that "consciously or not, I had been listening to the internal voices of my English anti-Semitism as I wrote my novel." Rush's criticism had obviously penetrated deeply, but why did the accusation fester for so long? An answer may lie in Davis's insight that "Jews are a source of fascination, perhaps even obsession, for le Carré." At one point the novelist offers a revealing admission: "In my perception of the Jewish identity—in my continuing dialogue with it, in private and in my novels—I have been aware from early on of a spiritual kinship that embraces what is creative in me and forgives what is despicable and shares with me the dignity and solitude and anger that are born of alienation."[13] Nowhere else, to my knowledge, has le Carré articulated so clearly his affinity to the Jewish people. It should also be noted that he connects his "spiritual kinship" to a creativity "born of alienation" or uprootedness.[14] Viewed from this angle, Harry Pendel is a variation of David Cornwell himself, including the latter's own experience of being a self-begotten son. We therefore should not be surprised that le Carré dismissed Rush's charge of inadvertent anti-Semitism as betokening nothing more than "the whole oppressive weight of political correctness."[15]

It still must be asked, though, how *The Tailor of Panama* accounts for Pendel's willingness to risk everything of personal value to him by abetting Andrew Osnard's larcenous scheme. Aside from describing the protagonist's financial straits and Osnard's threat of exposure, the novel repeatedly indicates that a mischievous "imp" overtakes Harry Pendel once he agrees to collaborate in inventing a plot with far-reaching consequences for the global balance of power. Initially, for the owner of P&B, it is simply a matter of "giving his fluence its head. Juicing up the story for the benefit of [a] wider audience" (*TP*, 50), but before long "the same imp that had obliged Pendel to make a scallywag of Delgado obliged him also to make a modern hero of Abraxas" (*TP*, 59).

The fabulist, in other words, becomes caught up by his own tale's literary requirements. "Why was he doing it?" queries le Carré's offstage narrator. "What was driving him? . . . A performer is a performer. If your audience isn't with you it's against you. Or perhaps, with his own fictions in tatters, [Harry] needed to enrich the fictions of others. Perhaps he found renewal in the remaking of his world" (*TP*, 64). Like the pseudonymous Ollie Hawthorne in *Single & Single*, a children's magician comparably intent on escaping his forsaken past, Harry Pendel comes fully to life only while giving free rein to his imagination, and the license he takes with historical facticity in the process is rewarded by "draw[ing the] sting" of things as they are (*TP*, 52).

Once le Carré's improvisator in *The Tailor of Panama* commits himself to connivance with Andrew Osnard, however, the simple morality tale he outlines over dinner at the Club Unión is overwritten with a new dimension. The main reason for this emergence of an increasingly labyrinthine metanarrative is the expectations of Pendel's wider audience as ready consumers of bogus intelligence. When their newly enlisted "listening post" in Panama asks for a job description of what information he is expected to relay, Osnard glibly sketches a sweeping fill-in-the-blanks template that encourages the widest possible reactivation of Cold War anxieties:

> Not a lot. Balance o' global power in the twenty-first century. Future o' world trade. Panama's political chessboard. Silent opposers. Chaps from the other side o' the bridge, as you call 'em. What's going to happen when the Yanks pull out? If they do. Who'll be laughing, who'll be crying, come midday December thirty-first, nineteen ninety-nine? Shape o' things to come when one o' the world's two greatest gateways goes under the hammer and the auction's run by a bunch o' wide boys? Piece o' cake. (*TP*, 68)

In giving such range to Harry's fertile capacity for invention, the recently arrived MI6 attaché to the British embassy in Panama is rehearsing what he already knows his besotted case officer in London, Scottie Luxmore, wants to hear. Introduced at the novel's midpoint, this bureaucratic functionary, who boasts of his instrumentality in the farcical Falklands War of 1982, lectures his understudy time and again on a world conspiracy supposedly brewing in the Republic of Panama. Because this lower-echelon factotum's suspicions and knee-jerk jingoism are the underlying target of le Carré's scathing satire, they deserve closer attention.

In one of his many fulsome perorations to Osnard, Luxmore soliloquizes on the dangers posed to Western democracy by the situation in Central America:

> "What is our *geopolitical* interest in Panama? Ask yourself that, if you will." He was away. "What is our *vital* interest? Where is the lifeblood of our great trading nation most at risk? Where, when we train our long lens upon the future well-being of these islands, do we recognise the darkest storm clouds gathering, young Mr. Osnard?" He was flying. "Where in the entire globe do we perceive the next Hong Kong living on borrowed time, the next disaster waiting to happen?" Across the river apparently, where his visionary gaze was fixed. "The barbarians are at the gate, young Mr. Osnard. Predators from

every corner of the globe are descending upon little Panama. That great clock out there is ticking away the minutes to Armageddon. . . . Who will win the greatest Prize Possession of the new millennium? Will it be the Arabs? Are the Japanese sharpening their *katanas*? Of course they are! Will it be the Chinese, the Tigers, or a Pan-Latin consortium underpinned with billions of drug dollars? Will it be Europe without us? Those Germans again, those wily French? It won't be the British, Andrew. That's a racing certainty." . . .

"Not only have the Americans signed a totally misbegotten treaty with the Panamanians—given away the shop, thank you very much Mr. Jimmy Carter!—they're also proposing to *honour* it. In consequence, they are proposing to leave themselves and, what is worse, their allies with a *vacuum*. It will be our job to fill it. To persuade *them* to fill it. To show them the error of their ways. To resume our rightful place at the top table. It's the oldest tale of them all, Andrew. We're the last of the Romans. We have the knowledge, but they have the power. . . . Our task—your task—will be to provide the *grounds*, young Mr. Osnard, the *arguments*, the *evidence* needful to bring our American allies to their senses. Do you follow me?" (*TP*, 168–70)

The riotous absurdity of these sententious extrapolations by Luxmore, who is given to sucking his teeth between oracular pronouncements, reinforces le Carré's indictment of the lingering appeal of "imperialist fantasies" in a new era of transnationalism and globalization (*TP*, 169). The game of "covert policymaking," he proposes, remains what it probably always was—an ideologically disguised grab for raw power and ascendancy (*TP*, 171). Luxmore, however, is only a hollow echo chamber for the fears that drive MI6's upper strata after the Cold War's end, specifically the apprehension that Britain had somehow been edged out of prominence on the world's stage by the upstart and well-heeled North Americans.

Like *Our Man in Havana*'s interludes in London, *The Tailor of Panama* includes behind-the-scenes glimpses of a "highly secret body known as the Planning & Application Committee" that effectively directs MI6's "Top Floor" (*TP*, 171, 175). The triumvirate includes media baron Ben Hatry, defense lobbyist Geoffrey Cavendish, and intermediary Tug Kirby. Periodically conferring with emissaries of the reactionary American "General Van" (*TP*, 245), these three men have succeeded in wooing Britain's "empire-dreamers, Euro-haters, nigger-haters, pan-xenophobes and lost, uneducated children" through Hatry-owned tabloids and television channels:

Nothing is more predictable than the media's parroting of its own fictions and the terror of each competitor that it will be scooped by the others, whether or not the story is true, because quite frankly, dears, in the news game these days, we don't have the staff, time, interest, energy, literacy or minimal sense of responsibility to check our facts by any means except calling up whatever has been written by other hacks on the same subject and repeating it as gospel. (*TP*, 241–42)

Le Carré's diatribe arraigns a culture of misinformation manipulated by a cabal of cynical moguls who shape public opinion at home and the practices of British embassies abroad. So it happens that when Osnard, in a rare moment of candor, confesses to wondering whether Pendel "isn't stringing us along," Luxmore as his indoctrinated supervisor urges conformity to the party line:

Listen to me, Andrew. That's an order. There *is* a conspiracy. Don't lose heart merely because you're tired. Of *course* there is a conspiracy. You believe it, I believe it. One of the greatest opinion makers in the *world* believes it. Personally. Profoundly. The best brains in Fleet Street believe it, or they very soon will. A conspiracy is out there[. I]t is being cobbled together by an evil inner circle of the Panamanian elite[. I]t centres on the Canal and we shall find it! (*TP*, 193–94)

The excursus suggests an institutionalized level of fiction-mongering that filters down to Her Majesty's minions, such that Osnard and his confidential source Pendel are obliged to ratify their handlers' preconceived notions of a globe-straddling conspiracy. The ramifications of groupthink are made explicit later when Ambassador Maltby tells Nigel Stormont, his head of chancery in Panama, that "the Buchan stuff is the most frightful tosh" but that they as dutiful civil servants need to carry on anyway as though it were true (*TP*, 261).

Such alarms regarding the postimperial advent of transnationalism are not limited to Ben Hatry's retrograde Planning & Application Committee. A similar paranoia infects Charlie Blüthner's surreptitious business coalition in Colón known simply as the "Brotherhood" (*TP*, 202). When Harry Pendel is invited to join this fraternity of expatriate entrepreneurs, he listens to a "wandering sage and longtime Servant of the Light" known only as Jonah expound with voluble profanity on a subversion of world trade that will be effected by an Asian takeover of the Panama Canal (*TP*, 206). Such inveterate and fundamentally racist suspicions on the part of Blüthner's captains of commerce in Central America parallel those that proliferate in Britain's Secret Intelligence Service after the Cold War's official end.

All the while, even as *The Tailor of Panama*'s protagonist is providing grist for MI6's propagandistic mill, a figurative "black cat" of moral outrage is sweeping away "the puny wall that had separated fact from fiction in Pendel's soul" (*TP*, 200, 197), especially when Osnard insists that Harry enlist Louisa as part of their scam. Pendel's response to a mounting crisis of conscience indirectly anticipates le Carré's early 2003 stand against the Iraq War in a sharp-edged article titled "The United States Has Gone Mad" as well as his publication that year of *Absolute Friends*, in which Cold War agent Ted Mundy redux comes to discover in his midfifties a long-suppressed anger at the "lies and hypocrisies of politicians," given the tendency of "a renegade hyperpower that thinks it can treat the rest of the world as its fiefdom" (*AF*, 301, 302). Fueled by a similarly seething sense of global injustice, Pendel abandons his reliance on fictionality in order to engage the world as it is. For him that means recognizing the constructed nature of all the relationships on the basis of which he has orchestrated his life to date, including his marriage to Louisa who "was a casualty he had created long ago, in collaboration with her mother and father and Brathwaite and Uncle Benny and the Sisters of Charity and all the other people who made up the person he himself had become" (*TP*, 267). So radical a break with his conjured past leads to what le Carré describes as a "resurrection":

> And suddenly Harry Pendel changed. He was not a different man but himself at last, a man possessed and filled with his own strength. In one glorious ray of revelation he saw beyond melancholy, death, and passivity to a grand validation of his life as an artist, an act of symmetry and defiance, vengeance and reconciliation, a majestic leap into a realm where all the spoiling limitations of reality are swept away by the larger truth of the creator's dream. (*TP*, 312)

The dynamics of this climactic epiphany are profoundly equivocal, however, not least because Harry's "life as an artist" has resulted (among other outcomes) in the suicide of Mickie Abraxas once MI6 credits Buchan's representation of his close friend as the intrepid but unheralded linchpin of Panama's "Silent Opposition." In order to assess the implications of this plot development, one needs to take into account its generative context.

Tragedy occurs when Harry Pendel can no longer exert unilateral control over the separation of art and life. After receiving a rambling telephone call from Mickie's mistress reporting his suicide at a fireworks festival in Guararé, Harry rushes to the scene in his four-track Toyota. En route he realizes that "in all his life he had only ever had one friend, and now he had killed him. . . . The Mickie he had invented was some sort of mistaken homage, an act of vanity on Pendel's part to create a champion out of his best friend" (*TP*, 305). Upon discovering that a despairing Abraxas has blown off half his head, Pendel proceeds to spirit away his bandage-swathed corpse, deposit it near an ancient Indian encampment, and fire two more bullets into the torso to corroborate the myth Harry has spun of a brave revolutionary, who now will appear to have met his end at the hands of professional executioners. Pendel thus enacts symbolically what he had earlier asserted—namely, that he "had murdered his own creation" (*TP*, 310)—but how are we to construe the revelation that reportedly validates his "grand vision"? On the one hand, a repentant Harry has accepted responsibility for endangering Mickie's life through his talent for "fluence," implying a renunciation of artistic license. On the other hand, by saving his friend from the disgrace and stigma of defeat usually associated with suicide, Pendel perpetrates another bit of stage management intended to convince forensic investigators that the Silent Opposition's leader was a marked man, thereby capitalizing on the fiction with which he had reinvented Abraxas as he might have been. Wherein consists, then, the essential core of Harry Pendel's *metanoia*?

My questioning of *The Tailor of Panama*'s ambivalent climax does not detract from the narrative's immense artistry and achievement. By developing the idea of secrecy's inherent fictionality, first explored in Greene's *Our Man in Havana*, the novel anticipates issues discussed in this study's introduction and previous chapter. At the same time, *The Tailor of Panama*'s denouement seems to suggest an unresolved tension in le Carré's fiction pertaining to the ethical latitude of creative invention when the forces against which it is marshaled make use of the same strategy, though usually for their darker purposes of institutional advantage.

Geoffrey Winthrop-Young remarks on an underlying parallel between James Wormold in Greene's *Our Man in Havana* and Harry Pendel in le Carré's *The Tailor of Panama*. "Like Wormold," he writes, "Harry is an increasingly desperate liar whose fabrications cater to the gullibility of a postimperial intelligence service eager to revive its bygone days." At the same time Pendel continues to embrace "the traitor's love of fiction" that sometimes amounts to "a fiction of love."[16] In support of that claim Winthrop-Young cites Harry's silent rumination while in bed with Louisa that "*everything in the world is true if you invent it hard enough and love the person it's for!"* (*TP*, 77). The only problem with such a rationale is that it neglects the consequences of falsifying and thereby betraying the lives of others.

While racing to retrieve the bloody remains of Mickie Abraxas, Pendel recalls at the beginning of the novel's final chapter his Uncle Benny's prayer of atonement: "*We live on the edge of ourselves, terrified of the darkness within. . . . We have harmed, corrupted, and ruined*[;] *we have made mistakes and deceived*" (*TP*, 327). Shortly thereafter, when US helicopter gunships are descending once more on Panama City, Harry finds himself abandoning in the dead of night his privileged suburb of Bethania and running toward the slums of El Chorillo. The childhood home of both Mickie and Marta, it is "the place . . . [where] nobody would ever again ask him to improve on life's appearance, [and] neither would they mistake his dreaming for their terrible reality" (*TP*, 332). So ends the novel. Its rendering of Harry Pendel's final action conveys, like Timothy Cranmer's in *Our Game*, the limbo of uncertainty in which he is immersed as an outsider but also as a would-be partisan during a period in which, ironically, a person's country of birth was being superseded as a marker of fixed identity.[17] Poised on the cusp of that change in a nascent age of transnationalism, *The Tailor of Panama*'s protagonist bears more than a faint resemblance to le Carré himself as one of its leading chroniclers.

* * * * *

Published three years later, *Single & Single* explores the divided loyalties of another self-begotten protagonist, although this time he is the disaffected son of a New World Order tycoon. Towering at six feet three inches over his diminutive father, who is vaingloriously known as Tiger, lawyer Oliver Single has been groomed to join his sire's West End firm as a junior partner. Concerning this proprietary investment company in the early 1990s, leading British periodicals are fond of quoting its founder's hyperbolic rhetoric:

> Single's is the "knight errant of Gorbachev's New East"—*Financial Times*— "boldly going where lesser houses dither." Single's is the "risk-taker extraordinaire"—*Telegraph*—"quartering the nations of the new-look Communist bloc in search of opportunity, sound development and mutual profit in the spirit of perestroika"—*Independent*. . . . Single's uses "a different set of tools, is nimbler, braver, smaller, younger, travels lighter" than the hoary juggernauts of yesteryear—*Economist*. (*SS*, 108–9)

Behind all the hype, however, is an old-fashioned con man who, having "earned his spurs as a defending barrister of the oppressed criminal classes" in Liverpool (SS, 154), currently specializes in money laundering for all newcomers to a market-based global economy, especially those in the former Soviet Union such as brothers Yevgeny and Mikhail Orlov. When Oliver learns of his father's illicit profiteering, he guiltily betrays him to veteran Customs officer Nat Brock, who has been on the track of homegrown facilitators of "human wickedness" for the past twenty years (SS, 89). This liaison agent's primary quarry is Bernard Porlock, an egregiously corrupt deputy superintendent at Scotland Yard and an opportunistic recipient of Tiger's bribes. In order to prosecute Porlock as part of a widespread network (known as Hydra) in England composed of "less-than-perfect coppers and overpaid white-collar civil servants [. . . and] bent MPs and silk-shirt lawyers and dirty traders with smart addresses" (SS, 105), the crusader is willing to offer amnesty to Tiger through his son, a conscience-stricken informant, if the House of Single's figurehead can be persuaded to provide incriminating evidence against Porlock.

Oliver's recourse, filled as he is with self-reproach, involves the same line of retreat pursued by Harry Pendel. First introduced four years after turning in his father, the heir apparent has requested resettlement in the Devon countryside, where he has embraced the life of a ludic performer after a failed marriage and the birth of a daughter named Carmen. Taking up residence at Elsie Watmore's boardinghouse and befriending her fatherless ten-year-old son, Sammy, the shambling man whose alias is Ollie Hawthorne works as a children's magician at birthday parties that feature his giraffe-shaped balloons and badinage with a wisecracking stuffed raccoon named Rocco.

Notwithstanding his attempt to escape into a fantasy world of unaccountability, the House of Single's scion soon finds that he cannot evade his past when a local banker reports an anonymous donation of more than 5 million pounds sterling to Carmen's trust fund, proof that Tiger has verified his errant son's whereabouts. Stunned by this discovery and haunted by "the deadness of his soul" (SS, 77), Oliver reluctantly contacts Brock again, coincidentally at a time when the news media are reporting the gangster-style murder of Alfred Winser, "chief legal officer to the West End finance house of Single & Single" (SS, 80), on a remote hillside in Turkey. This videotaped event, the novel's opening set piece, arises from complications related to the investment firm's participation in Russia's "black economy" shortly before President Mikhail Gorbachev's overthrow in August 1991.

Looking back at this twilight phase of glasnost, le Carré makes clear that he regards it as a fleeting but squandered opportunity for the West to have exercised principled leadership in management of the world's resources. In comments to reviewer Alan Cowell, he thus acknowledges that his book revolves around an ethos linked to a failure of geopolitical vision after the Cold War's end:

> As long as we had our Great Satan, we could see ourselves in some kind of moral light. But when that was removed, we were left with our own excesses. We have to create some kind of ethical standard for ourselves—I don't believe that has happened at all—some kind of self-restraint, some acceptance that the global village is not capable of infinite expansion.[18]

He adds, "We can't just be carpetbaggers," a term that aptly describes Tiger Single in his brokered deal with the Orlov brothers when all the principals meet in London to ratify the firm's lucrative contract with, in its founder's unctuous words, "farsighted pioneers of the new Russia" (SS, 113). After this preliminary fanfare Alix Hoban, the treacherous son-in-law of Yevgeny Orlov, outlines three business proposals for which the ex-Soviets are prepared to enter a partnership with the House of Single. Totaling $80 million in advance payments, not including subsequent commissions on gross profits, these transactions involve the sale of scrap ferrous metal; Azerbaijani, Caspian, and Kazakhstani oil; and huge quantities of Russian citizens' blood to the West's "victorious imperialists" (SS, 126). The last of these exports, according to Tiger's later marketing pitch to US senators, lobbyists, and health officials, is especially valuable as a commodity because it is "*white Caucasian*" (SS, 133). The fact that news of this prospective trade in Russian blood "dazzles" influential audiences in Washington, DC, Philadelphia, and New York obviously supports le Carré's criticism of the United States for its lack of ethical integrity in transnational relations during the early 1990s.

Although the reader can appreciate the novelist's indictment of the post–Cold War West's abdication, le Carré's portrayal of the Orlov brothers tends to be romanticized. Rugged survivors of the old Soviet monolith, both Georgians are wholly devoted to establishing with their wealth, derived in part from heroin trafficking on an industrial scale, a pastoral Eden in "the promised land of Mingrelia," where they dream of uniting four contentious villages in a wine-producing cooperative (SS, 142). This project lies near the Black Sea's coast in a mountain-encircled valley that they have named, significantly, Bethlehem. Presumably because the Orlov patriarchs have, as le Carré emphasized in his conversation with Cowell, "some kind" of larger vision beyond the mere amassing of money, he casts them in a positive light. This valorization is especially evident in the profiling of Yevgeny. During the signing of a contract for Russian iron, oil, and blood in Single & Single's boardroom, for example, he signals by eye contact his sympathetic rapport with Oliver, who is wrestling with reservations about the transaction's legality.[19] Then, shortly after the deal's consummation, Oliver is dispatched as an emissary to Mingrelia, where, bonding closely with Yevgeny, he learns from his hosts that their ancestors are the fabled Argonauts. The culture of this separatist region is idealized further by Yevgeny's celebration of its indigenous people and by his financial commitment to the province's agrarian rehabilitation.

At the other end of le Carré's moral spectrum in the novel is a triad of soulless villains who are invested in nothing more than self-enrichment. These figures are the already mentioned Alix Hoban, an ex-KGB apparatchik; Randy Massingham, the roving deal maker for Tiger Single; and Adam Mirsky, a Polish lawyer who in Brock's words now operates as an international "capitalist crook" (SS, 193). Conspiring against the Orlovs, these opportunists have formed a holding company named Trans-Finanz Vienna, which seeks to extort 200 million pounds from the London investment firm for lost earnings that they themselves have engineered. One could posit that, ethically speaking, le Carré is putting us on a slippery slope, for the simple reason that if motive—in this case, the Orlov brothers' dream of establishing a self-sustaining Mingrelian enclave versus the rapacious greed of the three villains—extenuates deeds, then Harry Pendel in The Tailor of Panama cannot be held responsible for the consequences of his actions. Rather than addressing this philosophical crux, however, le Carré opts in the second half of Single & Single to focus almost exclusively on the fraught relationship between a partly loyal son and his overbearing father.

The narrative's pace noticeably quickens as le Carré weaves back and forth between story lines; these lead to a revealing climax, but some readers who enshrine his earlier fiction will inevitably dismiss the ending as manufactured. A dramatic shift occurs when Tiger Single, a "knight errant of Gorbachev's New East," is unable any longer to stave off Trans-Finanz's assault on his combined assets and flees England, whereupon Oliver leaves his safe haven in Devon to rescue his imperiled father under Nat Brock's direction. In doing so, the son once again "feels the love rise in him like old poison" (SS, 169). First Oliver visits his neurotic mother and detested childhood home at Nightingales End ("This is the grave I was born in, he thought. This is where I lived in the time before I became a child" [SS, 197]). He then traces Tiger's flight to Zurich, where the magnate recently met with Kaspar Conrad, who for years served as confidential "keeper of the company purse" (SS, 248). Learning that Conrad

had abandoned his longtime client when Trans-Finanz's takeover of Single &
Single was imminent, the protagonist next follows his father's trail to Adam
Mirsky's fortresslike mansion in Istanbul. From that city, he is informed, Tiger
was taken away to Mingrelia for the exacting of blood revenge as the person
supposedly responsible, per Alix Hoban's cunning deception, for Mikhail Orlov's death when a freighter with him on board and three tons of refined heroin
en route from Odessa to Liverpool was intercepted by maritime authorities.
The penultimate chapter, which unfolds in a barrage of short declarative sentences, attempts to convey Oliver's headlong rush to Bethlehem to save a helpless parent, demonstrating once more his ineluctable devotion.

Regarding the novel's conclusion, notoriously censorious *New York Times*
critic Michiko Kakutani charged that le Carré seemed to rely on the "crudely
manipulative techniques favored by directors of Sylvester Stallone and Arnold
Schwarzenegger movies." She asserted that the "highly implausible" final chapter "reads like a cartoony [*sic*] script for James Bond" and ended her review
with this summative verdict: "It is a singularly inappropriate punctuation point
for a novel (and, for that matter, a body of work) predicated upon psychological subtlety, hardheaded realism, meticulous knowledge of tradecraft[,] and
wonderfully human heroes like the tortured Oliver Single."[20] This broad-brush
criticism, however, overlooks an intriguing dimension of le Carré's artistry
that has nothing to do with "hardheaded realism." (It is telling that Kakutani
cites her subject's "meticulous knowledge of tradecraft"; as my introduction
to this study began by observing, this is characteristic of those who esteem
le Carré primarily for the "authenticity" of his Cold War fiction.) And that
dimension involves a redemptive glimpse of who we can be to each other as
human beings, at least potentially, rather than as the fraudulent ciphers of any
system to which we may feel a misguided allegiance.

Such a claim, bluntly stated, means that there is a qualitative difference between le Carré's early corpus and his post–Cold War oeuvre. The difference
stems from his recognition that in a transnational world no longer divided by
a simplistic ideological binary, all previous frameworks of self-identification
and commitment can be imagined anew. In support of this idea, *Single & Single*'s last chapter presents two pivotal moments that entail a validation of the
protagonist as a conjuring magus and a revelatory insight about his father.

The first of these paired vignettes begins when Oliver, having arrived at the
Orlovs' farmhouse in Mingrelia, finds a bruised, half-naked Tiger curled up
in a fetal position and chained to a stable stall's post. After succeeding in getting him released, Oliver restores his battered father's dignity by sponging him
down with water from a bucket, all the while "trying to remember when Tiger

had last done this to him when he was a child," then "deciding he never had" (*SS*, 337), and finally dressing him in his bedraggled tailor-made suit. What transpires next, contrary to Kakutani's comparison of the novel's climax to shallow action movies, is a scene that calls to mind the sacramentalism of *Babette's Feast*, Gabriel Axel's 1987 film version of a short story by Isak Dinesen (Karen Blixen). Sensitive to the occasion's precariousness, Oliver returns with his father to the farmhouse, where he seats Tiger across from Yevgeny and pours each man a glass of wine. Having created an "atmosphere of conviviality," the "prodigal returned" then devotes himself to assisting Tinatin, Yevgeny's wife, in preparing a communal meal (*SS*, 337, 338). Before the food is served, the two old men remain by the fireside, and le Carré celebrates his protagonist's feat of reconciliation:

> The magician was coming alive. The illusionist, the eternal pacifier and deflector of ridicule, the dancer on eggshells and creator of impossible karma[,] was answering the call of the footlights. The Oliver of the rainswept bus shelters, children's hospitals, and Salvation Army hostels was performing for his life and Tiger's, while Tinatin cooked, and Yevgeny half listened and counted his misfortunes in the flames, and Hoban and his fellow devils dreamed their sour mischief and pondered their dwindling options. And Oliver knew his audience. He empathized with its disarray, its stunned senses and confused allegiances. He knew how often in his own life, at its absolutely lowest moments, he would have given everything he had for one lousy conjuror with a stuffed raccoon. (*SS*, 340–41)

The passage reinforces an earlier description of "Uncle Ollie's" craft as a "magician extraordinary" when he spins his practiced prologue to children at birthday festivities in Devon. On such occasions, by the time he as the impresario has finished his banter with Rocco, le Carré records the following:

> There's a shimmer in the room by now and a shimmer in Oliver's bearing also. His flushed head is thrown back, his rich black locks fly behind him like a great conductor's, his fluid cheeks are glazed with strenuous pleasure, his eyes are clear and young again and he is laughing, and the children are laughing louder. He is the Prince of Shimmer, the unlikely rainmaker in their midst. He is a clumsy buffoon and therefore to be protected; he is a nimble god who can call down laughter, and enchant without destroying. (*SS*, 37)

Although a few elements of this tableau in Bethlehem may appear gratuitous, the scene as a whole registers the concept of *kairos*, defined in both classical rhetoric and Christian theology as the "right" or "opportune" moment when within the flow of chronological time virtually anything becomes possible.[21] This temporal interstice—or, to invoke another paradigm, Hegelian *Aufhebung*—is that in which the conjurer Oliver is able to work his magic.

The second vignette arises from the first. After the prodigal son of Tiger Single effects a tenuous rapprochement between his father and Yevgeny, "a kind of madness grew, a shared illusion of normality" (*SS*, 341). Seizing on this interlude of "madness," over dinner Oliver calmly recites the facts of Mikhail Orlov's death and Alix Hoban's culpability, meanwhile "preserving with all the vocal tricks he knew the glasslike delicacy of the illusion" (*SS*, 343). Suddenly, however, everything changes when Oliver hears the distinctive sound of helicopters overhead, sees flak-jacketed figures charging into the farmhouse, and watches Nat Brock take into custody the now humbled and submissive Tiger. Le Carré then describes his protagonist's reaction to the scene:

> What am I seeing? Oliver wondered. What am I understanding now that I didn't understand before? The answer was as clear to him as the question. That he had found it, and it didn't exist. He had arrived at the last, most hidden room of his search[;] he had prized open the most top-secret box, and it was empty. Tiger's secret was that he had no secret. (*SS*, 344–45)

Like the revelation in *The Wizard of Oz* (1939) that the seemingly supernatural being of the title is actually a humbug, *Single & Single*'s climax exposes the freewheeling tycoon, the bombastic champion of New World Order opportunism and unbridled capitalism, as a vacuous poseur. In discovering this fact about his father, Oliver achieves an emotional independence that will enable him to chart a course in life other than the one previously scripted for him as Tiger's dutiful protégé and eventual successor.

If this dimension of le Carré's novel, which I have characterized as redemptive, strikes some readers as "highly implausible," in Kakutani's words, such a judgment depends largely on what they have decided to expect from his fiction. Those inclined to regard his Cold War corpus as definitive—indeed, almost statutory—are usually the same people who view him as a master "spy novelist," thereby pigeonholing le Carré as a genre author. In contrast, those who credit his objections to the superficiality of such literary branding will be sensitive to how le Carré's later oeuvre responds to a new era in world affairs.

When, even more so than before, the balance of things is weighted heavily in favor of exploitative economic systems and political institutions over hapless individuals, he invariably endorses the latter group, including their ability to play the role of *homo ludens*.

Greene's *Our Man in Havana* is the primary source for two different notions of madness in *The Tailor of Panama* and *Single & Single*. The first involves the conventional idea of insanity, such as when Greene writes of "a mad world" that during the height of the Cold War's nuclear standoff is preoccupied with testing a "new H-bomb on Christmas Island."[22] For that reason the protagonist is advised by his friend Dr. Hasselbacher, a veteran of World War I, that "reality in our century is not something to be faced."[23] In three books written during the 1960s, "antipsychiatrist" R. D. Laing argued the same point by maintaining that schizophrenia is at root a defensive response to a deranged milieu or culture.

Our Man in Havana presciently charts this kind of madness by having London's foreign-intelligence chief credit the bogus field reports of James Wormold, Agent 59200/5, on military installations in Cuba, even though he suspects that one of the drawings resembles the schematics of a vacuum cleaner. (The latest model that Wormold sells in his shop has the gimmicky trade name Atomic Pile Suction Cleaner.) In *The Tailor of Panama* there is a parallel example of institutional madness on the part of espionage agencies. When during his recruitment Harry Pendel confides his financial straits by saying, "There's no way out that *I* know of to save me, short of a mad millionaire," Andrew Osnard as MI6's representative responds, "Maybe my outfit's mad enough" (*TP*, 67). And so it quickly proves to be.

The other side of this exposure to the psychopathology of manipulative institutions is that the individuals whose services they enlist become infected by the contagion of fiction-mongering. For example, after Wormold signs on as Agent 59200/5 he begins, like Pendel, to invent a colorful cast of rebels that satisfies London headquarters' expectation of a looming insurgency. Perhaps not coincidentally, while celebrating his daughter Milly's seventeenth birthday at the Tropicana shortly before the novel's midpoint, he hears a cabaret ditty that Greene repeats three times as a leitmotif in the last half of *Our Man in Havana*:

> Sane men surround
> You, old family friends.
> They say the earth is round—
> My madness offends.

An orange has pips, they say[,]
And an apple has rind.
I say that night is day
And I've no axe to grind.[24]

The refrain seems to intimate that Wormold is being compromised by his involvement with England's Secret Intelligence Service, which pays him to communicate with his handler through old-fashioned book codes, write in invisible ink, and file weekly reports on a nonexistent Communist plot against Cuban dictator Fulgencio Batista. The ultimate folly of SIS is revealed in an epilogue after the protagonist realizes, pursuant to Dr. Hasselbacher's murder, for which he is indirectly responsible, that "falsity was an occupational disease."[25] The chief is at a loss about how to punish Wormold for his deceptions ("They could hardly charge him under the Official Secrets Act" because "he had invented secrets[;] he hadn't given them away").[26] Removing a monocle from his baby-blue glass eye, he decides to cover his operational myopia by appointing the former vacuum-cleaner salesman in Havana as a training-staff lecturer and recommending the conferral of an OBE, or Order of the British Empire. Given such blandishments, Beatrice Severn, formerly James Wormold's SIS-dispatched assistant and now his fiancée, worries in the novel's final line that "he would never be quite mad enough."[27]

The second paradigm of madness in Greene's 1958 novel that anticipates both le Carré's *The Tailor of Panama* and *Single & Single* is implicit in an early comment by the unidentified third-person narrator:

The cruel come and go like cities and thrones and powers, leaving their ruins behind them. They had no permanence. But the clown whom he [Wormold] had seen last year with Milly at the circus—that clown was permanent, for his act never changed. That was the way to live; the clown was unaffected by the vagaries of public men.[28]

Harry Pendel's failure as a "born impersonator" begins when in agreeing to become an intelligence source named Buchan for MI6, he imagines that he can reshape the lives of others without adverse consequences befalling them. His motives as a *homo faber* may be well-intentioned, but Pendel underestimates the corporate madness of those who are the primary audience for his inventions. That miscalculation, in turn, is related to why this protagonist's epiphany upon finding Mickie Abraxas's corpse in Guararé strikes me as equivocal. In contrast, Oliver Single recognizes the moral bankruptcy of his father's investment firm and betrays its practices rather than remaining complicit in them. That he should then, as self-deprecating "Uncle Ollie," take up the life of a ludic clown attests to his integrity and his longing for what Greene terms "permanence." The novel's concluding scene in the Orlovs' farmhouse affirms the healing magic involved in his choice, even though it cannot keep at bay the external forces that are intent on reprisal and a final settling of accounts.

Whether le Carré deliberately wrote *Single & Single* as an emendation or a refinement of *The Tailor of Panama* is impossible to know with absolute certainty, but in both texts he explores the options of creative and essentially conscientious individuals who are confronted with institutionalized forms of New World Order madness. Nowhere in these novels of the late 1990s is there even a fugitive glimpse, in President George H. W. Bush's formulation, of "A world where the rule of law supplants the rule of the jungle. A world in which nations recognize the shared responsibility for freedom and justice. A world where the strong respect the rights of the weak." Instead, this laudable ethical vision is nullified by the persistence of binary structures of thinking that have been molded by nearly half a century of ideological suspicion and paranoia.

Brian Morton's review of *Single & Single*, not to denigrate le Carré's achievement in *The Tailor of Panama*, concludes by averring that the follow-up narrative "puts le Carré . . . beyond the tortuous dialectic of the Cold War for good."[29] I could not agree more. After the publication of his seventeenth novel, which seems to resolve once and for all the ambiguities that complicate father-son relationships, le Carré moves on to address the global ramifications of the West's decades-long habit of profiteering from Third World nations' plight. This quantum shift in his oeuvre commences with *The Constant Gardener*. Though not pursued consistently until *A Most Wanted Man, Our Kind of Traitor*, and *A Delicate Truth*, the thematic realignment signals an advance in his fiction that distinguishes him as one of the most important ethicists among contemporary writers.

3

THE CONSTANT GARDENER AND *ABSOLUTE FRIENDS*

"Whoever Owns the Truth Owns the Game"

Do governments run countries anymore? Do presidents run governments? In the [C]old [W]ar, the right side lost but the wrong side won, said a Berlin wit. For the blink of a star, back there in the early nineties, something wonderful might have happened: a Marshall Plan, a generous reconciliation of old enemies, a remaking of alliances and, for the Third and Fourth Worlds, a commitment to take on the world's real enemies: starvation, plague, poverty, ecological devastation, despotism, and colonialism by all its other names.

But that wishful dream supposed that enlightened nations spoke as enlightened nations, not as the hired mouthpieces of multibillion-dollar multinational corporations that view the exploitation of the world's sick and dying as a sacred duty to their shareholders.

—John le Carré, "In Place of Nations"

BOTH OF THE novels discussed in the preceding chapter contain largely incidental examples of the news media's far-reaching power to shape public opinion. *The Tailor of Panama*, as noted, draws attention to the success of Ben Hatry's journalistic "empire" in exerting an "ever-growing stranglehold on the hearts and minds" of impoverished nations while stoking the fires of reaction against the perceived threat of globalization (*TP*, 242). Extending le Carré's mordant criticism there that "nothing is more predictable than the media's parroting of its own fictions" (*TP*, 241), *Single & Single* highlights the readiness of leading British periodicals to trumpet Tiger's boasts as the founder of a commercial firm willing to invest in "a market-oriented Soviet Union" (*SS*, 109). In le Carré's next two novels after the millennium's turn, the broadly propagandistic function of media is central to his now overtly political fiction. The key to this development in his corpus is the premise that "whoever owns" the putative "truth" about world crises "owns the game" (*AF*, 324).

This shift in le Carré's oeuvre is captured by his tirade in the *Nation* on April 9, 2001, part of which is quoted above as the epigraph, that First World countries with a vested interest in overseas exploitation have become the "hired mouthpieces" of "multibillion-dollar . . . corporations." Because this topical piece was published three months after the release of *The Constant Gardener* and begins by historically contextualizing the issue, it deserves closer examination.

"In Place of Nations" launches its excoriation of the pharmaceutical industry by establishing a geopolitical framework that enabled gross profiteering and market manipulation at a time of rampant AIDS infection in Africa:

> Times have changed since the [C]old [W]ar, but not half as much as we might like to think. The cold war provided the perfect excuse for Western governments to plunder and exploit the Third World in the name of freedom; to rig its elections, bribe its politicians, appoint its tyrants and, by every sophisticated means of persuasion and interference, stunt the emergence of young democracies in the name of democracy.
>
> And while they did this—whether in Southeast Asia, Central and South America[,] or Africa—a ludicrous notion took root that we are saddled with to this day. It is a notion beloved of conservatives and, in my country, New Labour alike. It makes Siamese twins of Tony Blair, Margaret Thatcher, Ronald Reagan, Bill Clinton[,] and George W. Bush. It holds to its bosom the conviction that, whatever vast commercial corporations do in the short term, they are ultimately motivated by ethical concerns, and their influence upon the world is therefore beneficial. And anyone who thinks otherwise is a neo-Communist heretic.[1]

This broadside makes le Carré's polemical voice abundantly clear in protesting how covert political interventionism during the Cold War led to a subsequent delusion that global business enterprises are guided by philanthropic motives. Explaining why he singled out Big Pharma in his eighteenth novel for an indictment of the "crimes of unbridled capitalism," le Carré cites the industry's monopolistic practices in the patenting process and its suborning of research testimony in medical journals. Crediting the efforts of a few valiant researchers for the *Washington Post* and the *New York Times* in advocating necessary reforms, he ends by remarking that "the sales of just one pharma giant, Pfiz-er, amounted last year to $29.6 billion and its profits to $3.7 billion." Nearly matching this sales figure but outdistancing Pfizer in terms of profitability, le Carré adds, "GlaxoSmithKline did even better, with lower sales of $27.5 billion and greater profits of $5.6 billion. And it's all for love of mankind."[2]

Sourced textual evidence on this issue proliferates throughout *The Constant Gardener*'s middle section (chapters 11–14), but initially the narrative takes shape as a detective mystery in which the dialogical give-and-take of interro-gation predominates. Two young officers from Scotland Yard's Overseas Crime Division are trying to discover who is responsible for the grisly murder of Tes-sa Abbott Quayle, a white activist for Kenyans' postcolonial rights and the wife of career Foreign Office diplomat Justin Quayle. Before this inquiry begins, le Carré records the press's predictable sensationalizing of her death: "'Bush Killers Slay British Envoy's Wife' ran the first reports, . . . written upward for the broadsheets and downward for the tabloids" (*CG*, 51). However, because Tessa was a close friend of Dr. Arnold Bluhm, her charismatic Congolese ally in relief work who had accompanied Tessa in investigating an outbreak of tu-berculosis on the eastern shore of Lake Turkana, racist suspicion begins to fall on him as the supposed killer. While efforts are being made to locate Bluhm, the slain activist becomes fodder for media reportage as

> . . . the Society Girl Turned Oxbridge Lawyer, the Princess Diana of the Af-rican Poor, the Mother Teresa of the Nairobi Slums[,] and the FO [Foreign Office] Angel Who Gave a Damn. An editorial in the *Guardian* made much of the fact that the Millennium's New Woman Diplomat should have met her death at [Richard] Leakey's cradle of mankind, and drew from this the disquieting moral that, though racial attitudes may change, we cannot plumb the wells of savagery that are to be found at the heart of every man's darkness. (*CG*, 52)

Pursuant to this reductive typecasting of the victim, "just as the press was run-ning out of steam, a Belgian daily ran a front-page story accusing Tessa and Bluhm of 'a passionate liaison'" on the eve of her murder. Parasitically extrap-olating from the flimsiest of circumstantial details, the Fleet Street hacks waste no time in stigmatizing Dr. Bluhm as a "seducer," "adulterer," "maniac," and "archetypal black killer" (*CG*, 55). Amid this gathering storm of lurid public-ity, the British High Commission in Nairobi receives a newsletter devoted to "rak[ing] mud regardless of race, color, truth or the consequences" that claims to unveil, in the wake of Tessa Quayle's murder, the Foreign Office's enabling of President Daniel Arap Moi's systematic corruption in Kenya (*CG*, 56).

All this media fallout, laced as it is with the rhetoric of scandal-mongering, indirectly impedes the Scotland Yard detectives' discovery of pertinent facts in the case. When they interview Sandy Woodrow, the head of chancery adept in "sleek evasions" (*CG*, 137), he prevaricates in order to keep the investigators from learning about two documents related to his personal involvement with Tessa. The first is a brief letter, written incongruously on "one insignificant sheet of Her Majesty's Stationery Office blue" (*CG*, 46–47), declaring his infatuation with the attractive activist and absurdly proposing elopement. The other text is an eighteen-page exposé that Tessa had entrusted to Woodrow for transmission to Sir Bernard Pellegrin, the Foreign Office's permanent undersecretary in London "with special responsibility for Africa" (*CG*, 22–23). Because Tessa's carefully researched treatise substantiated the malfeasance of diversified conglomerate Bell, Barker & Benjamin, better known as ThreeBees, in using Kenyans as guinea pigs for an antitubercular drug called Dypraxa before the clinical risks were fully verified, both Woodrow and Pellegrin connive in having it destroyed upon receipt. Their common motive for doing so is self-interested advancement: Woodrow wishes to curry favor with Pellegrin as a replacement for Porter Coleridge, the current high commissioner in Nairobi, and Pellegrin hopes to ingratiate himself with Sir Kenneth K. Curtiss, the CEO of ThreeBees, for a munificent appointment after his early retirement from public service.

The next round of interrogation by Scotland Yard agents is with Justin Quayle, recounted in flashback during his flight back to London immediately after his wife's interment in an African cemetery near the poverty-stricken slums of Kibera. Unlike the answers of "status quo man" Sandy Woodrow (*CG*, 45), Justin's responses to the detectives' questions are straightforward and candid, even though he knows that the detectives must entertain the possibility of his complicity in a contract killing based on Tessa's unconventionally close friendship with Arnold Bluhm. Quayle's answers differ from his supervisor's evasions in one other respect. Besides having nothing to hide, Justin freely admits that he failed his politically committed wife by "detaching [him]self" and "letting her go it alone" (*CG*, 124). Le Carré's protagonist is an "Old Etonian" (*CG*, 52), signifying the privileged class from which Her Majesty's Foreign Office was in the habit of recruiting its cadre of professional personnel, so this confession amounts to a decisive break with all his previous conditioning. In his career to date Justin had been trained to espouse a philosophy of "lofty nihilism": "Until now he had regarded strongly held convictions as the natural enemies of the diplomat, to be ignored, humored or, like dangerous energy, diverted into harmless channels. Now to his surprise he saw them as emblems of courage and Tessa as their standard-bearer" (*CG*, 133). This moral awakening on the part of Justin, "a well-dressed sleepwalker who had abdicated his sense of destination" (*CG*, 21), shatters all of his earlier preconceptions.

At this point in *The Constant Gardener*'s tapestry of forensic testimony, le Carré introduces an earlier cross-examination of Justin Quayle's personal beliefs. Invited a few years ago by Sir Bernard Pellegrin's lackeys to read his vacuous lecture on "Law and the Administered Society" to aspiring lawyers enrolled in a Cambridge summer seminar during its author's last-minute summons to Washington, DC, Justin was pressed by Tessa in the question-and-answer session afterward to "imagine a situation where you personally would feel obliged to *undermine* the state" (*CG*, 127). Although the recently returned emissary from Bosnia temporizes at first, he quickly comes to her rescue when he detects the conservative audience belittling Tessa's question. Justin suppresses peer ridicule of his interrogator by saying the following:

> You *have* put your finger on precisely the issue that literally none of us in the international community knows how to answer. Who *are* the white hats? What *is* an ethical foreign policy? All right. Let's agree that what joins the better nations these days is some notion of humanistic liberalism. But what *divides* us is precisely the question you ask: [W]hen does a supposedly humanistic state become unacceptably repressive? What happens when it threatens our national interests? (*CG*, 129)

Articulated in this passage are the queries around which, in one way or another, all of le Carré's post–Cold War fiction revolves. The novel's unidentified narrator, best described as a dispersed and ventriloquistic consciousness, characterizes Justin's rejoinder as "metaphysical fluff," which indicates only the protagonist's adherence at this juncture to a Foreign Office mentality. If Tessa, in his estimation, "doesn't know how the game is played" (*CG*, 131), Justin Quayle knows only too well, and what attracts him irresistibly to the young lawyer is her integrity and independence. However the career diplomat might conceive of himself as "a fully paid-up pessimist" (*CG*, 133), in other words, he recognizes a moral alternative to the discursive conceits, circumlocutions, and lies by which the establishment he serves tries to justify its transnational policies. Justin thus hovers on the brink of discovering his existential authenticity, a journey that the rest of *The Constant Gardener* traces.

Quayle's responses not only to Scotland Yard detectives but also to his future wife contrast sharply with the hollow rhetoric typical of the bureaucratic world in which he has been immersed for most of his adult life. Le Carré amply documents babble of this kind. One example comes through the distinctly neurotic voice of Gloria Woodrow, the neglected wife of Nairobi's head of chancery. Once she and Sandy have sequestered Justin in the ground-floor quarters of their suburban home after the news of Tessa's death, the novelist mimics Gloria's breathless telephone conversation with her friend Elena:

> But at least the poor man would have his aloneness, which everybody absolutely *had* to have when they lost someone, El, and Gloria herself had been *exactly* the same when Mummy died, but then of course Tessa and Justin did have—well, they did have an *unconventional* marriage, if one could call it that—though speaking for herself Gloria had never doubted there was real fondness there, at least on Justin's side, though what there was on Tessa's side—frankly, El darling, God alone knows, because none of *us* ever will. (CG, 29)

Such rambling effusions, punctuated here by false emphases, typify what Martin Heidegger termed *Gerede*, usually translated as "idle talk" or "chatter."[3] The speech patterns of Gloria Woodrow, "famously loquacious, especially when there wasn't much to say" (CG, 29), stand in sharp counterpoint to the incisiveness of Tessa's retort to Gloria's womanizing husband when he fatuously asks on behalf of British business interests in Kenya, "How can we help a poor country if we're not rich ourselves?" (CG, 43): "Specious, unadulterated, pompous Foreign Office bullshit, if you want its full name, worthy of the inestimable Pellegrin himself. Look around you. Trade isn't making the poor rich. Profits don't buy reforms. They buy corrupt government officials and Swiss bank accounts" (CG, 44).

Shortly after his wife's murder Justin Quayle is faced with his employer's insistence on appropriating the files of Tessa's investigative research and is taught a forceful lesson in the mendacity of his chosen profession. The three functionaries who attempt to confiscate Tessa's trove of raw data, preposterously claiming that it constitutes intellectual property to which the Foreign Office is entitled, are Sandy Woodrow, Alison Landsbury, and Bernard Pellegrin, all of whom pitch their cases in comparably disingenuous fashion. The most maladroit of this group is Justin's field supervisor, Woodrow, who summarily invokes "rules of confidentiality" and "Pellegrin's order" as binding constraints (CG, 71). The next to ply him is Landsbury, the head of personnel in London, who after sham condolences reminiscent of Gloria

Woodrow's saccharine way of expressing her sentiments adopts a "frigid managerial stare" and, criticizing Tessa for "*meddling*," bluntly insists that the bereaved husband surrender his wife's laptop computer (*CG*, 173, 175). The last to weigh in over an expensive lunch at his club after Quayle's meeting with Landsbury is Sir Bernard. Affecting his customary "decent chap's image" (*CG*, 178), Pellegrin pretends to commiserate but soon lapses into his truncated style of "High Tory telegramese" in order to secure possession of "so-called confidential information that you shouldn't have—in your head or anywhere else—it belongs to us, not you" (*CG*, 182, 188). All these face-to-face interactions, le Carré comments, amount to a "master class in sophistry" (*CG*, 188).

From this point on *The Constant Gardener* presents more tangled skeins of textual evidence as Justin Quayle emerges from his somnolent state of being "*totally* loyal to London guidance" and questions the compromises by which he has negotiated his comfortable existence (*CG*, 77). Under the alias of Peter Paul Atkinson, supposedly a *Daily Telegraph* reporter, Justin makes his way from England to his wife's villa on the Mediterranean island of Elba. There, with the assistance of a precocious twelve-year-old Albanian refugee whom Tessa had taken under her wing, he begins to trawl through a voluminous cache of information in the form of press clippings, handwritten notes, email correspondence, solicitors' letters, unbiased scholarship, and extracts from medical journals that Tessa had used to compile the exposé she sent to Sir Kenneth Curtiss. Both the protagonist and le Carré's readers thus become accomplices in reconstructing the steps by which Tessa Abbott Quayle ferreted out a transnational violation of human rights.[4]

That process of collaborative detection becomes the avenue by which we are invited to participate in a vicarious project of radicalization. In a trenchant article on Fernando Meirelles's 2005 film version of *The Constant Gardener*, which hews closely to the novel, Todd McGowan contends that because of his willingness to track down the institutional forces behind his wife's murder, Justin escapes from his cocoon of ideological subservience and hazards the plunge into "a temporality of the real."[5] Such an ontological reorientation, maintains this critic, involves the individual's acceptance of his or her *Dasein* in its authentic attitude of "Being-towards-death."[6] Quayle's spiritual journey commences when he can no longer tolerate the artifices by which the Foreign Office tries to suppress discovery of the truth about Tessa's final days. He therefore ventures out beyond the pale of his circumscribed life as his employer's British representative on the East African Donors' Effectiveness

Committee and as an expert gardener absorbed by the challenges of growing yellow freesias in Nairobi's scorching climate. Once he learns that Tessa's
murder was "a corporate job" (*CG*, 84), le Carré's protagonist commits himself unsparingly to investigating why she was targeted for assassination.

The next stage of Justin's moral development comes when he interviews a
researcher in Germany who had provided his wife with incriminating information about Karel Vita Hudson (KVH), the manufacturer of Dypraxa, and
learns that former KVH-ThreeBees intermediary Markus Lorbeer informed
both companies of Tessa's inquiries into their dispensing the drug in Africa.
For that discovery Quayle is savagely beaten by unknown assailants. Pursuant
to this reprisal, which in his mind means that he has "*passed the exam I've
been shirking all my life*" (*CG*, 321), a convalescent Justin flies from Zurich to
Winnipeg after he has become "conscious of a dawning sense of his own completion" (*CG*, 344). The first of only two references to the concept of existential
"completion" (the second appearing on the novel's final page), the term suggests that he has now succeeded in acquiring a sense of meaningful purpose
and engagement.

In this regard we should note that Quayle's subsequent actions become far
more intentional than was the case earlier. In Saskatchewan, for instance, no
longer believing in himself "and all I stood for" (*CG*, 346), Justin searchingly
interrogates Dr. Lara Emrich, once a partner in KVH's production of Dypraxa,
whose reluctant revelations about her ex-lover Lorbeer then direct Quayle
back to Africa's heartland. Soon after, while being sought by the Foreign Office in Kenya as a renegade to the cause he once abetted, the former career
diplomat elicits a full confession from Sandy Woodrow about Pellegrin's suppression of Tessa's exposé. Despite being forewarned by Tim Donohue, MI6's
station head at the Nairobi embassy, that "whatever it is you're looking for,
you won't find it, but that won't prevent you from getting killed" (*CG*, 429), le
Carré's protagonist pursues his quest to its ineluctable end.

The last stage of Justin Quayle's odyssey takes him to a confrontation with
Markus Lorbeer and then to the site of his wife's murder. Although informed
by Donohue that the deposed Porter Coleridge is championing his cause in
London, so that if Justin returns there he "might *just* be able to tip the balance" by testifying before the Ethical Trials Committee of the World Health
Organization (*CG*, 431), he is guided instead by a more fundamental accountability to Tessa. En route to where she was killed, Justin compels the guilt-
haunted religious fanatic Lorbeer, now salving his conscience by serving as a
famine-relief worker in Sudan, to admit his betrayal of both Tessa and Bluhm
to KVH-ThreeBees. The confession of this Lutheran pietist's son is a classic

example of what Jean-Paul Sartre calls *mauvaise foi*, or "bad faith," indicating Lorbeer's self-deceiving belief that he was merely a victim of circumstances beyond his control and therefore incapable of exercising independent choice.[7] Having won a moral victory by forcing Lorbeer to recognize his complicit role in Tessa's death, her husband flies to Lake Turkana's eastern shore.

There he realizes the liberating efficacy of what Heidegger designates as *Gelassenheit*. Because the concept derives from one of the philosopher's less well-known texts, some background may prove helpful. His *Discourse on Thinking* (1959) encompasses a "Memorial Address," delivered in 1955, and "Conversation on a Country Path about Thinking," written in 1944–1945. The former postulates "two kinds of thinking, each justified and needed in its own way: calculative thinking and meditative thinking." Analytical, restless, outcome-oriented, and scientific, calculative thinking "never collects itself" to contemplate "the meaning which reigns in everything that is." In contrast, meditative thinking, which Heidegger associates with "rootedness," is characterized by a willingness "not to cling one-sidedly to a single idea" and by two other traits: "releasement toward things" and an "openness to the mystery."[8]

The "Conversation" demonstrates heuristically a revitalized way of thinking. Couched in an open-ended exchange involving a scientist, a scholar, and a teacher, this section evolves as "hermeneutical circles that are nourished *by* the dialogue itself. The dialogue, that is, the *interplay* between the interlocutors, shows the movement and counter-movement" that constitute "the experience of *Gelassenheit*."[9] The "Conversation" thereby suggests that "releasement" proceeds only from embracing one's temporal finitude while accepting a "non-willing" negation of self that recognizes a "higher[-]acting" agency.[10] This essentially religious tenet, which Heidegger took from the Christian mystical tradition of Meister Eckhart, is related to the previously noted stance of "Being-towards-death" that contrasts sharply with the inauthentic posturing of Sandy and Gloria Woodrow, Alison Landsbury, and Sir Bernard Pellegrin.

The Constant Gardener's closing tableau dramatizes its protagonist's hard-won achievement of *Gelassenheit*. After forcing Lorbeer to admit responsibility for Tessa's assassination by corporate hirelings, Justin travels to the place of her death, a Kenyan region vulnerable to marauding Sudanese tribesmen, Ugandan and Somalian bandits, and Muslim extremists intent on seizing control of scarce natural resources. While at this matrix of violence for historically disenfranchised populations and in meditative communion with her spirit, Quayle hears the approaching sounds of Tessa's killers. As they close in on him, le Carré writes, "Although he had been expecting something of the kind ever since he had returned to Nairobi—even in a remote way wishing for it, and had therefore regarded Donohue's warning to him as superfluous—he greeted the sight with an extraordinary sense of exultation, not to say completion" (*CG*, 476–77). This ending, rather than signifying a passive suicide, implies that Justin has attained the centered equipoise of initiation into the freedom of fully realized accountability. What he has remained faithful to is not only his wife's political code of values but also an "openness to the mystery," in Heidegger's phrase, that characterizes authentic Being.

If this coda invites interpretation as an individual triumph, it is yet overwritten by the reifying power of textuality and developments reported in the media. Le Carré thus begins his novel's conclusion with the following sardonic comment:

> Out of the finely steered gossip of Whitehall and Westminster; out of parroted television sound bites and misleading images; out of the otiose minds of journalists whose duty to inquire extended no further than the nearest deadline and the nearest free lunch, a chapter of events was added to the sum of minor human history. (*CG*, 462)

Regarding the key figures behind the quashing of Tessa Abbott Quayle's investigative research on Big Pharma's exploits in Africa, le Carré includes several press disclosures: Sandy Woodrow, "contrary to established practice," soon succeeded the discredited Porter Coleridge as British high commissioner in Nairobi, and an indigenous newspaper ironically acclaimed him "A Quiet Force for Understanding"; Bernard Pellegrin was appointed to a "senior managerial post" with KVH because of his "fabled skills at networking"; and the "latter-day Houdini" of London, Sir Kenneth Curtiss, was elevated to the House of Lords after a face-saving dissolution of ThreeBees (*CG*, 462, 463). All these headlines and manufactured representations confirm the postulate that "whoever owns the truth owns the game."

Meanwhile, Justin Quayle is calumniated as a husband who, "deranged by grief and despair" on supposedly learning that "his trusted friend Arnold Bluhm was also his wife's murderer," committed suicide by firing one round of "an assassin's short-barreled .38 pistol" into his head (*CG*, 464). So ends the public record concerning the novel's principal characters. Le Carré provides a tenuous glimmer of hope that the ensconced manipulators of truth might eventually be tarnished by the release of the evidentiary documents that Justin mailed to Tessa's uncle throughout his quest.

The permanent government of England, on which her transient politicians spin and posture like so many table dancers, had once more done its duty: except, that is, in one small but irritating respect. Justin, it seemed, had spent the last weeks of his life composing a "black dossier" purporting to prove that Tessa and Bluhm had been murdered for knowing too much about the evil dealings of one of the world's most prestigious pharmaceutical companies, which so far had contrived to remain anonymous. (*CG*, 464)

Rather than confirming the outcome of parliamentary and judicial inquiries into the matter, though, le Carré writes that "a string of cross-petitions by . . . lawyers ensured that the case would run for years" (*CG*, 466).

Viewed from a broad perspective, *The Constant Gardener* explores the human costs of corporate greed and the unethical compromises it inspires. Given le Carré's empathy for Third and Fourth World countries as beleaguered victims of "colonialism by all its other names," per this chapter's epigraph, it is therefore ironic that in his eighteenth novel Africa and its people constitute a largely mute backdrop for a white Eurocentric drama of personal transformation. Nowhere in the narrative, for example, is Dr. Arnold Bluhm, "the Westerner's African" and reportedly an eloquent orator at the United Nations on "medical priorities in disaster situations" (*CG*, 23), heard to speak on his own behalf. Also deprived of a voice is Wanza, "surname unknown" (*CG*, 140), a young Kenyan woman who before dying from the deleterious side effects of Dypraxa gives birth to a child in Uhuru Hospital that Tessa breastfeeds after her own son Garth's stillborn delivery. Such silencing of the few Africans singled out for identification in the novel brings to mind Chinua Achebe's landmark and widely anthologized critique of Joseph Conrad's *Heart of Darkness* titled "An Image of Africa."

Recognizing these and other lacunae, Diana Adesola Mafe points out certain archetypes that surface in le Carré's "mise-en-scène of Africa." Foremost among them is the depiction of Tessa Abbott Quayle as the totemic White Queen or White Goddess who, in such vignettes as her suckling Wanza's fatally ill son Baraka, becomes a "default model of white normativity." Although Mafe concedes that in portraying Dr. Arnold Bluhm as secretly gay le Carré departs from the stereotype of the Dangerous African Male, she concludes that "the underlying problem with *The Constant Gardener* is precisely its dominant representation of Africans as victims, either of the West or of each other."[11]

This critic's point about the replication of archetypes is well-taken, but she neglects to take into consideration le Carré's appalled reaction to the discoveries that he, like his protagonist, made while researching Big Pharma's transnational practices. In a note appended to the novel, for instance, he admits, "As my journey through the pharmaceutical jungle progressed, I came to realize that, by comparison with the reality, my story was as tame as a holiday postcard" (*CG*, 480). The quotation's simile could be wrested out of context to suggest that le Carré is yet another Western writer who exploits the *idea* of Africa as an exoticized construct of Otherness, but to read *The Constant Gardener* this way would be to ignore its larger import as part of the author's post–Cold War corpus—namely, his mounting outrage at the politically ratified deceptions by which corporations, under the pretense of humanitarian outreach, take capitalistic advantage of the emerging phenomenon of globalization.

Nine months after the novel's release came the tragedy of 9/11. On October 13, only thirty-two days later, le Carré published in Toronto's *Globe and Mail* a prediction titled "We Have Already Lost." While agreeing that "Osama bin Laden and his awful men . . . must be hunted down," the article also included a prescient observation:

> It's not a new world order, not yet, and it's not God's war. It's a horrible, necessary, humiliating police action to redress the failure of our intelligence services and our blind political stupidity in arming and exploiting fanatics to fight the Soviet invader, then abandoning them to a devastated, leaderless country. As a result, it's our miserable duty to seek out and punish a bunch of modern medieval religious zealots who will gain mythic stature from the very death we propose to dish out to them.
>
> And when it's over, it won't be over. The shadowy bin Laden armies, in the emotional aftermath of his destruction, will gather numbers rather than wither away.

At the time of my writing this, the major powers that backed President George W. Bush's Coalition of the Willing in 2003 find themselves scouring the Middle East for Arab partners to oppose the Islamic State of Iraq and Syria (ISIS), reportedly repudiated even by Al Qaeda for its nihilistic extremism. Nor is it accidental that thousands of recruits to this organization are said to be citizens of the same Western nations who, disenchanted with a prevailing culture of hedonistic materialism, have aligned themselves with the latest embodiment of a far sterner set of priorities. "And when it's over," presaged le Carré, "it won't be over." If nothing else, his bold prognosis of October 2001, when few if any other writers of his stature were going on record with the same opinion, indicates le Carré's canny awareness of the intimate connection between First World governments' intervention in subaltern countries' affairs and its repercussions years later in a fully realized environment of transnationalism.

* * * * *

While momentum was gathering for the invasion of Iraq, le Carré was still drafting *Absolute Friends*.[12] On January 15, 2003, he contributed to the *Times of London* a blistering diatribe titled "The United States of America Has Gone Mad." Contending that the deflection by "Bush and his junta" of "America's anger from bin Laden to Saddam Hussein was one of the great public[-]relations conjuring tricks of history"—a description recalling tropes woven throughout *The Tailor of Panama* and *Single & Single*—he begins by proposing that this recrudescence of US "historical madness" is "the worst I can remember: worse than McCarthyism, worse than the Bay of Pigs[,] and in the long term potentially more disastrous than the Vietnam War." Le Carré's second paragraph then indicts a collusion between media and corporations in promoting another "colonialist adventure":

> The reaction to 9/11 is beyond anything Osama bin Laden could have hoped for in his nastiest dreams. As in McCarthy times, the freedoms that have made America the envy of the world are being systematically eroded. The combination of compliant US media and vested corporate interests is once more ensuring that a debate that should be ringing out in every town square is confined to the loftier columns of the East Coast press.

Bridging his critique in *The Constant Gardener* of Big Pharma's exploitation of Africans and his theme in *Absolute Friends* that bonds of personal commitment take precedence over contrived political demarcations between "Absolute Good and Absolute Evil," the newspaper article anticipates the overtly polemical tenor of his nineteenth novel's final 150 pages. Reviewers were divided about how to appraise this new register in le Carré's fiction, which his detractors regarded as violating the aesthetic integrity of his work.

Jeanne A. LeBlanc, for example, asserted that *Absolute Friends* demonstrated le Carré's "increasingly tendentious" stance in his allegedly unsubtle corpus of post–Cold War fiction.[13] The more celebrated *New York Times* critic Michiko Kakutani summarily declared the work "didactic" and "ridiculously contrived."[14] Other voices expressed the same negative judgment. Writing for the

Guardian, Steven Poole, while lauding the novel's bravura opening, criticized it as "an angry disquisition on contemporary geopolitics" that indulged in "strident editorialising."[15] And in London's *Sunday Telegraph* George Walden pronounced *Absolute Friends* "ham-fisted" because of its "simplistic political opinions."[16]

At the same time, le Carré's new book won over an equal number of admirers, among the most discerning of whom were Robert McCrum and Philip Hensher. In the *Observer*, refusing to concede any inherent incompatibility between an author's convictions and the representation of a protagonist's historically shaped experience, specifically a weariness with flawed ideologies of all stripes, McCrum posited that "few could fail to be thrilled by the unbridled rage that fuels his storytelling. If he was seething when he wrote *The Constant Gardener*, he is now incandescent."[17] Hensher concurred. Beginning his review for the *Spectator* with an incisive insight into spy novels' "obsessive grip on our imagination, even after the end of the Cold War" (a point to which I shall return in this study's conclusion), he maintained that *Absolute Friends* was "certainly among le Carré's best" tales.[18]

What, then, can be said about this polarization of opinion? One obvious answer is that the anti-American rancor dispersed throughout the novel but heavily concentrated in its last third elicited divergent responses along political lines at a time of tremendous upheaval and insecurity worldwide. Without dismissing the possibility of such partisanship as a contributing factor, a more probing analysis would take into consideration three other facets of le Carré's narrative.

The first involves the text's compositional history (see note 12). Le Carré told an interviewer that "*Absolute Friends* did not just pop out of a box but came quite naturally from the other books. . . . The source of my despair is that of somebody who was engaged in the Cold War seeing everything come round again."[19] The closing words of his statement are echoed within the novel itself toward the beginning of chapter 11, the point at which le Carré resumed work on his manuscript shortly before the March 2003 invasion of Iraq. Asking "what had happened" to his now politically incensed protagonist Ted Mundy at age fifty-six "that hadn't happened before," the author writes, "It's old man's impatience coming on early. It's anger at *seeing the show come round again* one too many times" (*AF*, 301; emphasis added). The phrase I have italicized crops up again in slightly altered form in an interview on February 4, 2004. In response to a question about life's incomprehensibility, le Carré replied as follows:

I still find it a mystery. At my age, it's watching the movie come 'round again. I think the fact that after we had ended the Cold War . . . we set about demonizing Islam, that we set about preparing ourselves for unlimited wars in the future[—]I continue to find that deeply depressing. And I suppose that's what I was fighting against in *Absolute Friends* and that, for as long as I can, is what I will continue to fight against.[20]

The reviewers who condemned the novel as an egregious jeremiad failed to recognize that by means of "Mundy *redux*" le Carré was expressing not only his own reactions to recent events but also those of his protagonist's generation who were dismayed by England's diminished integrity on the world's stage (*AF*, 302). It thus is significant that in its opening pages *Absolute Friends* invokes Britain's history of colonialist imperialism and Prime Minister Neville Chamberlain's "shameful Munich Agreement of 1938" (*AF*, 4), both of which prepared the ground for subsequent debacles in international affairs.

A second point overlooked in negative criticism of the novel concerns the spokesman for antiwar views in chapter 11. A shadowy villain known only as Dimitri, supposedly a "mad billionaire" who directs the "New Planet Foundation" (*AF*, 337, 319), is less a character in his own right than a Buchanesque ogre given to profanity-strewn monologues about the Western powers' seemingly insatiable appetite for waging wars.[21] Here are two samples of his denunciatory rhetoric:

> That war on Iraq was illegitimate, Mr. Mundy. It was a criminal and immoral conspiracy. No provocation, no link with Al Qaeda, no weapons of Armageddon. Tales of complicity between Saddam and Osama were self-serving bullshit. It was an old colonial oil war dressed up as a crusade for Western life and liberty, and it was launched by a clique of war-hungry Judeo-Christian geopolitical fantasists who hijacked the media and exploited America's post-9/11 psychopathy. (*AF*, 320–21)

> Makes no difference the Cold War's over. Makes no difference we're globalized, multinational or what the hell. Soon as the tom-toms sound and the politicians roll out their lies, it's bow and arrows and the flag and round-the-clock television for all loyal citizens. It's three cheers for the big bangs and who gives a fuck about casualties as long as they're the other guy's? (*AF*, 324)

Even though Dimitri's fulminations correspond in large measure to the novelist's own op-ed statements regarding the US-led invasion of Iraq, le Carré deliberately undermines this speaker's credibility. Later, for example, Dimitri, whose unlimited funding originates in Riyadh, is revealed to be a seasoned anarchist whose professed interest in subsidizing Ted Mundy's debt-ridden Academy of Professional English in Heidelberg is only a ruse for establishing a base from which to launch terrorist attacks in Europe. Described as being "seventy if a day" (*AF*, 322), Dimitri is also said to have "bombed for the Spanish anarchists against Franco, the Basques against the Spanish[,] and the Red Brigades against the Italian Communists. He ran with . . . all fifty-seven varieties of Palestinian[s], and played both sides of the net for Ireland" (*AF*, 379). In short, this demiurge of insurrection cannot be trusted. Le Carré's novel thus sets us up to question *all* formulaic expressions of political conviction, even when they coincide substantially with his own more nuanced views.

The third dimension of *Absolute Friends* neglected by many of its detractors pertains to an observation by Michael Denning in *Cover Stories: Narrative and Ideology in the British Spy Thriller*. A central appeal of the genre, he argues, is that "it serves as a way of narrating individual political agency in a world of institutions and states that seem to block all action and paralyze all opposition."[22] Although that claim may be true of some Cold War espionage novels (Denning's study was published in 1987), it does not accurately describe the usual pattern of le Carré's fiction. Alec Leamas's death atop the Berlin Wall at the end of *The Spy Who Came In from the Cold* attests to the nullifying supremacy of ideologically entrenched superpowers, and the situation is even bleaker in most of le Carré's post–Cold War narratives. However sympathetic Ted Mundy is in *Absolute Friends* to the indictments by Sasha, his Conradian "secret sharer," of "the octopus of corporate imperialism" (*AF*, 276, 309), both men are brutally murdered by clandestine security forces dispatched on behalf of the transatlantic War on Terror, and their limited degree of political agency is abrogated by spurious media reports on the "Siege of Heidelberg" (*AF*, 438). Despite, then, his novel's undeniable freight of liberal sentiments, le Carré invites us to reflect on what "conviction" means any longer in a world dominated by ubiquitous forms of state-supported indoctrination. It is as though what William Butler Yeats lamented in "The Second Coming" (1920) shortly after World War I—"The best lack all conviction, while the worst / Are full of passionate intensity"—has undergone such a reversal that eighty years later any and all "conviction," no matter how shallow, is fraught with a "passionate intensity."

We are first alerted to this thematic undercurrent when Sasha, discoursing a decade or so after his initial bonding in an East Berlin commune with expatriate Ted Mundy, delivers the following homily:

If we are to build a better world than this, I asked myself, where do we turn, whose actions do we support, how do we frustrate the endless march of capitalist-imperialist aggression? . . . Conviction without action has no meaning for me. *Yet what is conviction? How do we identify it? How can we know that we should be guided by it?* Is it to be found in the heart, or in the intellect? And what if it is only to be found in the one and not the other? (*AF*, 216; emphasis added)

After Sasha, as a mole in the East German Stasi, has conspired with Mundy in a "classic Cold War double-agent operation" before the Berlin Wall's fall (*AF*, 235), le Carré's aging protagonist reflects on how "convictions until now were essentially what he borrowed from other people" (*AF*, 302). That all changes, however, when Mundy, a "naturally pretended man" (*AF*, 232), reaches the limits of his tolerance for political lies. "It's about becoming real after too many years of pretending," he decides. "It's about putting the brakes on human self-deception, starting with my own" (*AF*, 303).

Le Carré takes this critique of "conviction" one step further. Before presenting Dimitri's speeches about "the corporate state and its monopoly of information" (*AF*, 325), he recounts Mundy's solicitation by an urbane CIA representative named Orville J. Rourke, familiarly known as "Jay," who later left that governmental agency and "signed up with a politically motivated group of corporate empire-builders four years ago. Oil chaps, most of them. Strong attachment to the arms industry. And all of them very close to God" (*AF*, 421). This updated report on Rourke by Nick Amory, "Mundy's longtime [MI6] advisor in matters of self-preservation" (*AF*, 23), then leads the formerly "pretended" but now undeceived man to ponder the latter-day phenomenon of unswerving and unquestioning "belief":

What would it be like really and absolutely to *believe*? . . . Like Jay Rourke's chums. To *know*, really and absolutely *know*, that there's a Divine Being not set in time or space who reads your thoughts better than you ever did, and probably before you even have them? To believe that *God* sends you to war, *God* bends the path of bullets, decides which of his children will die, or have their legs blown off, or make a few hundred million on Wall Street, depending on today's Grand Design? (*AF*, 424)

Mundy's reflection reprises Dimitri's harangue about "a clique of war-hungry Judeo-Christian geopolitical fantasists" in President George W. Bush's administration "who hijacked the media and exploited America's post-9/11 psychopathy," but the clear implication is that such "conviction" amounts to little more than a sanctimonious justification for pursuing hidden agendas. Le Carré is thus evenhanded in challenging the role of self-interest as it shapes the rhetoric of both Dimitri and Rourke.

Before this scenario developed, however, the author of *Absolute Friends* was intent only on "writ[ing] a story about a young Englishman who by accident and through his background and because of his natural naïveté had drifted into anarchism" (see, again, note 12). The novel's introductory chapter masterfully profiles its fifty-six-year-old protagonist as a ludic performer, much like Ollie Hawthorne in *Single & Single*, who sports a "clown's bowler" and a removable Union Jack on his jacket's breast pocket while serving as a tour guide to "one of Mad King Ludwig's castles in Bavaria" (*AF*, 4, 3). Under cover of this "Laurel and Hardy" getup (*AF*, 3), former double agent-turned-jester Ted Mundy, "all things to all men and nothing to himself" (*AF*, 5), salts his docent's spiels with jibes about George W. Bush, Donald Rumsfeld, and Tony Blair soon after the Iraq War's declared end. Meanwhile, intent on "separat[ing] himself from his country's hated colonialist reputation" (*AF*, 12), Mundy has become the lover of a young Turkish woman named Zara and a surrogate father to her eleven-year-old son, Mustafa, in the Muslim ghetto of Munich. A disaffected "son of Empire" (*AF*, 36), in other words, has renounced that British legacy and devoted himself instead to protecting some of the most recent victims of cultural injustice.

When Sasha reappears at Mundy's current place of employment as in a "hall of mirrors" (*AF*, 19), the two friends' paths in life have diverged since their Cold War years as collaborative spies.[23] Chapters 2–10 then present a retrospective that emphasizes how both men are disillusioned sons of fathers whose "convictions" reflected the vagaries of mid-twentieth-century history. Mundy is the only surviving child of a retired major of infantry who, at the time of Pakistan's partition from India in 1947, was mustered out of service for assaulting a fellow officer prepared to reveal that Mundy's deceased mother was not, as his father maintained, an aristocratic colonialist lady but instead the semi-illiterate Nellie O'Connor from County Kerry, Ireland, a nursemaid employed by the Anglo-Indian Stanhope family. When the son returns from abroad at age sixteen with his disgraced father, he is understandably deracinated. One of le Carré's best lines in *Absolute Friends* captures his uprooted protagonist's sense of dislocation: "The England that awaits the young Mundy is a rain-swept cemetery for the living dead powered by a forty-watt bulb" (*AF*, 43). Once there, the teenager distinguishes himself as a cricketer and a student of German at a boarding school in Weybridge, after which he is awarded a scholarship to study modern languages at Oxford University. Upon his father's death shortly later, the "nineteen-year-old Steppenwolf in search of a cultural safe haven" migrates aimlessly to "the Free University of Berlin, crucible of the new world order" (*AF*, 50, 62), though hardly the same one proclaimed by President George H. W. Bush.

The point of this rehearsal of Ted Mundy's background is that both he and Sasha are, effectively, orphans by dint of their fathers' ignoble careers. Major Arthur Henry George Mundy succumbed to alcoholic nostalgia after the British Empire's collapse in India, but Sasha describes his paternal forebear as someone who all too readily adapted himself to the shifting currents of World War II. Originally a Lutheran minister in Germany who sided with the Nazis, the "Herr Pastor" then became a "Christian Bolshevik" when such a political realignment proved expedient (*AF*, 85, 86). After Sasha's birth his father "made the spiritual transition from East to West with his customary agility. Having caught the eye of a Missouri missionary organization of dubious connections," the Communist cleric from Leipzig, pursuant to further religious instruction in the United States, reportedly secured a curacy in "the old Nazi stamping ground of Schleswig-Holstein," where from the pulpit he routinely extolled Lutheran theology and "free[-]market Christian capitalism" (*AF*, 87). Repudiating his father as an ideological turncoat, Sasha becomes an ardent searcher for any political creed that will combat "the multiple diseases of fascism, capitalism, militarism, consumerism, Nazism, Coca-Colonization, imperialism and pseudo-democracy" (*AF*, 104). When he resurfaces in the protagonist's life more than a decade later, Sasha, like Mundy, is a ripe prospect for recruitment as a spy both because of his orphan status (recalling that of the otherwise very different Jonathan Pine in *The Night Manager*) and because of his disillusionment with the fate of liberal ideals in the late 1960s' reactionary aftermath.

By the time that *Absolute Friends* picks up the story again in chapter 11, Mundy and Sasha have already cooperated for several years with British Intelligence while Ted, under cover as a British Council overseas supervisor of an acting troupe, relays critical information gathered by Sasha as a Stasi insider. Clandestinity, however, exacts a price, which in Mundy's case is a kind of induced schizophrenia. Unable to reconcile the different versions of himself that he presents to others, the man who agreed to become a Carmelite for MI6, as his handler Nick Amory wittily puts it, finds that his marriage to Kate Andrews cannot endure under the strain of his frequent missions abroad and her rising eminence as a Labour Party candidate for parliamentary election. Sasha, meanwhile, also pays a price for his alliances. Gradually realizing East

Germany's "wholesale betrayal of the sacred socialist dream" (*AF*, 269), he discovers from his Stasi patron that the now dying Herr Pastor, ironically, had all along been a dedicated operative for East Germany. When the two friends are reunited after the turn of the century, both are looking for a new foundation on which to reintegrate their fragmented lives.

Sasha's beguilement by Dimitri's denunciations of the US-led attack on Iraq in 2003 as a "war of lies" attests to an inveterate ideologue's desperate need to believe in the viability of a continuing cause (*AF*, 305). In a perceptive review Christian Caryl observes that "nowhere do[es] Sasha or Mundy come even close to formulating a coherent counterprogram, and in this sense the book reflects the diffuseness and confusion of the contemporary radical left just as much as it skewers the Bush administration."[24] This riposte to those who criticized le Carré's allegedly one-sided and "strident editorialising" takes into account not only the deflation of Dimitri as a cunning terrorist who will say anything to further his objectives but also Sasha's idealistic gullibility in crediting his benefactor's plans for a system of global reeducation. Warier than his friend of "Dimitri's Grand Vision" (*AF*, 343), Mundy, throughout his interview with Sasha's "latest Svengali" at a remote Austrian lodge, has an unnerving sense that the whole setup is an exercise in theater (*AF*, 380). This impression grows on him when, listening to his host's soliloquies, he "has the feeling of sitting too close to the stage, and seeing the cracks in Dimitri's makeup, and the pins in his wig, and the wires when he spreads his wings" (*AF*, 323). Subsequently verifying these intuitions, Mundy also learns at the end of chapter 12 that his bankrupted Academy of Professional English in Heidelberg, which Dimitri has pledged to rescue with an initial outlay of half a million dollars, will be the site for Jay Rourke's apprehension of Sasha as a purported terrorist.

If deceptive role-playing, saturation surveillance, and remote monitoring occur where Mundy meets with Dimitri, they are even more pervasive in chapters 13–14 when Mundy waits in his renovated school to find out whether Sasha is knowingly conspiring with Dimitri's anarchist plans as Rourke has alleged. Upon confirming in a nearby park that his friend is not in fact complicit, the "naturally pretended man" at last becomes his own person. After arranging a charter flight to Turkey for Zara and Mustafa, as well as another for himself later, and seeing them safely off, Mundy returns to his Heidelberg academy for a conference with Nick Amory. Away from the hidden cameras and microphones recently installed there, the protagonist's old mentor then brings his former Cold War agent up-to-date on the changes that have ensued since

9/11 in Britain's "Special Relationship" with the United States: "'There's a new Grand Design about in case you haven't noticed, Edward,' he announces. . . . 'It's called *preemptive naïveté*, and it rests on the assumption that everyone in the world would like to live in Dayton, Ohio, under one god, no prizes for guessing whose god that is'" (*AF*, 419–20). For the veteran MI6 case officer, who opines that "lying for one's country is a noble profession as long as one knows what the truth is, but alas I don't anymore" (*AF*, 422), the advent of a mentality that regards any and all forms of perceived "anti-Americanism" as a sufficient excuse for military action is a frightening sign of the times. For this reason, despite his personal disapproval of Sasha, Amory provides Mundy with fake passports so that both of his former double agents can escape their shared predicament.

The scenario ends later that evening when both Mundy and Sasha are gunned down in a hail of bullets by Rourke and other defenders of "America's policy of conservative democratic imperialism." Le Carré's wry phrase is garnished in the novel's concluding chapter by a recitation of what journalists are allowed to report about events that transpired during the so-called "Siege of Heidelberg," which figures as "the equivalent of a closed film set" (*AF*, 438). Dimitri's maxim that "whoever owns the truth owns the game" again proves accurate in this context. The sanctioned media outlets in Germany thus announce that Sasha was "a former Baader-Meinhof" member and that Mundy, after a failed career with the British Council, was a "Muslim sympathizer" (*AF*, 440, 444).

Balanced against this avalanche of misrepresentation is a lone article subtitled "The American Rightists' Conspiracy Against Democracy" that appears on a "not-for-profit website pledged to transparency in politics" (*AF*, 448, 447). In this widely discredited piece the pseudonymous author, "a long-serving field operative of British Intelligence who had recently resigned his post" (*AF*, 448), reveals the truth about what occurred at Mundy's academy, but Nick Amory's exposé is promptly denigrated by Downing Street spokespeople. The eventual outcome of these clashing renditions in the media, much like that at the end of *The Constant Gardener*, is left in doubt, but the closing sentences of *Absolute Friends* are quietly elegiac. Both main characters are buried alongside their mothers, "Sasha the German in Neubrandenburg, and Mundy the Englishman on a sun-baked hillside in Pakistan." Le Carré adds, "An intrepid journalist tracked down Mundy's final resting place. The mist, she reported, never quite lifts, but the broken Christian masonry makes it a popular place for children to stage their mock battles" (*AF*, 453). The implications of that final image elegantly convey the book's overall vision.

In a short essay focused partly on *Absolute Friends*, Jost Hindersmann postulates that "espionage novels are fever thermometers of world politics."[25] He
then cites le Carré's query, "How far can we go in the rightful defense of our
Western values without abandoning them along the way?", as what anchors
all the novelist's post–Cold War narratives. Vittorio Hösle concurs by show-
ing the congruency of *Absolute Friends* with le Carré's earlier work.[26] From
such discussions we can infer that le Carré's nineteenth novel addresses pivotal
issues concerning the political legacy of 9/11, particularly the rising tide of
ideological "conviction" as a substitute for thoughtful policy in the conduct of
international relations.

At the start of this chapter's second half, I pointed out le Carré's indictment of
the US response to Al Qaeda's attack on the World Trade Center and the Pentagon, and I then noted that *Absolute Friends* frames Ted Mundy's story in terms
of Britain's history of imperialism. What has not been made explicit in my discussion so far is how these otherwise separable elements are intertwined. Two
scholarly articles help to explain how this fusion manifests itself within the novel.

Anne McClintock's essay in the October 2014 issue of *PMLA*, which con-
denses the first section of her book *Imperial Ghosting: Perpetual War in the
Twilight of U.S. Power*, clarifies the above-noted linkage in *Absolute Friends*.
Beginning by asking how imperialism casts a spectral shadow on the present,
McClintock writes as follows:

> What does it mean to say that we live in tragic times? The 9-11 attack was
> certainly a tragedy, but whose tragedy was it? What constitutes a national
> tragedy in the first place? . . . What are the consequences of sacralizing one
> national calamity (the 9-11 attack) as a world-historic tragedy while ghost-
> ing the other foundational violences of United States history, which have
> returned to haunt the post–9-11 era as unspeakable premonitions and accu-
> satory revenants?[27]

Despite proclamations by Bush appointees such as Deputy Secretary of State
Richard Armitage that "history begins today," McClintock observes, the United States of America's proclaimed doctrine of exceptionalism does not exempt
it as a nation-state from the phantasms of past depredations. These reminders
resist the official "administration of forgetting," defined as "the calculated and
often brutal amnesias by which a state contrives to erase its own atrocities."
Even though the "founding tenet of American empire is that it is no empire
at all," McClintock reminds us of the US record of imperialistic aggression,
sometimes amounting to attempted genocide, as in the cases of indigenous

populations in Mexico, Latin America, Hawaii, the Philippines, Japan (Hiroshima and Nagasaki), Southeast Asia, and the Middle East. To think of such repeated episodes simply as "tragic," she argues, is to nurture a mindset that makes possible their ritualistic repetition. "But does the idea of history as tragic," queries McClintock, "not itself involve a form of ghosting, allowing state violence to be shorn of historical complexity and political agency," per Bush-Blair declarations, "so that ethical culpability is more easily cloaked, accountability concealed, and guilt disavowed?"[28] *Absolute Friends* develops that theme by meshing its main narrative of the espionage careers of Mundy and Sasha with the amnesiac West's rationale for invading Iraq in 2003.

A second and concurrently published essay by Phyllis Lassner explains how *Absolute Friends* as well as *A Most Wanted Man* (2008) constitute a distinctive variation on le Carré's Cold War fiction. Arguing that these later novels convey a strong critique of British deference to US foreign policy after the World Trade Center and Pentagon attack, Lassner suggests that they cultivate "a parodic narrative voice that makes [le Carré's] political diatribe all the more controversial by mocking it."[29] Mikhail Bakhtin's ideas about deprivileged and dialogized heteroglossia become the theoretical anchor of her main thesis:

A decade after the end of the Cold War and the fall of the Soviet empire, with the launch of the [W]ar on [T]error and Britain's capitulation to American policy, the double and triple crosses that victimize le Carré's protagonists in *Absolute Friends* and *A Most Wanted Man* become the material of paradoxical polemics, which both mock and mourn the desperately defensive illusion that Britain has a moral imperative and influential position on the world stage.[30]

Lassner then explores how *Absolute Friends* relies on a multivocal dialectic "between characters' spoken and unspoken thoughts" to focus on the issue of "Britain's passive . . . collaboration with American foreign policy."[31] By means of indirect discourse, le Carré moves freely beyond the rigidities of entrenched ideologies, including Sasha's virulent anti-Americanism, and prompts readers to question *all* formulaic expressions of political conviction.[32]

Both *The Constant Gardener* and *Absolute Friends*, le Carré's two longest novels since *A Perfect Spy*, explore in different ways the crippling consequences of Britain's more than three-centuries-long experiment in colonialist imperialism. However Justin Quayle wishes at the outset to insulate himself from this legacy, he ultimately succeeds in accepting his contingent responsibility for that inheritance and, as a result, reaches a new plateau of self-understanding.

The situation is more complicated in the case of Ted Mundy. As an orphaned "son of Empire," he, like Sasha, struggles to forge a way ahead beyond the ideological blindness of his father's generation but only to be manipulated by the emergent Anglo-American champions of a New World Order. In each of these cases the concept of individual political agency—or, more accurately, its efficacy—seems to be shuffled aside as a nostalgic anachronism of Cold War thinking. Moreover, death at the end of both narratives seems the only escape for their respective protagonists. Despite the starkness of their endings, *The Constant Gardener* and *Absolute Friends* celebrate the moral rectitude of Quayle and Mundy's stands against unprincipled state institutions of deception. For that reason the two men stand out as unsung heroes among the pantheon of le Carré's other, invariably compromised, fictional characters.

4

THE MISSION SONG AND
A MOST WANTED MAN

Covert Surveillance, Deniable Syndicates, and
Extraordinary Rendition

Our society is one not of spectacle, but of surveillance[. U]nder the surface of images, one invests bodies in depth; behind the great abstraction of exchange, there continues the meticulous, concrete training of useful forces; the circuits of communication are the supports of an accumulation and a centralization of knowledge; the play of signs defines the anchorages of power[. I]t is not that the beautiful totality of the individual is amputated, repressed, [or] altered by our social order[;] it is rather that the individual is carefully fabricated in it. . . . We are much less Greeks than we believe.

—Michel Foucault[1]

THE BURGEONING ACADEMIC field of surveillance studies has made abundantly clear the omnipresence of third-party monitoring in our present era of global terrorism.[2] Jeremy Bentham's eighteenth-century panopticon model for overseeing the behavior of penitentiary inmates has long since been replaced by infinitely more sophisticated methods of tracking the interactions of ordinary citizens. Given today's multimodal forms of electronic surveillance, some scholars, such as Kevin D. Haggerty, have questioned the continuing ascendancy of Bentham's panopticon, famously theorized by Michel Foucault in *Discipline and Punish: The Birth of the Prison*, as a useful paradigm for preemptive information gathering.[3]

Meanwhile post-9/11 monitoring continues to be particularly widespread in Britain. According to authoritative testimony cited in a BBC News report in November 2006, "compared to other industrialised Western states, the UK was 'the most surveilled country'" and "the worst . . . at protecting individual privacy."[4] David Murakami Wood, one of the sources for that finding, has elsewhere linked this development to the worldwide expansion of a capitalist economic order, concluding that "the globalization of surveillance needs to be met by a globalization of human values like autonomy and dignity, combined with global democracy and the transparency and accountability of states and corporations to people rather than the other way around. At present, this appears an unlikely direction."[5] In his recent fiction John le Carré wholeheartedly agrees with that assessment.

The Mission Song and *A Most Wanted Man* are closely attuned to the emergence of new technologies employed in state-sponsored surveillance. These platforms for intercepting signals intelligence, or SIGINT, as the espionage industry dubs it, require a new kind of spy for providing human intelligence, or HUMINT—specifically, a versatile translator-interpreter capable in real time of rendering the polyglot communications of individuals targeted as "persons of interest."[6]

In *The Mission Song*, le Carré's twentieth novel, twenty-eight-year-old Bruno Salvador, the illegitimate son of a Congolese mother and an Irish Roman Catholic missionary, figures as an unwitting pawn in that scenario. The reason for describing him so involves his subaltern status in a country not his birthplace. Bruno's biography predicts his susceptibility to exploitation. Transported after his father's death to the United Kingdom as an orphaned "secret child" (*MS*, 8), he eventually becomes a highly talented multilingualist and interpreter. Fluent in Swahili, Kinyarwanda, Lingala, Bembe, Shi, French, and English, Salvo (as he is called) prides himself on his "mynah-bird ear and jackdaw memory" as an "assimilated, mid-brown Briton" (*MS*, 13, 23). This self-identification was bolstered five years earlier by his token and, except in the bedroom, largely dysfunctional marriage to Penelope Randall, an "upper-echelon Oxbridge journalist" who at age thirty-two is "a rising star in the firmament of a mass-market British tabloid capable of swaying millions" (*MS*, 2). During that interim Salvo, as he boasts at the outset of his first-person narrative, is in regular demand by London law courts and at negotiations involving Third World countries' natural resources.[7] The latter assignments have earned him "glowing references from many of our"—note the collective pronoun— "nation's finest corporate names." Salvo then expatiates on his contributions as follows:

> In six years of honest labour in the world of commerce I have applied my services—be it in the way of cautiously phrased conference calls or discreet meetings in neutral cities on the European continent—to the creative

adjustment of oil, gold, diamond, mineral, and other commodity prices, not to mention the diversion of many millions of dollars from the prying eyes of the world's shareholders into slush funds as far removed as Panama, Budapest, and Singapore. Ask me whether, in facilitating these transactions, I felt obliged to consult my conscience and you will receive the emphatic answer, 'No.' The code of your top interpreter is sacrosanct. He is pledged to his employer in the same manner as a soldier is pledged to the flag. (MS, 1–2)

The ironies of this opening declaration complicate The Mission Song's narrational context as revealed in its final chapter, but here we need note only the biracial protagonist's desire to be of utility to his adopted country. Given his specialized linguistic skills, Salvo is "called upon to do [his] patriotic duty on a confidential basis by a government department whose existence is routinely denied" (MS, 1). In a part-time capacity he thus becomes "an indoctrinated employee of the all-powerful British Secret Service" (MS, 238–39).

A naif in the mold of Henry Fielding's Joseph Andrews and Voltaire's Candide, le Carré's stateless narrator accepts unquestioningly the demands of his MI5 job as an eavesdropper on international conversations. "Crouching in a soundproof cubicle, one of forty, in a secure underground bunker known as the Chat Room," Salvo quickly becomes adept at audio surveillance. Somewhat breathlessly he recounts his voyeuristic exposure to malfeasance in the making:

One minute I'm listening to a top-ranking Acholi-speaking member of the Lord's Resistance Army in Uganda plotting by satellite phone to set up a base across the border in East Congo, and the next sweating it out in Dar-es-Salaam docks with the clatter of shipping in the background, and the cries of hawkers, and the in-out hum of a wonky table-fan that's keeping away the flies, as a murderous bunch of Islamist sympathisers conspire to import an arsenal of anti-aircraft missiles in the guise of heavy machinery[.] And the very same afternoon being sole ear-witness to a trio of corrupt Rwandan army officers haggling with a Chinese delegation over the sale of plundered Congolese minerals[.] Or bumping through the honking traffic of Nairobi in the chauffeured limousine of a Kenyan political mogul as he wangles himself a massive bribe for allowing an Indian building contractor to cover five hundred miles of new road with a single paper-thin surface of tarmac guaranteed to last at least two rainy seasons. (MS, 40)

By his faithful translation of these intercepted telecommunications, Salvo strives to ingratiate himself as a valued member of the British government's sprawling security apparatus. In this respect, consonant with le Carré's long-standing diagnosis of the spy's basic motivation, Bruno Salvador is yet another orphan in search of acceptance by a surrogate "family."

Bruno's next assignment, however, substantially deepens his immersion in operational surveillance. Based on his exemplary performance in MI5's Chat Room, Salvo is nominated by supervisor Robert Anderson, whom Bruno venerates as "rectitude personified" (MS, 42), for a weekend engagement that allegedly will "do a bit of good for your country" (MS, 44), an overture that does not go unnoticed. Under the alias Brian Sinclair he therefore consents to act in the role of a freelance interpreter "temporarily employed by an internationally based syndicate," which the novel subsequently designates simply as the Syndicate, "registered in the Channel Islands and dedicated to bringing the latest agricultural techniques to the Third and Fourth Worlds" (MS, 47). Concurrently, Salvo has realized the vacuity of his marriage to Penelope and, by sheer accident, fallen in love with a black African hospital nurse named Hannah, who also hails from East Congo. In a London still unsettled by the terrorist bombings of its subway system on July 7, 2005, their liaison becomes the connection by which Bruno Salvador hopes to reclaim his indigenous heritage and identity. That investment, though, is still balanced against his lingering hopes of validation as an "assimilated, mid-brown Briton" doing his level best on behalf of queen and country. The rest of le Carré's novel elaborates on that tension of allegiances.

The Mission Song's middle section revolves around its protagonist's gradually dawning discovery that he is participating in what Foucault memorably calls the modern state's "subtle, calculated technology of subjection."[8] While ensconced in a basement listening post between the formally convened sessions of a secretive six-hour conference at an unidentified North Sea island retreat, Salvo is supposed to monitor the private dialogues of three African power brokers invited by the anonymous Syndicate to support its plans for foreign intervention. According to Maxie, the venture's brusque paramilitary facilitator, the British entity is committed to "delivering democracy at the end of a gun barrel to the Eastern Congo" (MS, 84):

> "Congo's been bleeding to death for five centuries," he went on distractedly. "Fucked by the Arab slavers, fucked by their fellow Africans, fucked by the United Nations, the CIA, the Christians, the Belgians, the French, the Brits, the Rwandans, the diamond companies, the gold companies, the mineral

companies, half the world's carpetbaggers, their own government in Kinshasa, and any minute now they're going to be fucked by the oil companies. Time they had a break, and we're the boys to give it to 'em." (*MS*, 85)

Maxie's explanation of the conference's purpose, however, is a ruse meant to control the dissemination of (dis)information. Only much later do we and Salvo alike learn that the clandestine summit has been orchestrated, through a silver-tongued intermediary known simply as Philip, by Lord Jack Brinkley, a "former New Labour minister" and reputed "champion of all things African" (*MS*, 65). The endeavor's declared objective is to install a man known as "the Mwangaza," a "self-proclaimed Congolese saviour" (*MS*, 104), as a political leader by means of a surgical coup.[9] Yet Brinkley is interested solely in gaining exclusive commercial access to the region's vast mineral resources, particularly the stockpiles of coltan ore, which is essential to the manufacture of cell phones, on behalf of a consortium of plutocrats spanning the globe. Such a layered, hierarchical, and pervasively *secret* structure, of course, ensures the Syndicate's strategic latitude for deniability.

At the heart of this drama is le Carré's focus on the discursive slipperiness of language, especially as manifested, reviewer Neil Gordon notes, in "diplomatic obfuscation and corporate newspeak."[10] Much of this evasion is obvious to Salvo when it surfaces in Western print media, but while translating the *viva voce* speeches of African participants at the North Sea conclave, he seems largely unaware of their underlying geopolitical import, despite his boasted "third ear" and proficiency in dialects (*MS*, 60). Salvo's credulity in this regard is a result of his lover Hannah's high esteem for the Mwangaza as "*an apostle for truth and reconciliation*" along with his own sense of awe at the charismatic populist's oratory, which promises "harmonious coexistence and prosperity for all Kivu" (*MS*, 104, 129). When this inspirational figure then summons the translator to his side at the gathering as an example of the Middle Path movement's "all-inclusiveness" (*MS*, 134), the displaced narrator-protagonist is beguiled by a utopian vision that, if realized, will restore him to his roots. Little does Salvo know at this juncture, as he will subsequently, that the Mwangaza, the owner of a "ten-million-dollar villa in Spain" with "plasma television screens in [*sic*] every toilet," has already cut a deal with the denounced Kinshasa "fatcats" that concedes to them the "People's Portion" of the Syndicate's financial payout (*MS*, 175). In his mediatory role at the conference, however, such duplicity is inconceivable to Salvo, who for personal reasons wants to believe in the probity of both parties he represents.

The protagonist's alertness to rhetorical dissimulation is also blunted by the fractious battle of words between two African warlords who have been invited to lend their bribed support of the Mwangaza's accession to power in the Democratic Republic of the Congo (i.e., East Congo). The first such magnate is the elderly and AIDS-stricken Dieudonné, signifying the "Given One of God," who as a Munyamulenge is a racial icon to whom Salvo feels an instant attraction (*MS*, 110). The other warlord is Franco, "an old-style Bembe" thug who once served Mobutu Sese Seko, the longtime dictator of Zaire, and thereafter opposed Dieudonné's tribal faction as a sworn member of the Mai Mai (*MS*, 111). The rancor of these principals' verbal sparring causes Salvo to dismiss the sardonic comments of the third participant, Honoré Amour-Joyeuse ("Haj"), an ethnic Shi from the city of Bukavu and the Sorbonne-educated "heir to an East Congolese trading fortune" who is representing his father Luc as a former comrade of the Mwangaza (*MS*, 113).

Inclined to regard Haj's jibes at the conference's plenary sessions as symptomatic of nothing more than obstructionist cynicism, Salvo will later realize the canniness of the Bukavu entrepreneur's suspicion toward the Syndicate's intentions when, in his underground bunker during a recess, he listens to the sounds of Haj being tortured by Felix Tabizi, a Lebanese middleman for the Mwangaza, at the behest of the meeting's British organizer. *The Mission Song* thus literalizes the idea of Foucauldian subjection as it is associated with audio surveillance, a linkage explored less graphically in such films as Francis Ford Coppola's *The Conversation* (1974) and Sydney Pollack's *The Interpreter* (2005).

There are no unsung heroes in le Carré's twentieth novel, however, only some characters who are less mendacious and predatory than others. After eavesdropping on a private consultation between Haj and Dieudonné, for example, Salvo alerts Philip to Haj's disclosure that he has put his father, based in the city of Goma, in touch with a Dutch friend from business school in Paris named Marius van Tonge, one of "eight bright young partners in a multinational venture-capital house called the Union Minière des Grand Lacs" (*MS*, 205). Haj, in other words, is loosely affiliated with a rival conglomerate that threatens the Syndicate's vested interest in profiting from East Congo's natural resources. Moreover, we are told that the Union Minière is backed by a neoconservative "Who's Who of American corporate and political power, indistinguishable from government" (*MS*, 206). Transnationalism devolves into a reactivated form of economic imperialism. The more immediate point, though, is that Haj, portrayed as an outspoken critic of the Syndicate's plans, is linked to a de facto colonialist enterprise little different from what he condemns. Furthermore, as compensation for his physical abuse, Haj demands an additional $3 million, a leveraged extortion that Lord Brinkley reluctantly approves.

At this juncture le Carré's characteristically dutiful and compliant protagonist undergoes the beginning of a decisive change. Having been privy to Haj's humiliation through surveillance, Salvo feels a new rapport with the man roughly his own age who had earlier disparaged the translator as a "zebra" because of his mixed race (*MS*, 150). When the conference participants meet for the final session to sign a contract prepared by the Syndicate's lawyer, Salvo deliberately establishes eye contact with Haj and ponders their gaze's telegraphic significance:

Was he telling me, "You bastard, you betrayed me"? Was *I* reproaching *him* for betraying himself, and Congo? Today, with more days and nights than I need to reflect on the moment, I see it as one of wary mutual recognition. We were both hybrids: I by birth, he by education. We had both taken too many steps away from the country that had borne us to belong anywhere with ease. (*MS*, 214)

By acknowledging his hybridity through a comparison of himself to his Shi counterpart, the culturally deracinated Salvo takes an initial step in abandoning his self-identification as an "assimilated, mid-brown Briton" and moves tentatively toward "completion" (*MS*, 231). The latter word might seem to carry the same implications as found in *The Constant Gardener*, but here it signals no induction into a state of *Gelassenheit*. What immediately ensues, however, does make clear that, if nothing else, the narrator-protagonist has chosen sides, even though doing so gains him nothing in the end. After exchanging business cards at the close of the conference with Haj, the latter's bearing a hand-scrawled email address, he tapes several incriminating recordings and notepads to his torso, securing them from detection under his shapeless tweed jacket, before flying back to England along with the rest of Lord Brinkley's arm's-length team.

Salvo's actions after his return fail to inspire confidence in what he has learned about the ways of the world. Trying to decide how most effectively to prevent the Syndicate's pending coup, scheduled for two weeks after the clandestine summit, he ignores Hannah's counsel to approach a man named Baptiste, a "Congolese nationalist who is passionate for a united Kivu" (*MS*, 247), and instead reports what he has discovered to Lord Brinkley at his Knightsbridge residence. Naively assuming that the publicly touted "champion of all things African" has "no notion of what had been perpetrated under his aegis"

(*MS*, 257), Bruno is quickly outflanked by the seasoned politician and accused of attempted blackmail. He fares no better in a nocturnal meeting with Baptiste. After preparing a twenty-page exposé of the Syndicate's plot for his MI5 supervisor Robert Anderson, a document rather grandly titled "*J'Accuse!* after Émile Zola's spirited defence of Colonel [Alfred] Dreyfus" (*MS*, 276), Salvo at least has the sense to buffer his oral narrative to Baptiste as originating from a reliable but unnamed source. Far from crediting his story, however, the Mwangaza's supporter summarily denounces him as a liar intent on subverting the Congo's long struggle for freedom from foreign exploitation.

Salvador's next recourse is Anderson, whom he regards as the epitome of integrity, but again his judgment proves misguided. Meeting with the fifty-eight-year-old at his choral society's weekly practice, Salvo presents him with a copy of *J'Accuse!* After closely reading it, Anderson temporizes about what he is expected to do with the information. When pressed to surrender his "feloniously obtained" recordings and notepads (*MS*, 295), the subaltern balks, prompting this response from his supervisor: "And has it never occurred to you that it might be God's will that the world's resources, which are dwindling even as we speak, do better in the hands of civilised Christian souls with a cultured way of life than some of the most backward heathens on the planet?" (*MS*, 297). Salvo's rejoinder that he is not sure who constitute the "heathens" then triggers this outburst from Anderson regarding the Kivu region of East Congo:

> A rogue country, Salvo—a country that is incapable of settling to an orderly way of life—a country that abandons itself freely to genocide and cannibalism and worse is *not*[,] . . . in my considered opinion, entitled to respect under international law . . . any more than is a *rogue element* in our *own* society—such as *yourself*, Salvo—entitled to indulge his naivety at the expense of his adoptive country's best interests. . . . I'll ask you one more time, and that's it. *Where are the illegally held materials?* (*MS*, 298)

Now knowing exactly where he stands in the eyes of his erstwhile mentor, Salvo is at a loss about how to proceed next in order to circumvent the Syndicate's staged coup and installation of the Mwangaza as a puppet figurehead.

From this point onward *The Mission Song*'s resolution sputters, seemingly by design, to an anticlimactic ending that suggests le Carré's skepticism about the climate of international affairs and the disposition of the British Foreign Office in 2006. On the day after Salvo's disillusioning colloquy with Anderson, he resorts to contacting Fergus Thorne, his alienated wife Penelope's editor in chief whose newspaper had lost a costly lawsuit a few years ago involving Lord

Jack Brinkley's financial dealings. When Salvo tries to present Thorne with the digital tapes of Haj's interrogation and Brinkley's approval of his demand for an additional $3 million, he discovers that Hannah, anticipating her lover's misplaced loyalty to England, has taken them in order that copies might be sent to Haj's email address.[11] Meanwhile, the novel's attention shifts to unconfirmed news reports from Kinshasa that fighting has erupted between opposed militias in East Congo, a clash attributed to a renewed Rwandan insurgency. Amid the frenzy of television coverage it becomes evident to Salvo that the Syndicate's coup, moved forward from its original timetable, has gone disastrously awry. There ensues a disclaimer from a junior minister aligned with Lord Brinkley's political party:

> "Our hands are clean as a whistle, thank you, Andrew," she informs her inquisitor in the feisty language of New Labour at its most transparent. "HMG [Her Majesty's Government] is nowhere in this one, trust me. All right, so one or other of the men is British. Give me a break! I'd have thought that you'd have had a bit more respect for us, frankly. All the signals *we're* getting say this was a botched, incompetent bit of private enterprise. It's no good saying, 'Who by?' all the time because I don't *know* who by! What I *do* know is, it's got amateur written all over it, and whatever else you may think we are, we're not amateurs. And I believe in free speech too, Andrew. Goodnight!" (*MS*, 316–17)

Once more, as in *The Constant Gardener*, media proclamations distort or mask the truth of events, all the while vilifying such enablers of a failed operation as Maxie and the Mwangaza as its alleged masterminds. Utterly lost in this reshuffling of face cards is any deeper excavation of behind-the-scenes players. Concerning "Lord Brinkley and his multinationally backed anonymous Syndicate and its designs on the Eastern Congo's resources" (*MS*, 317), therefore, virtually nothing is reported. So much, implies le Carré, for the investigative rigor of the press in delving into the intricacies of global deception.

The Mission Song's denouement leaves things deliberately inconclusive. After the coup fails, Philip, as Lord Brinkley's deputy, apprehends the protagonist and makes clear that he (Philip) can have both Hannah and Salvo deported on the basis of visa violations and immigration irregularities. Regarding the biracial Salvo, who sought cultural assimilation by his services to England's security establishment, Philip asserts that "the man who calls himself Bruno Salvador is not now and never has been a British subject, loyal or otherwise. In short, he doesn't exist" (*MS*, 326). Salvo is now forced to recognize that all along he has been a dupe of the adopted social order in terms of which his self-perceived identity has been fabricated. This outcome places Salvo in an ontological limbo. Incarcerated within a (deniable) detention impoundment somewhere in Britain, le Carré's protagonist reveals that as a "man adrift" he is composing his narrative for Noah, Hannah's young son in Uganda, with whom he hopes to be united one day (*MS*, 330).

This ending, however, is problematic. Is Salvo in his sequestration boasting about his former employment by MI5, possibly trying to impress a prospective stepson, or is he arriving at an honest reckoning with his inglorious past? All that we are finally given to know is that Salvo's case is still pending, apparently for years to come. A letter from Haj, transmitted via Robert Anderson, welcomes the "zebra" to Bukavu upon his release, should that ever occur, but otherwise nothing indicates what may yet transpire.

Compared to *A Most Wanted Man*, le Carré's next novel, *The Mission Song* seems less consequential and rewarding despite its racially mixed narrator's firsthand account of his immersion in a hegemonic Western nation's culture of subjection. This impression may result in part from the text's conjuration of Africa as a backdrop, not unlike what was discussed earlier regarding *The Constant Gardener*, even though here the Congolese principals are very much endowed with voices. The author freely acknowledged this dimension in an article he contributed to the *Globe and Mail* after *The Mission Song*'s release. Admitting that contrary to his usual research practice he had not visited Bukavu or Africa's Great Lakes region before composing his twentieth novel, le Carré wrote: "But *The Mission Song* isn't really set in [the] Congo. . . . It's a romantic satire, for heaven's sake, written with both feet firmly off the ground. It's about Tony Blair's England, and good old-fashioned colonial exploitation, and political hypocrisy and shameless public lies, and other scores I had to settle."[12]

Once again the issue of polemics in his post–Cold War fiction surfaces. If the Congo, as le Carré went on to admit, figures only as an "abstraction" in *The Mission Song*, then it is little wonder that its epigraph from Joseph Conrad's *Heart of Darkness*—"The conquest of the earth, which mostly means the taking it away from those who have a different complexion or slightly flatter noses than ourselves, is not a pretty thing when you look into it too much"—and its "Acknowledgements" nod to Michela Wrong's *In the Footsteps of Mr. Kurtz: Living on the Brink of Disaster in Mobutu's Congo* appear adventitious. These limitations noted, *The Mission Song* is hardly "clunky" or "simplistic," as the habitually dismissive Michiko Kakutani charged.[13] Instead it constitutes another experimental foray in le Carré's mounting engagement with the complexities of transnationalism, however difficult he finds it at times to detach himself from overt condemnation of the "political hypocrisy and shameless public lies" that nullify the paradigm shift's potential for bringing about a more equitable world.

* * * * *

No such complications haunt *A Most Wanted Man*, which is set in Hamburg, a city that le Carré knew well from residing there while working for MI6 during the early 1960s. Nearly half a century later, however, that hub of mercantilism in northern Germany has become a hotbed of xenophobic suspicion and surveillance because it was the staging ground for some of the 9/11 Muslim hijackers, including "Mohammed Atta, who steered the first plane into the Twin Towers" (*MW*, 3). For that reason Hamburg's "grandly named Office for the Protection of the Constitution—in plain language, domestic intelligence service"—is on high alert, as mandated by the centralized espiocracy in Berlin's Ministry of the Interior and Office of the Chancellor, regarding any new immigrants seeking refuge within the country's borders (*MW*, 43).

Into this web of heightened vigilance enters an emaciated twenty-three-year-old vagrant named Issa Salim Mahmoud (*Issa* is the Arabic equivalent for *Jesus*), who later reveals that he is Chechen and has managed to escape from torture in an Istanbul prison and incarceration in Copenhagen en route to Hamburg. When the destitute stranger materializes on the doorstep of Leyla Oktay and her son Melik, who are Turkish émigrés seeking naturalized German citizenship after many years of probationary status, Leyla unhesitatingly extends hospitality to Issa. Only subsequently do the Oktays learn that their mysterious guest is the illegitimate son of Colonel Grigori Borisovich Karpov in the Red Army and that, disavowing his progenitor's wartime crimes, Issa wishes to lay claim to more than $12.5 million deposited over the years to an illicit "Lipizzaner" account held by "the private banking house of Brue Frères PLC, formerly of Glasgow, Rio de Janeiro, and Vienna, and presently of Hamburg" (*MW*, 18). Issa's sole motive for doing so is to donate all the tainted money to various approved Muslim charities while he is permitted to pursue medical studies in the West.

From this point onward *A Most Wanted Man* unfolds through a shifting overlay of three equally weighted perspectives and subnarratives linked to Issa's arrival.[14] The first is that of Annabel Richter, a morally scrupulous young lawyer who is affiliated with a nonprofit immigrant-support organization called Sanctuary North and whose view of justice encompasses an ethic of empathy. Like Tessa Quayle in *The Constant Gardener*, Richter champions the cause of those seeking asylum from persecution and oppression, and she does so in large measure because her attorney father preached the standard juridical doctrine of an emotionally uninvolved "professionalism." Rejecting this counsel as spurious, and deeply remorseful for having earlier allowed it to sway her decision to surrender a client named Magomed for deportation, Annabel is fiercely intent on protecting Issa's interests after being consulted by the Oktays about his plight. When a document in their guest's possession directs the Sanctuary North advocate to an otherwise unknown "Mr. *Lipizzaner*" (*MW*, 24), she contacts Tommy Brue, at age sixty the sole legatee of Brue Frères PLC and the novel's second perspective on the events surrounding a mysterious Chechen's arrival in Hamburg.[15]

Unlike Annabel Richter, who is young enough to be his daughter, Tommy Brue has embraced a resigned (non)ethic of expediency concerning both his banking career and his disintegrating second marriage. Even though he knows that his father, Edward Amadeus Brue, collaborated with British intelligence in laundering deposits from Russian profiteers after the Cold War's end in order to be awarded an OBE in his declining years, Tommy has kept such discreditable accounts a closely guarded secret, known (supposedly) only to him and his father's former secretary and mistress. Tommy is similarly pragmatic about his union with Viennese wife, Mitzi—ten years his junior but still at age fifty, "thanks to high maintenance and the attentions of a fashionable surgeon, . . . a ravishing thirty-nine, or almost" (*MW*, 94). Tommy no longer can satisfy her conjugal expectations, so he tolerates her casual weekend infidelities with a family friend. Having arrived at this downhill phase of his life, fraught as it is with personal shortcomings and compromises, the last scion of Brue Frères PLC prides himself by way of compensation on his public persona:

> If he was a dying species, he was also secretly rather pleased with himself on account of it: Tommy Brue, salt of the earth, good man on a dark night, no highflier but all the better for it, first-rate wife, marvelous value at the dinner table and plays a decent game of golf. Or so the word went, he believed, and so it should. (*MW*, 20)

That carefully constructed bulwark against an admission of failure begins to crumble, however, when he is confronted with Annabel Richter's unyielding claims on behalf of her disenfranchised client. Moved by the human-rights activist's stubbornness in defense of her convictions—a refusal to play the world's game that reminds Tommy Brue of the generational antiauthoritarianism of his disaffected daughter, Georgie, by his first marriage—the private banker begins to question the code of expediency by which he has regulated his life to date. Tommy's willingness to do so makes him, in quite another sense than Issa, "a most wanted man."

The third narrational perspective is that of Günther Bachmann, a veteran agent runner reminiscent of Leonard Burr in *The Night Manager*. Gruff and disdainful of bureaucracy, Bachmann is profiled as the "polyglot offspring of a string of mixed marriages contracted by a flamboyant German-Ukrainian woman, and reputedly the only officer of his service not to possess an academic qualification beyond summary expulsion from his secondary school." With a pedigree far different from that of "Old Etonian" Justin Quayle in *The Constant Gardener*, the one-time field recruiter is further said by age thirty to have "run away to sea, trekked the Hindu Kush, been imprisoned in Colombia[,] and written a thousand-page unpublishable novel" (*MW*, 45). Now in his midforties, Bachmann leads a sixteen-person team of technologically sophisticated researchers, watchers, and listeners headquartered in World War II riding stables and innocuously named the Foreign Acquisitions Unit of Hamburg's domestic intelligence service. In this downgraded capacity he must deal with bumbling supervisor Arnold Mohr, who is eager to impress Berlin's Joint Steering Committee by immediately seizing Issa as a suspected terrorist. Thanks to the intervention of Michael Axelrod, his left-leaning federalist supporter who opposes the machinations of arch-neoconservative Dieter Burgdorf, Bachmann wins a ten-day reprieve to use Issa as bait for compelling Dr. Faisal Abdullah, a high-profile Islamic scholar living in Germany, to cooperate by betraying the militant groups abroad to which the charities he oversees funnel funds from time to time.

Like all of le Carré's fiction, then, *A Most Wanted Man* establishes a dichotomy between primary characters presented as humanly authentic persons and secondary figures depicted as ciphers of a supervening ideology or institutional cause. Given the work's background framework of the War on Terror's extralegal practices, it is not surprising that the secondary characters outnumber the few primary characters who wrestle with issues of conscience. Initially this imbalance is not unduly pronounced when shortly after Issa's arrival from abroad Dr. Otto Keller, "the most protective of all protectors" (*MW*, 97), convenes a top-secret meeting of the Joint Steering Committee, which "had become a house bitterly divided" between "those determined to defend civil rights at all costs, and those determined to curtail them in the name of greater national security." At this conference Axelrod, a rival of Burgdorf, "the German intelligence community's most vocal evangelist for greater integration with its American counterpart" (*MW*, 99), is able to negotiate a grace period for Günther Bachmann to pursue his operational plan for turning Dr. Abdullah.

Several days later, however, after the resurfacing of an MI6 spook named Foreman (formerly Findlay) from the Cold War's last days who arranged Colonel Karpov's deposits to a Brue Frères account, the geopolitical tide shifts. At
a second emergency meeting of the Joint Steering Committee, to which Dr.
Keller invites various "swiftly risen managers of the post-9/11 boom market in
intelligence and allied trades" (*MW*, 236) as supposedly neutral observers, the
US contingent is notable for its overbearing influence. These proponents of the
Bush doctrines include, for example, boisterously "majestic Martha, the Agency's formidable number two in Berlin," accompanied by "sweetly courteous"
British sycophant Ian Lantern and "six-foot-something Newton, alias Newt,
one[-]time deputy [CIA] chief of operations at the U.S. embassy in Beirut and
Bachmann's opposite number there" (*MW*, 237, 239).[16] Their presence at the
strategy session tips the wavering consensus in Germany's security establishment toward the immediate apprehension of Issa.

Well before this political crisis for Günther Bachmann arises, however, *A
Most Wanted Man* concentrates on the personal interaction between Annabel
Richter and Tommy Brue. Already conscience-stricken by his firm's oversight
of Lipizzaner accounts arranged by his father, the sole surviving partner is
intent on liquidating them, even if that means the fiscal collapse of Brue Frères
PLC. When first contacted by Richter by telephone, the private banker suspects blackmail, which he once dealt with while based in Vienna, but upon
meeting the young lawyer in Hamburg's nearby Atlantic Hotel he is disarmed
by her directness and obvious sincerity. Subsequently, after interviewing Issa at
the Oktays' residence, Brue protests to Richter that "I don't *do* protection. I'm
a bank. I don't *do* permits of residence. I don't *do* German passports or places
at medical school!" (*MW*, 84–85). His vehement disclaimers equating himself
with a disinterested institution dissolve, however, when Annabel points out to
Tommy that "without your fucking bank, my client wouldn't be here." Persuaded by the blunt truth of Richter's retort, the self-possessed manager of illegal
fiduciary accounts senses increasingly "the feeling of going over to her side"
(*MW*, 85). A few pages later le Carré records the following observation about
his otherwise improbable hero:

> But here, out of the blue, either his good heart became too much for him,
> or he just forgot for a moment that he was a hard-headed banker born and
> bred. An eerie sensation swept over him that someone else—someone real,
> someone prepared to embrace spontaneous humanity rather than treat it as
> a threat to sound financial management—had commandeered him and was
> speaking out of him:

"But if there's anything personal I can do in the meantime—to help, I mean—
quite honestly, anything at all within reason—I'd really be very happy to. Delighted, in fact. I'd regard it as a privilege." (*MW*, 90)

Brue then drafts a check for 50,000 euros for expenses connected with Issa's
temporary safeguarding. His unexpected magnanimity persuades the previously skeptical Richter that their value systems regarding the "seraphic" refugee may coincide (*MW*, 73). It should be noted, however, that, in overcoming
their conditioned prejudices about each other to find common cause, neither
of these guardians is entirely certain of Issa's self-representation, religious or-
thodoxy, or even sanity.

Issa Salim Mahmoud is intentionally portrayed as an enigma. Although he
wears a bracelet with "the talismanic golden Koran hanging from it to protect
him" (*MW*, 73), for instance, Melik Oktay observes that his family's Chechen
guest "doesn't *think*" or "*act* like a Muslim" (*MW*, 71). We also are led to question whether the survivor of torture might not be partially deranged when we
see him, safely billeted in Richter's harbor-front loft apartment, flying paper
airplanes from the top of a stepladder. The fugitive is also prone to delusions
about his female protector. "Maybe you will convert to Islam," he says to Annabel more than once, "and I will marry you and attend to your education. That
will be a good solution for both of us." Despite these singularities about Issa,
both Richter and Brue recognize a moral imperative to do what they can on
behalf of a "damaged and traumatized child who's had no childhood" (*MW*,
131). Their response of genuinely caring about his plight is based on painful
personal experience—in Annabel's case, the memory of her former client Magomed sent to an almost certain execution; in Tommy's case, the recollection
of his six-day-old grandson's death two years ago. This is a distinctly *human*
factor that sets them apart from the officials of international security policy.
Beyond the constraints of their respective professions, in other words, the idealistic young lawyer and the initially resistant banker acknowledge a transcendent mandate to provide succor to the world's helpless.

The larger significance of Brue's voluntary involvement in Issa's welfare
can be illuminated by drawing on Luc Boltanski's recently translated book
Mysteries and Conspiracies. A widely published professor of sociology at the
École des Hautes Études en Sciences Sociales in Paris, this theorist begins his
study by noting that crime and detective stories gave rise to espionage fiction,
which emerged as a popular literary genre concomitantly with three other developments in the late nineteenth and early twentieth centuries: (1) the rise
of the nation-state, which was endowed with the responsibility of "unifying"

or "*constructing* reality, for a given population on a given territory"; (2) sociology's emergence as a discipline devoted to identifying the forms of causality that "punctuate the lives of persons and groups or even the course of
history"; and (3) psychiatry's invention of "a new nosological entity, paranoia,"
that obsessively questions the underpinnings of an officially proclaimed "reality."[17] At a time when the global expansion of capitalism was undermining
"the logic of the *territory*, a unified space bounded by borders enclosing a ho-
mogeneous population that the state is expected to protect," there arose a generalized metaphysics of suspicion regarding "apparently legitimate political
power-holders" conceived as "marionettes manipulated, with or without their
knowledge and consent, by other forces that possess much more extensive, but
hidden, powers." Foremost in this subversive group were anarchists, socialists,
terrorists, and, notably, international (i.e., stateless) bankers whose "*flows*" of
"*liquid* currency" destabilized their host countries' territorial economy and,
ultimately, nationalistic autonomy.[18]

Given this theoretical framework, all the more remarkable is expatriated
banker Tommy Brue's decision to risk everything that has hitherto defined
him for the sake of an exigent refugee whose claims on his intervention cannot
be empirically confirmed. His boldness in jettisoning the inherited context
of Brue Frères PLC for conceptualizing his agency leads to an unanticipated
epiphany at the novel's exact midpoint:

> Now at last he was able to understand himself. He had mistaken his need. He
> had invested himself in the wrong market. . . . And now he had found *this*,
> which was an important and rather astonishing clarification of his nature for
> him. Waning testosterone was not the issue. The issue was *this*, and *this* was
> Annabel.
>
> And it was for *this*, as much as for any other reason, that he had lied to Messrs.
> Lantern and Foreman. They had talked about his father as if he was their
> property. They had bullied the son in the name of the father, and thought
> they owned him, too. They had strayed too close to ground that was his and
> Annabel's alone, and he had kept them out. In doing so he had consciously
> and deliberately entered her danger zone, which he now shared with her. And
> in consequence, his life had become vivid and precious to him, for which he
> thanked her from the heart. (*MW*, 161)

For Brue, however, the realization of "*this*" is only the beginning of his battle.
What he yet needs to forge, after Richter's kidnapping by Bachmann's team, is

a way to circumvent the host of state operatives now seeking to exploit him as a conduit to Issa. In this endeavor he succeeds, at least temporarily, by adopting his opponents' tactics of dissimulation and pretending to collaborate in the War on Terror, even to the extent of signing a copy of the Official Secrets Act. An emboldened Brue then demands and receives from Ian Lantern an official letter indemnifying Richter against retaliatory prosecution, as well as a German passport for Issa Karpov. A few chapters later, after a pivotal account of all those "laboring in the secret vineyard" of post-9/11 intelligence (*MW*, 235), Brue convinces a wary Dr. Abdullah, coded as "Signpost" by his many surveillants, to meet with him, Issa, and Annabel after hours at his bank in order to finalize the electronic transfer of $12.5 million in illicit Lipizzaner funds.[19]

Just before this transaction occurs, however, le Carré introduces an interlude or *epoché* in the sense of a momentary suspension in the plot's action, that harks directly back to the literary tradition of romance. Having already contemplated the possibility that "I'll sell the bank while there's still a bit to sell, and get myself a life. Might even pop over to California for old Georgie's wedding" (*MW*, 259), Tommy Brue, meeting again with Annabel Richter at the Atlantic Hotel before their appointment at Brue Frères, shows her the documents he has secured from Lantern and invites her to meet his previously estranged daughter, Georgina, in the "Golden State," a mythical land of perpetual promise, to celebrate the arrival of his first grandchild. The proposal, to which the beleaguered lawyer readily agrees, signifies the romantic trope of a new beginning, one that escapes the trammels of past compromises and subjection associated with the political realm.

At the end of *A Most Wanted Man*, however, the collective weight of what Timothy Melley calls the National Security State crushes this tentatively advanced scenario of redemptive possibility.[20] After overseeing the transfer of Colonel Karpov's millions, Brue ushers his guests to the bank's front entrance, where in the evening shadows is hidden a small army of Joint Steering Committee interceptors prepared to abduct both Issa and Dr. Abdullah. Just as Günther Bachmann, disguised as a taxi driver, is about to take custody of "Signpost," a white minibus slams into his cab at nearly the same time as two black-windowed Mercedes Benzes box him in and prevent his interference. In the collision's aftermath a dazed Bachmann watches as four or five masked men force their Muslim captives into the escape vehicle. Staggering down the road with a smashed arm, the maverick agent then spots Arnold Mohr conversing with Newton, his former US counterpart in Beirut. As his feckless

supervisor wanders away to take a phone call, an outraged Bachmann asks
Newton, "Where have you taken him?" Replies Newton:

"Abdullah? Who gives a shit? Some hole in the desert, for all I know. *Justice
has been rendered, man. We can all go home.*" . . .

"*Rendered*?" he [Bachmann] repeated stupidly. "What's rendered? What justice are you talking about?"

"*American* justice, asshole. What do you think? Justice from the fucking hip,
man. No-crap justice, *that* kind of justice! Justice with no fucking lawyers
around to pervert the course. Have you never heard of *extraordinary rendition*[?] No? Time you Krauts had a word for it! Have you given up speaking
or what?"

But still nothing came out of Bachmann, so Newton went on:

"Eye for a fucking eye, Günther. Justice as retribution, okay? Abdullah was
killing *Americans*. We call that original sin. You want to play softball spy
games? Go find yourself some Euro-pygmies."

"I was asking you about Issa," Bachmann said. (*MW*, 321–22)

Newton's apoplectic exposition of the Bush administration's extrajudicial practice of flying suspected terrorists to "black sites" in Europe and Asia for what
is euphemized as "enhanced interrogation" but is actually torture by proxy—
grotesque methods like "waterboarding" and "rectal rehydration"—utterly
obliterates the idyllic alternative represented by Brue's earlier invitation to
Richter to join him and his reconciled daughter in California. In the novel's
concluding paragraph these main characters are last seen standing absently
together near a crossroads, not unlike Timothy Cranmer in the final pages of
Our Game, as a hesitant Bachmann hobbles toward them. All three now know
firsthand that "renditioning" has usurped the "rendering" of impartial justice.
In such a world, implies le Carré, the option of romantic escape no longer
exists, however we might still assume a meaningful distinction between the
private and public spheres.

The collapsed segmentation of those hypothetically discrete realms, argues
Melley, is a consequence of the postmodern emergence of covert and perpetual warfare. Global conflicts once decided on actual battlefields have yielded, he
maintains, to the Cold War's pervasive architecture of secrecy, or "public deception as a *fundamental* element of U.S. policy,"[21] which since the early 1960s

has expanded exponentially, as has the number of intelligence and counter-terrorism agencies engaged in its perpetuation.[22] This scholar further notes that these developments have contributed to a masculinization of the covert sphere and a corresponding feminization of the domestic sphere conceived in the abstract as a threatened "homeland." In light of Melley's model, le Carré's presentation of two households in A Most Wanted Man suggests his critique of secrecy's encroachment on the democratic principle of privacy's supposed inviolability.

The first household is the recently widowed Leyla Oktay's modest domicile in a ghetto for Turkish émigrés, the novel's opening setting, located in Hamburg's unlovely industrial district. When she welcomes vagrant Issa into her "tiny brick house that, after decades of family scrimping, [Leyla] now owned almost free of debt" (MW, 5), the stage is set for Germany's hypervigilant security establishment to pay close attention to what transpires at the residence, even though the state's watchers never physically enter its premises. The Oktays' presumptive "home" in a "foreign" land, in other words, becomes the site for around-the-clock surveillance by the administrative forces of post-9/11 suspicion based on its occupants' ethnicity. As such, they are easy targets for police action because of the government's pervasive Islamophobia.

In sharp contrast is the second household, the lace-curtained "Snow White house . . . , set beside one of Hamburg's most desirable canals" (MW, 198), the home of Frau Ellenberger, deceased Edward Amadeus Brue's former secretary and lover whom Günther Bachmann visits under the guise of a pseudonymous bureaucrat. When Bachmann coaxes Frau Elli, as Tommy Brue calls her, into divulging information about her former employer's dealings with Colonel Karpov through British intelligence intermediary Foreman (Findlay), she lapses into "an unconscious act of retrospective ventriloquism" (MW, 203) eerily reminiscent of Miss Havisham in Charles Dickens's Great Expectations. Manipulated by Bachmann into reliving this phase of her past, during which the man she knew as Teddy Findlay is said to have "worked his evil magic" on Brue senior's banking integrity (MW, 209), Ellenberger expresses a sexual jealousy of these male interlopers' corruptive influence on her much older paramour.

Regarding the Red Army colonel she thus says, "On Mr. Edward he acted like a revitalizing drug. 'Karpov is my Spanish fly,' he once remarked to me. Karpov's irreverence towards the conventional norms of life struck a kindred spark in Mr. Edward's heart" (MW, 205). And when her lover received telephone calls from Findlay, even "in the middle of a private moment," he was in the habit of directing Frau Elli to "go and powder your nose" or, in the event of Findlay's request for a face-to-face meeting, of saying, "Not tonight, Elli. Go and cook a chicken for your mother" (*MW*, 209). These chauvinistic dismissals, prompted by Karpov and Findlay's androcentric bonding with Edward Brue, fuel Ellenberger's repressed resentment, but they also alert us to the masculinized domain of secrecy's penetration of the feminized realm of domesticity.[23]

While dramatizing the travesty, then, of "extraordinary rendition," *A Most Wanted Man* exposes the gendered basis of a putative distinction between public and private amid the West's zealous management of a seemingly interminable War on Terror. No longer immune, given these circumstances, is the paradigm of *home* as a privileged space of inviolability. Both Leyla Oktay and Frau Ellenberger, despite their vastly different cultural backgrounds, experience either siege or invasion in their domiciles by what might be termed the *plenipotentiary* of a New World Order, which ignores nations' geographical borders and territorial mandates. Such appears to be the trade-off by secular democracies in their ongoing campaign against stateless terrorist organizations hoping to establish, as in the case of ISIS, a theocratically governed "homeland."

The insurmountable conundrum, of course, is that in this ongoing confrontation between two antithetical and absolutist ideologies there is no middle ground. Both sides in the global conflict replicate each other's strategies in a process that Boltanski terms "*symmetrization*," which includes situations wherein "threats of conspiracy, made palpable by sporadic, adroitly orchestrated acts of terrorism, result in the maintenance, through fear, of a diffuse belief in the presence of an enemy that is at once threatening, concealed[,] and multiform."[24] In such a geopolitical milieu, the supposed sanctity of domestic privacy is overridden by imperatives decreed by the National Security State's appointed protectors. The question raised by le Carré in the April 2013 issue of *Harper's*, as documented at the beginning of this book's introduction, is consequently more pertinent than ever before: "How far can we go in the rightful defense of our Western values without abandoning them along the way?"

From an Anglo-American perspective, of course, the atrocities committed by Taliban militants in methodically killing 145 people, 132 of whom were schoolchildren, on December 16, 2014, in Peshawar, Pakistan, all the while chanting "Allah is great!" are morally incomprehensible. The West was also appalled on January 7, 2015, when Islamists Cherif and Said Kouachi, trained years earlier in Yemen, attacked the Paris offices of *Charlie Hebdo*, a satirical magazine that had pilloried the prophet Mohammed, and cold-bloodedly executed a dozen staff members while wounding eleven others. Immediately after this event thousands of security forces tracked down the Kouachi brothers before preempting imminent depredations by ISIS sleeper cells in Belgium. Such short-term successes against the perpetrators of jihadist violence, however, are hardly a cause for congratulatory vindication. In terms of tactics, everything about the War on Terror is recursive.

More important, a kind of cultural amnesia justifies the extent to which the liberal democracies of the West have been willing to abrogate their foundational principles in this intractable conflict. All but erased from active memory are egregious violations of human rights that occurred at the Abu Ghraib prison in Iraq, the Bagram prison in Afghanistan, and the Guantánamo Bay detention camp in Cuba, not to mention the indiscriminate deaths that result from high-altitude Predator drones bombing terrorist encampments throughout the Middle East. Ever since the Cold War, contend both Timothy Melley and Eva Horn in remarkably congruent books, Westerners have been influenced to accept a metaphysics of secrecy that legitimizes geopolitical campaigns by their respective "homelands" against incursions by "enemies of the state." In closing this chapter on *The Mission Song* and *A Most Wanted Man*, I want to relate some of these critics' insights to key issues at stake in le Carré's pair of novels.

Melley's *The Covert Sphere: Secrecy, Fiction, and the National Security State* begins by recognizing how apposite to the present era are developments that occurred shortly after the CIA's founding on July 26, 1947, under President Harry S. Truman's National Security Act. At the center of these redirected efforts was George F. Kennan, "arguably the chief architect of the Cold War," who as head of the State Department's Policy Planning Staff "insisted that the United States embrace 'covert political warfare' and 'propaganda as a major weapon of policy.'"[25] Toward realizing these ends, less than a year later Kennan drafted a classified memorandum that upon its official endorsement transformed the fledgling agency's primary mission from one of gathering empirically verifiable intelligence about threats abroad to a paramilitary role of producing "strategic fictions, deceptions, and propaganda for a range of purposes, including the deliberate creation of uncertainty about what is real and true."[26] In this latter capacity, notes Melley, over the next two decades the CIA "spent tens of millions of dollars funding an astonishing array of journals, exhibits, societies[,] and other creative and critical works that projected what it viewed as a strategically favorable view of Western liberal capitalism."[27] From the 1970s onward such generous subsidization was increasingly offered to unaffiliated novelists, filmmakers, television producers, and "think tanks" in order to bring into public consciousness the *idea* of conspiracies, covert action, and systematic governmental deception. Ironically, then, the CIA engaged in the business of promoting "a regime of half-knowledge"—or, oxymoronically, "*open secrecy*"—that Melley links to the rise of "postmodern epistemological skepticism."[28]

By so inoculating, as it were, what Jürgen Habermas calls the "public sphere" as a forum for the rational discussion of civic policy, this arm of the National Security State mobilized a generalized apprehension regarding overseas threats while also inducing a conditioned amnesia on the domestic front.[29] For the foundation of his critique, Melley acknowledges indebtedness to Michael Rogin's 1990 article "'Make My Day!': Spectacle as Amnesia in Imperial Politics." Concentrating on the reductive praxis of "demonology" as it figures in sustaining the doctrine of American exceptionalism, Rogin posits that the United States was led down a forking path of irrationalism, uncertainty, and suspicion blazed by the selfsame forces that were energized by the prospective advent of a New World Order. In the process there came into being what Melley describes as a "*covert sphere* . . . shaped by both institutional secrecy and public fascination with the secret works of the state."[30]

Paradoxically, fictional portrayals of this realm in popular media simultaneously render it visible and make it dismissible as "mere entertainment." Another effect accrues, however, argues Rogin. When covert operations function as "imperial spectacle," a collective amnesia results wherein "that which is insistently represented becomes, by being normalized to invisibility, absent and disappeared." The participle *disappeared*, we might note in passing, aptly sums up what happens to the victims of "extraordinary rendition" according to Newton's rant in *A Most Wanted Man*. Rogin states that such "motivated forgetting" involves at the geopolitical level the ability "both to have [an] experience and not to retain it in memory."[31] We are immersed, that is, in a postmodern heterotopia of "hyperreality," as Jean Baudrillard first maintained in a 1981 treatise, in which a "precession of simulacra" shapes the public's understanding of the way things supposedly are.[32]

Drawing on many of the same evidentiary sources as Melley's study, Eva Horn's *The Secret War: Treason, Espionage, and Modern Fiction* complements the preceding analysis by proposing that the dynamics of betrayal are deeply imbued in the *structure* of secrecy itself. Given the ideal of transparency in modern democracies, state secrets "generate conjectures" and "trigger narratives designed to make sense of events that are removed from knowledge"; thus fictional accounts (i.e., literature and film), more than either journalistic or historical accounts, "illuminate secrecy's structure because they reconstruct its logic, its subtle and mysterious economy of light and dark, truths and lies, presence and absence."[33] Horn's understanding of what she calls the "poetic," or heuristic, nature of fiction makes her analysis infinitely more insightful than that of Frederick P. Hitz, a former CIA inspector general, who in *The Great Game: The Myth and Reality of Espionage* relies on a binary cleaver to maintain that narrative fictions are invariably unreliable, nonveridical distortions of what "really" happened. Altogether lost on Hitz is le Carré's career-long distinction between historiographic "authenticity" and fictional "credibility" in "*extrapolat[ing]* the theme of espionage."[34]

Horn's nuanced critique is valuable for two other reasons. The first involves her diachronic methodology. Tracing the emergence of modern notions of treason and betrayal since the early twentieth century, she points out the stages by which secret intelligence became "a type of knowledge that is primarily geared not toward truth but toward effectiveness in the face of an enemy." The National Security State of today, while manufacturing cover *stories* of "plausible deniability," thus legitimizes its routine practice of "engineering deceptions, disseminating disinformation, or providing false clues" by mimetically replicating the strategies of its perceived adversaries.[35] Moreover, these exercises in dissimulation necessitate the continual production of phantasmal "enemies," often via the creative license of fiction, that threaten a nation's welfare. When the chicanery of such actions is occasionally exposed, as in the case of fraudulent claims about Iraq's possessing "weapons of mass destruction," the public's skepticism about governmental integrity is reinforced but also "normalized," to use Rogin's term, thereby accustoming us to what is proclaimed necessary to protect the "homeland."

The second reason why Horn's book deserves serious attention is her excavation of an underlying linkage between the "secrecy effect" and the "reality effect." The former term signifies a political culture's "employment of clandestine means and practices [that] may be officially admitted" but the details of which "are, as much as possible, hidden deep within the administrative infrastructure and the pervasive reticence of . . . intelligence agencies." The secrecy effect, however, turns into a reality effect preoccupied with a "narrative unfolding of the complex distribution of light and shadow, the knowable and the unknowable[,] within a given political situation." This largely unplumbed interconnection is the focus of le Carré's post-Cold War fiction as he explores, in Horn's words, how "the doubling of reconnaissance and deception in modern intelligence agencies results in an abysmal logic of suspicion."[36]

In light of these conceptual frameworks, both *The Mission Song* and *A Most Wanted Man* dramatize pivotal crises of conscience faced by two usually acquiescent individuals, Bruno Salvador and Tommy Brue, when they find themselves enmeshed in the transnational maze of suspicion. By taking a moral stand amid circumstances that lend themselves to easy compromise, neither protagonist, in the end, "wins," which in any event is an outdated pre–Cold War construct. Instead, both Salvador and Brue, despite their different cultural backgrounds, are left suspended in an indeterminate interspace that represents le Carré's sense of where most of us, confronted with the intransigent and competing ideologies of twenty-first-century geopolitics, are now mired. The unpropitious alternatives, le Carré suggests, are a servile deference to the National Security State's authoritarian mandates or a doomed defiance of those norms. Despite this impasse Salvador and Brue struggle to do the right thing, even though in the end they are co-opted, at least for the moment, by the self-elected guardians of governmental secrecy.

If thwarted in their campaigns of resistance, the *vir bonus* figure in one of these novels bequeaths a testimonial of his experience. *The Mission Song* includes a glimmer of hope for the future in the form of Salvo's narrative for Noah, written while Bruno is under officially deniable detention in England, that contextualizes his decision to "go rogue" as an underling in Her Majesty's security apparatus. Whatever complications this addendum might involve in terms of le Carré's narratological schema in *The Mission Song*, as discussed earlier, it nevertheless holds out the possibility that Noah will learn from Bruno Salvador's trial of self-definition and accountability.

The finale of *A Most Wanted Man* is far more tenuous. As helpless witnesses to Issa's abduction by American renditionists, Annabel Richter and Tommy Brue are left so mute by this raw display of transnational power and intervention that Tommy's attempt to console Annabel in the novel's last sentence by putting his arm around her shoulders goes wholly unacknowledged. Nonetheless, the fact that they have previously managed to establish a bond of mutual trust suggests that after this crushing defeat they might become so radicalized that, through a combination of her legal expertise and his financial resources, they might redouble their efforts to combat such catastrophes in the future. Le Carré's twenty-third novel, *A Delicate Truth*, will present a slightly more hopeful vision of the odds for success in opposing the Secret State's hegemony, but meanwhile he characteristically sides with the cause of humanistic liberalism, however attenuated that position may have become with the expansion of a New World Order.

5

OUR KIND OF TRAITOR AND
A DELICATE TRUTH

"Who Were We Doing All This Secrecy Stuff For?"

The State is a concept based upon the power principle, and a denial of responsibility. It is thus itself criminal. . . . Its own blacker evils are hidden under a veil of hypocrisy, whitewashed by propaganda, and when laid bare covered by the *raison d'état*, a term stretched to enrobe the basest ignominy.

—Nicolas Freeling[1]

THE RAMIFICATIONS OF state-promulgated secrecy, as *Our Kind of Traitor* and *A Delicate Truth* demonstrate, entail another effect besides that of cultural paranoia and, as Eva Horn postulates, a "reality effect." For lack of a more precise theoretical term, we may think of this phenomenon as *muffling*, which in turn is linked to a blurred distinction between friends and enemies, or what since the late 1970s has come to be known as "frenemies."[2] Both consequences ultimately derive from the "regime of half-knowledge" that Timothy Melley relates to the rise of "postmodern epistemological skepticism." Their irruption into the lives of ordinary citizens not professionally involved in the geopolitical intrigues of Whitehall and Westminster attests to the pathology of the *raison d'état* as conceived above by Nicolas Freeling. The other side of this coin, as *Our Kind of Traitor* and *A Delicate Truth* show, is that credible stories of such infection cannot be told without reliance on a whorled, highly oblique mode of narration, which itself, ironically, is a by-product of or a reaction to institutionally promoted campaigns of secrecy.

Before I begin to discuss *Our Kind of Traitor* in light of this thesis, three observations from a throng of favorable reviewers provide helpful perspectives. James Naughtie notes that the novel unfolds by means of an intricate narrative pattern in which even the innocuous play of language has become "a barometer of decay." Given this degradation in dialogical exchange, it is not always easy to determine who at any given point is actually speaking. A medley of polyvalent voices, presented sometimes in italics as emanating from the main characters' unarticulated thought, proliferates within what at the outset is framed as a conventional third-person narrative. Reinforcing this insight, Yvonne Klein posits that le Carré's novel "represent[s] something of a departure from anything he's done before. . . . It's impossible to determine absolutely whose voice . . . tells the story, especially since the point of view seems quite fluid."[3] A third review by Peter Millar captures especially well the kind of narrational obliquity that distinguishes *Our Kind of Traitor*:

> Le Carré writes in that curious tense he has made his own, . . . a sort of pluperfect conditional third person, in which almost every piece of information is transmitted to the reader through the eyes or emotions of another character, often at another time. It is recognisable, inimitable[,] and aggravatingly impossible to paraphrase. There is no facile linear narrative, just a fluid, conversational weft of events that have happened, should have happened, might have happened[,] and probably will happen. Or won't.[4]

Such recognition of the novel's "fluidity" bear out how it attempts to reflect the ever expanding sphere of deception and deterioration of trust fostered by state secrecy, particularly during the post-9/11 era. Not only do the demarcations between public and private collapse; now the virus of secrecy invades even the inwardly turned consciousness of le Carré's protagonists.

One way of gauging the significance of this development in le Carré's fiction is to invoke Frank Kermode's Charles Eliot Norton Lectures at Harvard University in 1977–1978. Kermode maintained that all narratives are "capable of darkness" informed by "radiant obscurity"—that is, of harboring a hermetic reserve of parabolic meaning that eludes discursive understanding. Every "story," therefore, contains a gnostic core that solicits and in fact compels interpretation. The hermeneutical challenge, as Kermode conceived it, lies in acknowledging the riddling nature of what we might refer to as the unsayable. Penetrating this domain is difficult because fictional narratives interweave proclamation with concealment, ultimately requiring something like "acts of divination" to construe them.[5] An ineluctable secrecy thus inheres in texts that we are seduced into exploring by virtue of their clandestine import.

Christopher J. Knight has characterized Kermode's model of narrational secrecy as an example of modern apophaticism, a tradition that harks back to an ancient distinction between *kataphasis* (affirmation or saying) and *apophasis* (negation or unsaying).[6] The first can be equated in a general sense with how and what a text proclaims, the second with how and what it conceals. Historically the two modes have existed in dialectical tension each other. However, during epochs when the foundations of logocentrism and belief are uncertain or, it might be added, when they are eroded by a milieu of normative suspicion, apophaticism predominates. Such, contends Knight, is the cultural matrix in which we have been immersed since the late nineteenth century. The result is a widespread "rhetoric of indirection."[7] Secrecy of this sort is a pivotal issue, I shall argue, in *Our Kind of Traitor*. Furthermore, le Carré's way of narrating his "story" connects him to the literary expression of apophaticism.

Secrecy in this novel manifests itself at two overlapping levels. One level, of course, is its bureaucratic incarnation in MI6. The stock-in-trade of this extension of state power is privileged nondisclosure regarding its ownership of information. The second and more interesting level encompasses unaffiliated individuals who, for reasons unclear even to themselves, agree to auxiliary participation in covert activities. Typically their involvement leads to a degeneration of relational openness with one another. Subtending both of these levels is the motif of England's having lost its moral bearings and integrity after the Cold War's end.

Our Kind of Traitor develops this theme by recounting the efforts of Hector Meredith, a Secret Intelligence Service operative in his midfifties who believes that "we are suffering, as an ex-great nation, from top-down corporate rot" (*OK*, 119), to arrest his country's slide into marginality on the world's stage. Maintaining that "good intelligence [is] about the only thing that gets us a seat at the international top table these days" (*OK*, 86), Meredith enlists protagonists Peregrine (Perry) Makepiece and Gail Perkins upon learning that the lovers were approached by Dmitri (Dima) Vladimirovich Krasnow while they were on vacation in Antigua. Krasnow, the European director for the Arena Multi-Global Trading Conglomerate of Nicosia, Cyprus, and self-described "World Number One money-launderer" (*OK*, 111), is seeking political asylum for himself and his family in exchange for incriminating evidence against British power brokers in collusion with the Russian mafia.

In this role Meredith is reminiscent of Leonard Burr in *The Night Manager*, who also combats the cancer of complicity by his country's leaders with a transnational underworld. For the sake of exposing this network's tentacles in the United Kingdom, Hector Meredith deliberately targets Aubrey Longrigg, a former MI6 officer and "leading member of Her Majesty's Opposition, a Shadow Minister tipped for stratospheric office at the next election," whose "remit, according to the Party handout, will be *to put British trade into point position in the international financial marketplace*" (*OK*, 158).[8] As "Chairman designate of the new parliamentary subcommittee on banking ethics" (*OK*, 162), Longrigg has entered a silent partnership with an emergent Russian syndicate known as the Seven Brothers that controls billions of dollars in illicit funds. Determined to thwart these "vulture capitalists," per the veteran spymaster's repeated description of them (*OK*, 126), Meredith takes advantage of Perry Makepiece and Gail Perkins when they come his way as accidental intermediaries for Dima. To his credit Meredith apprises both neophytes of the risks they are running in consenting to act as go-betweens in this high-stakes game of ferreting out extremely sensitive information.

In contrast to the way he portrays the combative evasions of William J. Matlock, MI6's assistant chief and Meredith's supervisor, le Carré ennobles Meredith's rhetoric of honest proclamation. After a preliminary vetting of his recruits' voluntary report by a pair of his "professionally inquisitive listeners" (*OK*, 12), Hector presents an unvarnished account of what Perry and Gail will face if they choose to cooperate with his investigation. On the eve of a prearranged meeting with Dima at a French Open tennis match in Paris, their handler asserts the following:

> We shall tell you as little as we can get away with, but whatever we do tell you will be the truth. . . . What you don't know you can't fuck up. Every new face has got to *be* a new face to you. Every first time has got to *be* a first time. . . .
>
> So it's familiarization, it's confidence-building, it's establishing trust in all weathers. You in us, us in you. But you are *not* spies. So for Christ's sake don't try to be. Don't even *think* about surveillance. You are *not* surveillance-conscious people. (*OK*, 183–84)

Meanwhile, "status quo man" Matlock, a more truculent version of Sandy Woodrow in *The Constant Gardener*, charges his freewheeling director of special projects with being an "*absolutist*," thereby sounding the note of bureaucratic dismissal and vested self-interest: "We're not a crusade, Hector. We're not hired to rock the boat. We're here to help steer it. We're a *Service*" (*OK*, 175). Meredith, however, has little stomach for such temporizing. After patiently documenting the fact that at least three unscrupulous opportunists besides Longrigg—Westminster lobbyist Giles de Salis, a retired captain of the Royal Navy; Signor Emilio dell Oro, an Italian-Swiss factotum; and lawyer Evelyn (Bunny) Popham, a "courtier and pimp to the Surrey oligarchs" (*OK*,

166)—are involved in a larcenous scheme of self-enrichment, he wins provisional consent to pursue his case against Longrigg pending its ratification by a quorum of the Cabinet Office's specially appointed Empowerment Committee. Behind-the-scenes secrecy, then, is set into motion by Perry Makepiece's vaguely patriotic act of submitting to MI6 a surreptitious recording and a twenty-eight-page transcript of his dealings with Dmitri Krasnow at an Antiguan resort while on holiday.

This decision by le Carré's male protagonist constitutes a key crux in *Our Kind of Traitor*. Shortly after his thirtieth birthday Peregrine Makepiece is beginning to grow restless with his course in life. "His first name," we are told, "traditionally the property of the English upper classes, derive[d] from a rabble-rousing Methodist prelate of the nineteenth century." Despite this incongruous line of descent, Perry has won "ultimate academic success" at Oxford as the "State-educated son of secondary-school teachers," yet he questions "just what the first third of his natural life ha[s] achieved, apart from providing him with an excuse for not engaging in the world beyond the city's dreaming spires" (*OK*, 1). Experiencing a generational displacement not unlike that of T. E. Lawrence, Makepiece, a politically liberal don who recently "delivered a series of lectures on George Orwell under the title 'A Stifled Britain?'" (*OK*, 2), exorcises his inner demons by participating in cross-country marathons, alpine mountain climbing, and semiprofessional tennis in order to recapture a fugitive sense of being "at the *hard centre of life*" (*OK*, 3). Further indicative of Perry's unrest are two other details: a year earlier he had argued in a *London Review of Books* article on Wilfred Owen, Edmund Blunden, Siegfried Sassoon, and Robert Graves that "*the sacrifice of brave men does not justify the pursuit of an unjust cause*" (*OK*, 87); and only a month ago, in the novel's fictive timeline, he "composed a full-page advertisement in the *Oxford Times*, endorsed by a hastily assembled body of his own creation calling itself 'Academics against Torture', urging action against Britain's Secret Government and the assault-by-stealth on our most hard-fought civil liberties" (*OK*, 89). Peregrine Makepiece, in other words, is a man in search of redefinition and deeper commitment.

Viewed from another angle, Perry is eager to discover a modern-day exemplar of ruggedly masculine individualism. Dima, having survived fifteen years of imprisonment in a Siberian gulag in his youth for murdering a "Sovietsky apparatchik" who had raped his mother (*OK*, 104), seems to fit the disaffected academician's construct of "*a formed man*, another definition that he aspired to himself, but for all his manly striving did not feel he had yet attained" (*OK*, 8; emphasis added). The passage suggests Perry's quest for

"Connection with a capital C" (*OK*, 65). The fact that rogue informant Dmitri Krasnow, who now seeks only "fair play" in England (*OK*, 111), strikes Peregrine Makepiece as fulfilling his expectations of such a paradigm implies that his own country lacks comparably heroic role models. He therefore finds himself magnetically drawn to Dima on behalf of the Russian's overtures to the British government.

In this developing scenario Gail Perkins, le Carré's female protagonist, is every bit Perry's equal at the outset. Although her family background differs strikingly from his, both are profiled as "*de facto* orphans. If Perry's late parents had been the soul of high-minded Christian socialist abstinence, Gail's were the other thing"—actors prone to "wayward" indulgences who separated when their daughter was thirteen years old (*OK*, 3). Notwithstanding this sociological disparity in their origins, the two lovers have become upwardly mobile professionals intent on forging an independent future for themselves. For Perkins, an ambitious "young barrister on the rise" (*OK*, 2), this aspiration involves suppressing at least one secret about her past, which she has never divulged to Perry—namely, that in her late teens she had an abortion. Otherwise both protagonists are evenly matched in terms of their competitive drive to succeed in markedly different spheres of endeavor. Like Perry, however, Gail harbors a latent need that has gone unsatisfied by all her accomplishments to date. When the couple is besieged by Dima and soon trusted as adjuncts to his extended family, Gail's sympathy quickly gravitates to his seventeen-year-old daughter Natasha's plight of illegitimate pregnancy. Both main characters thus find themselves enticed into acting as mediators for the Krasnow clan.

Such vicarious identification—hedged around by confidentiality, given Dima's hope of bartering criminal intelligence for sanctuary in England—soon compromises Perry and Gail's previous openness with each other. Unable to fathom Perry's "slide into involuntary kinship" with Dima as betokening anything more than a romanticized form of male bonding (*OK*, 93)—"Who is Perry hoping for a glimpse of?" wonders Gail. "Of Dima, his Jay Gatsby? Of Dima, his personal Kurtz? Or some other flawed hero of his beloved Joseph Conrad?" (*OK*, 82)—she fails to grasp until much later that "it's about being in touch with the real world" (*OK*, 215). Meanwhile, Gail finds her voice becoming muffled, at times falsely histrionic, when she and Perry are being debriefed by Hector Meredith's team members regarding their interactions with Dmitri Vladimirovich Krasnow. As the two lovers rehash those circumstances, a gulf of self-questioning widens between them. "Is that really how Perry and I talk to each other?" ponders courtroom-trained Gail at one point, "listen[ing] to her voice rattling back at her from the brick walls of the basement room" (*OK*, 11, 16), another variation on echolalia in le Carré's fiction. Perry, caught up in the high drama of an undercover operation, takes it upon himself to become Gail's protector after drafting their supposedly joint affidavit on Dima. Once drawn into that venture by Meredith's "professionally inquisitive listeners," Gail asks herself, "Who were we doing all this secrecy stuff for? Who were we fooling except ourselves?" (*OK*, 56–57). The widening gap between Perry and Gail is a result of their participation in state-sanctioned secrecy.

This rupture is all the more disturbing to Perkins because after five years as a couple "the two of them were separately and together at life's crossroads with some pretty heavy thinking to do" (*OK*, 5). The decision with which they are confronted looms over their vacation: "What should Perry do with his life, and should they do it together?" Moreover, "should Gail give up the Bar and step blindly into the azure yonder with him, or should she continue to pursue her meteoric career in London?" (*OK*, 4). After meeting Dima and learning of his family's predicament, Gail discovers that Jekyll-like Perry is transmogrifying into "Mr. Hyde of the British Secret Service" (*OK*, 77), and she recognizes that a chasm is opening between them as partners. *Our Kind of Traitor*, in other words, is primarily concerned not with recounting a thrilleresque tale of Dima's defection to the West but rather with exploring the dynamics of secrecy as they impinge on two "orphans" who become enmeshed in the machinery of post–Cold War espionage.

The miasma of that world soon becomes apparent when Gail and Perry cross through the looking glass. All three members of Hector Meredith's handpicked MI6 team involved in the protagonists' debriefing after Antigua exemplify the "Great Wall between . . . outer and inner selves" that immersion in tradecraft erects (*OK*, 162). Gail and Perry's minder named Ollie Devereux, "the best back-door man in the business" (*OK*, 135), is thus a chameleonic figure of indeterminate age whose accent changes as readily as his disguises. Interrogator Luke Weaver is presented in greater depth as being a casualty of "*déformation professionnelle*" (*OK*, 86), a phrase that contrasts him with Perry's impression of Dima as "*a formed man*." After the interrogator's last posting in Bogotá, Colombia, during which Weaver had an affair with a colleague's wife and endured torture in the jungle by a drug lord who was previously his informant, MI6's "Queen of Human Resources" has apprised Luke—"all spoken in a gabble between brackets"—that he is "headed for the shelf" (*OK*, 122–23). Meanwhile, he remains trapped in a loveless second marriage to his "irretrievable wife," Eloise, and pretends unconvincingly to be an attentive father to their ten-year-old son (*OK*, 226). The third member of Meredith's team, "Iron Maiden" Yvonne (*OK*, 138), is a coolly detached researcher who claims rather improbably, as she is rebuffing Luke's timid sexual advances, that in private life she is the happily married mother of a toddler. What all these operatives have in common, then, is a disjunction between "outer and inner selves" that is a direct consequence of their devotion to state-supported secrecy.

Despite *Our Kind of Traitor*'s heroizing him as an incorruptible crusader, Hector Meredith is not exempt from personal failures that seem linked, at least inferentially, to his all-consuming battle against "the forces of darkness" (*OK*, 243). We thus are told that his "only son Adrian, not for the first time, had crashed a stolen car at high speed while under the influence of class-A drugs" (*OK*, 125), a repeat offense for which he has now been imprisoned. Moreover, Hector's "beloved daughter," Jenny, while pursuing a PhD on Leon Trotsky, nearly married a manipulative "sadist," and in ancipation of this planned union Meredith had bought them a recession-indexed house in Bloomsbury, the same one he now uses for auditing the testimony of Makepiece and Perkins on their dealings with Dima Krasnow (*OK*, 134–35). Toward the novel's end it is also revealed that "according to Ollie, Hector's wife Emily had ceased to live with him in London after Adrian's crash. She preferred the arctic cottage in Norfolk, which was nearer to the prison" (*OK*, 289).

The middle section of *Our Kind of Traitor* develops two thematically interlaced strands in light of its title. The first revolves around Dima's "synergy of confession" as he braces himself to narrate his life story to Perry in a rickety and windblown upper chamber of Three Chimneys, the dilapidated Caribbean estate that he purchased for $6 million (*OK*, 93). The second details all the deceptions by which Aubrey Longrigg and his cohorts have managed to circumvent ethical standards of accountability. Juxtaposed, the accounts delineate completely different kinds of "traitors."

Before surrendering himself to Perry and Gail's mediation on his behalf with British authorities, Dima must buffer the shame that accompanies his self-perceived treachery. Without extenuating his involvement in the Russian underworld, he begins by cathartically recalling human rights violations in Guantánamo, Kabul, and Mumbai from which he once profited indirectly. "I done enough death in my life" (*OK*, 101), he summarizes in disgust at his own opportunism. Dima's narrative arc then takes him back to his imprisonment as a young man when he was inducted into the elite *vory*, "a brotherhood of criminals of honour sworn to abide by a strict code of conduct" and enforce justice in the gulag (*OK*, 105). Only a few weeks before *Our Kind of Traitor* begins, however, the money launderer found himself unable to protect a protégé named Misha from assassination by an unscrupulous Moscow syndicate. To avenge Misha's murder, Dima is prepared to reveal the syndicate's foreign beneficiaries, including several dignitaries in England. Even so cursory an overview indicates that Dmitri Krasnow is an incomparably more principled person than Aubrey Longrigg.

Meanwhile, in presentations that he makes to "Billy Boy" Matlock for approval of his operation against Longrigg and his fellow insider crooks, Hector Meredith's *bête noir* is exposed as a wholly corrupt betrayer of his nation's ideals. Even before being shown incriminating evidence of the New Labour MP Longrigg's collusion with the Russian mafia—including video clips of his attending a lavish reception on board a yacht anchored near Dubrovnik whose other guests are such influence peddlers as Giles de Salis, Emilio dell Oro, and Bunny Popham—Matlock signals his aversion to authorizing Meredith's investigation:

All right, granted, the Service has a statutory interest in international crookery and money-laundering. We fought for a piece of it when times were hard, and now we're landed with it. I refer to that unfortunate fallow period between the Berlin Wall coming down and Osama bin Laden doing us the favour of 9/11. We fought for a piece of the money-laundering market the same as we fought for a larger slice of Northern Ireland, and whatever other modest pickings were available to justify our existence. But that was *then*, Hector. And this is *now*, and as of today, which is where we are living, like it or not, your Service and mine has better things to do with its time and resources than get its knickers caught in the highly complex wheels of City of London finance, thank you. (*OK*, 151)

So speaks the voice of managerial expediency. Matlock's peroration also reveals that in the "fallow period" of intelligence gathering during the 1990s, MI6, like any other market-sensitive corporate enterprise, had to diversify in order to survive. In later objections to Meredith's case against Longrigg, it thus is not surprising that Matlock, in an outburst that recalls supervisor Robert Anderson's to Bruno Salvador in *The Mission Song*, should say: "What's *wrong*, when you come down to it, with turning black money to white, at the end of the day? . . . So where would you rather see that money? Black and out there? Or white, and sitting in London in the hands of civilized men?" (*OK*, 176).[9]

Although no love is lost between Meredith and Matlock, the latter, as MI6's assistant chief, actively subverts his director of special projects in the novel's climax by exploiting secrecy's predictable leakage. In addition to Aubrey

Longrigg, then, he qualifies as "our kind of traitor" tainted by exposure to the "Whitehall-Westminster jungle" (*OK*, 133).[10] Before this revelation, however, the narrative's setting shifts to France and Switzerland, where the countdown to Hector Meredith's tentatively approved operation begins. After "Perry's conversion to the cause" (*OK*, 180), Dima is scheduled to sign over his financial network to the Seven Brothers in Paris on June 8, 2009, two days after which he must ratify the arrangement in Berne.

In order to rescue Dima and his family immediately after the transaction, Meredith commissions Perry and Gail, under their respective code names of Milton and Doolittle, to rendezvous seemingly by accident with the Russian defector at the Roland Garros Stadium, where tennis star Roger Federer is playing against challenger Robin Söderling.[11] The upshot of this staged reunion is that they are able to facilitate a face-to-face meeting between Hector and Dima, after which the two principals agree on a future course of action for their mutual benefit. This plan involves sequestering Dima and his family in the nondescript rural village of Wegen, Switzerland, while Meredith is "locked in a life-and-death bureaucratic duel" for their safe escape to England (*OK*, 237).

To no surprise, and with all the predictability of a collapsing house of cards, Hector Meredith's last-minute efforts to negotiate on behalf of his witness fail when he is cunningly outflanked by Matlock. Resentful of Meredith's verbal thrashing of him earlier and concerned about "his own position in the future scheme of things," Matlock relies on a calculated whisper campaign to scuttle the mission's chances of success. Le Carré frames this development in a series of speculative rhetorical questions:

> What great City eminence might Billy Boy . . . have invited to lunch— famously parsimonious though he might be—and sworn to secrecy, knowing that in the great eminence's book a secret is what he tells one person at a time? Knowing also that he has gained himself a friend should events take a tricky turn?
>
> And of the many ripples that might fan out from this one little pebble tossed into the City's murky waters, who knew which of them might lap against the super-sharp ear of that distinguished City insider and rising parliamentarian, Aubrey Longrigg? (*OK*, 281–82)

The central image of a secret's serial divulgence fanning out like ripples on a pond captures perfectly its mode of transmission and deniable consequences.

In the case of Dima Krasnow, the star deposer against some of England's most venal politicians, these outcomes amount to a sentence of death.

The concluding paragraphs of *Our Kind of Traitor* record this eventuality through a strategic syncope that involves the silencing of Hector Meredith's whistle-blower. While Perry and Gail are chaperoning the Krasnow family dependents at a chateau, patriarch Dima, crediting the cultural mythology that the "English gentleman" believes in "fair play" (*OK*, 26), dies when the privately chartered airplane transporting him along with Luke Weaver to supposed safety in the United Kingdom implodes shortly after takeoff. Le Carré writes the following:

> And there was no explosion. Or none that reached Perry's ears. Later, he wished there had been. Just the thump of a gloved fist into a punchball and a long white flash that brought the black hills rushing at him, then absolutely nothing, either to look at or to hear, until the ta-too-ta-toos of police and ambulances and fire brigades as their flashing lights began to answer the light that had gone out. (*OK*, 305–6)

This null sound effect is reminiscent of Joseph Conrad's offstage report of Stevie's obliteration by a Greenwich Park bomb in *The Secret Agent* (1907). In both cases the events' muffled reality indicts institutionalized forms of secrecy and their official guardians for these deaths.

"No group," ends *Our Kind of Traitor*, "has claimed responsibility" (*OK*, 306). Of course not, and why should we expect anything else when, as Meredith opines, "A lot of people in my Service make a profession of not seeing things in black and white" (*OK*, 119)? The novel's third-person coda supplants its earlier concentration on the protagonists' dialogical interplay, reinforcing the idea of how their initiation into a governmental culture of secrecy has rendered them mute witnesses of its cost in human lives. "The State is a concept based upon the power principle, and a denial of responsibility," declares Freeling in this chapter's epigraph. "It is thus itself criminal." Le Carré's novel agrees with that assessment in dramatizing how the post–Cold War recrudescence of a politics of duplicity strips ordinary people of autonomy.

Shortly before this finale, realizing that his cause is probably lost, Hector Meredith calls Perry Makepiece and disconsolately admits that from time to time he reads the works of philosopher Leszek Kolakowski, who maintains that "Evil" is "not rooted in social circumstance" but constitutes "an *absolutely* and *entirely* separate human force" (*OK*, 288). The maverick MI6 officer then mentions Kolakowski's Law of the Infinite Cornucopia, which posits that even though there is "an infinite number of explanations for any single event" (*OK*, 289), the fallible pursuit of truth is itself ennobling. Although Meredith, in his dejection, does not mention the last point, we come close here to the monitory impulse behind le Carré's lifelong vision, but pervading it is an ongoing inquiry into secrecy's invidious genesis and corruptive power.

* * * * *

A Delicate Truth, set almost entirely in England, extends further its author's critique of the state's inherent criminality while also obliquely responding to philosopher Leszek Kolakowski through Hannah Arendt's concept of the banality of evil in *The Human Condition*. At a time when the responsibility for national security was being outsourced to private defense contractors, another extension of a corporate model, le Carré condemns the emergence of a "Deep State . . . of non-governmental insiders from banking, industry[,] and commerce who were cleared for highly classified information denied to large swathes of Whitehall and Westminster" (*DT*, 252).[12] His anger at that development, as reviewer Fintan O'Toole points out, is conveyed by le Carré's depiction of three British stalwarts. These "real men of England" (*DT*, 278) seek to make public the debacle of a counterterrorism venture dubbed Operation Wildlife, which had been engineered three years earlier by Jay Crispin, a dodgy "forty-something television version of the officer-class business executive" engaged in "peddling raw *intelligence*" as a blue-chip commodity in "the free world's . . . marketplace" (*DT*, 50, 289, 66).[13]

In contrast to le Carré's Cold War canon, observes O'Toole, *A Delicate Truth* suggests that patriotism today *requires* a person of conscience to betray the state.[14] The underpinnings of such an obligation differ radically from the ethic expressed by Control to Alec Leamas in *The Spy Who Came In from the Cold*, when the West was engaged in ideological combat with the Soviet bloc:

> We do disagreeable things, but we are *defensive*. . . . We do disagreeable things so that ordinary people here and elsewhere can sleep safely in their beds at night. . . . Of course, we occasionally do very wicked things. . . . And in weighing up the moralities, . . . you can't compare the ideals of one side with the methods of the other. . . .

I mean you've got to compare method with method, and ideal with ideal. I would say that since the war, our methods—ours and those of the
opposition—have become much the same. I mean you can't be less ruthless
than the opposition simply because your government's *policy* is benevolent,
can you now? . . . That would *never* do. (*SW*, 14–15)

Articulated in this speech is the familiar, easily abused argument that the
end justifies the means. One problem with this consequentialist proposition,
however, is that it relativizes moral values and does little to ensure evenhanded justice. Codified laws by themselves, of course, do not guarantee justice, least of all when elected officials or their supporters pontificate about
the latter concept based on private agendas, but they do serve as an imper-
fect bulwark against flagrant injustice.[15] When this system is widely compromised, *A Delicate Truth* implies, a patriot has no other choice but to commit
what once was deemed treason by exposing the government's extrajudicial
circumventions.

Le Carré dramatizes such a situation by focusing on three honorable and
conscience-stricken opponents of Britain's "Deep State": Toby Bell, a "gifted,
state-educated only child of pious artisan parents from the south coast of England who knew no politics but Labour" (*DT*, 47); Christopher (Kit) Probyn, a
middle-ranking "low flyer" in the Foreign Office (*DT*, 93); and David Jebediah
(Jeb) Owens, a Welsh soldier in British Special Forces who participated in "a
privately funded stealth operation" (*DT*, 88). Aided by Jeb's feisty widow Brigid, who was formerly employed by Northern Ireland's Royal Ulster Constabu-
lary, these men devote themselves to revealing the malfeasance of the recently
elected MP Fergus Quinn, "Scottish brawler" and "marooned Blairite of the
new Gordon Brown era" (*DT*, 4, 57). Having hitched his ambitions to a political star in decline, Quinn was anxious at the time to resurrect his prospects
by entering into a surreptitious partnership with Jay Crispin, the founder of
a start-up organization calling itself Ethical Outcomes Incorporated, whose
team of American mercenaries hoped to capture a high-value terrorist arms
buyer on the shores of the Crown colony of Gibraltar.

Both conspirators are self-serving opportunists. Married to a "rich Cana-
dian alcoholic wife whom his Party's spin doctors have ruled unfit for public
presentation" (*DT*, 81), politician Quinn spends most of his time as junior
minister of state to the Foreign Office attending to whatever will advance his
career, no matter how suspect the enterprise. When appearing on television,
Quinn is fond of portraying himself as "the people's scourge of Whitehall's

bureaucracy" (*DT*, 5), yet behind his securely locked office doors he enter-
tains half-cocked proposals that will cast him as a Churchillian leader in England's counterterrorism effort. His evil genius and "secret sharer" (*DT*, 72),
Crispin, is even more craven. Outwardly suave and prepossessing, this British
CEO of Ethical Outcomes has launched his latest enterprise by courting the
financial backing of Mrs. Spencer Hardy of Houston, Texas, "better known as
the mountainously wealthy Miss Maisie, born-again benefactress of America's
Republican far right, friend of the Tea Party, scourge of Islam, homosexuals,
abortion[,] and . . . contraception" (*DT*, 85). Le Carré's swipe at this neoconservative dowager from the United States speaks for itself, but the primary targets
of his scorn are Britons like Crispin and Quinn whose parasitic mendacity
contributes to their nation's moral bankruptcy.

The gulf separating this pair of chameleons from le Carré's triad of valorized
heroes is immense.[16] Thirty-four-year-old Toby Bell, erstwhile private secretary to MP Quinn, is described as "the most feared creature of our contemporary world: a solitary decider" (*DT*, 47). Like Perry Makepiece in *Our Kind
of Traitor*, Toby is an anomaly in terms of England's centuries-old class structure.[17] Having "battled his way into the Foreign and Commonwealth Office,
first as a clerk, and thence by way of evening classes, language courses, internal
examinations[,] and two-day leadership tests," Toby still wishes to "make a
difference . . . in his country's discovery of its true identity in a post-imperial,
post–Cold War world" (*DT*, 48). His private life is admittedly a shambles. Having indulged, according to his "enigmatic mentor and self-appointed patron"
Giles Oakley (*DT*, 49), in "an inappropriate dalliance with the spouse of the
Dutch military attaché" during his first overseas posting in Berlin when the
Iraq War was imminent (*DT*, 52), Bell acquired a reputation as a womanizer.
Several years later, while "steeling himself to perform an act of espionage so
outrageous that, if detected, it would cost him his career and his freedom" (*DT*,
47), he is in the process of being abandoned by his live-in girlfriend, Isabel,
someone else's estranged wife. Despite the unevenness of his personal relationships, this rising star in the Foreign Office is renowned for his calmness and
composure in crisis situations. Largely because Toby Bell is upward bound in
that bureaucratic structure, his decision to tape-record Quinn, then his supervisor in the Ministry of Defence, clandestinely planning Operation Wildlife is
all the more a sign of his foundational patriotism.

Unlike Bell at the time of that ultrasecret mission, Kit Probyn is in the twilight of his relatively undistinguished career as a civil servant. Finishing out his
tenure in a backwater department known as Logistical Contingencies, he yet is
regarded by Human Resources as a "*cool head*" and by Quinn as a "safe pair of

hands" (*DT*, 6). When summoned in his late fifties to the new junior minister of state's inner sanctum, Probyn agrees, against the backdrop of "a twelve-foot portrait of an eighteenth-century Empire-builder in tights" (*DT*, 5), to serve as field liaison in what Quinn describes as an "extremely delicate assignment" that "involves depriving the terrorist enemy of the means to launch a premeditated assault on our homeland" (*DT*, 7). Susceptible to the post-9/11 rhetoric of alarmist fear-mongering, Kit, using the alias Paul Anderson, interfaces in Gibraltar with team commander Jeb Owens where, unbeknownst to him until three years later, the ill-conceived Operation Wildlife results only in the deaths of a Muslim illegal immigrant from Morocco and her infant daughter at the hands of trigger-happy American mercenaries. In the aftermath of that unpublicized event, Probyn receives knighthood and an appointment as high commissioner in the Caribbean.

In his private life Sir Probyn, as his surname suggests, is the soul of probity. Fiercely devoted to his wife, Suzanna, now in full remission from cancer, and his daughter, Emily, a physician rebounding from a disastrous love affair, Kit relishes his honorary role as "the first non-Cornishman ever to be elected Official Opener and Lord of Misrule for Master Bailey's Annual Fayre" in the village of St. Pirran, to which he and Suzanna have recently retired (*DT*, 130). In this bucolic setting the master of ceremonies first learns from an itinerant leatherworker, the seemingly deranged Jeb, that misguided Operation Wildlife culminated in the death of two innocents written off as collateral damage.

The third member of le Carré's heralded triad, Jeb Owens, figures as a tragic victim of circumstances far beyond his control. Pursuant to the fiasco on Gibraltar's shores, during the initial stages of which both he and Probyn advised Minister Quinn in London by encrypted cell phone against proceeding with the nighttime operation, Owens refused bribery by one of Crispin's cronies and returned to Britain a shattered man.[18] Appalled at having participated in a covert act of extraordinary rendition, given its murderous casualties, the tormented Jeb has separated from his family in a Welsh hamlet and has become a drifter selling handcrafted leather goods from a converted van. After accidentally encountering "Paul Anderson" in St. Pirran, however, the ex–Special Forces soldier and Sir Christopher, the latter now ashamed of the reason for conferral of his title and the Caribbean posting, join forces to expose Quinn's self-serving adventurism by means of firsthand testimony supplemented by photographs of the slain mother and child. Yet before that collaborative dossier of evidence can be assembled, Owens is killed and hastily cremated. The metropolitan police investigate the incident and declare his death a suicide, despite overwhelming evidence to the contrary. Such is the fate of an isolated whistle-blower, indicates *A Delicate Truth*, who was brave enough to oppose the machinations of a "Deep State."

While tracing these fortuitous interactions among his three leading male characters, le Carré goes out of his way to illustrate the labyrinthine complexity of Whitehall's new infrastructure, or "sprawling intelligence octopus" (*DT*, 58), in the wake of 9/11. Toby Bell becomes aware of this increased bureaucratization and corresponding escalation of governmental secrecy when, after assignments in Berlin, Madrid, and Cairo, he is "whisked back to London and yet again promoted ahead of his years" to the position of private secretary to MP Quinn (*DT*, 55). In an attempt to fathom Quinn's furtive ways and wary distrust of subordinates, Bell relies on his earlier civil-service colleagues for background information. From Anglo-Indian friend Diana, now officially his director of regional services, Toby discovers that Quinn managed to survive an unspecified but major scandal in his previous appointment. Another Defence Ministry veteran named Lucy confirms this report off the record.

Bell taps other old friends engaged in the profession of intelligence gathering. From "career spy" Matti, "drinking pal and . . . embassy colleague in Madrid," he learns more concretely that "your man went off the reservation" while "all those bent lobbyists and arms salesmen [were] beavering away at the fault lines between the defence industry and procurement'" (*DT*, 61). Subsequent confidences by "Treasury boffin" Laura reveal that "Defence was in a state of corporate rot long before [Quinn] came on the scene" (*DT*, 63, 65). "Half its officials," she explains nervously over dinner, "didn't know whether they were working for the Queen or the arms industry, and didn't give a hoot as long as their bread was buttered" (*DT*, 65). When Toby then consults longtime rival Gregory, now slaving away at a secondary appointment, as well as former counterpart Horst of the German Foreign Service, he finds out only that his current master had once been under a cloud of suspicion but was exonerated by an internal investigation. What le Carré emphasizes through these grapevine intimations and hesitantly disclosed rumors is the post-9/11 infection of rampant secrecy.

Toby Bell's subsequent decision to surreptitiously audiotape MP Quinn's preliminary briefing of "Paul Anderson" and Jeb Owens before Operation Wildlife attests to le Carré's faith in a vanishing breed of "solitary decider[s]" in an age of amoral corporatism. Even the Nixonian technology that Bell employs for this purpose is a throwback to an earlier time: a "Cold War–era, pre-digital, industrial-sized tape recorder—an apparatus so ancient and lumbering, so redundant in our age of miniaturized technology[,] as to be an offence to the contemporary soul" (*DT*, 103). In contrast to his BlackBerry, which later betrays his independent sleuthing, this antiquated device allows Bell to document Quinn's complicity with Crispin in perpetrating a wholly deniable act of extraordinary rendition. The junior minister of state's specious rhetoric while trying to allay Owens's concerns about the Gibraltar undertaking corresponds to that posted on the website of Ethical Outcomes:

> With our brand-new international team of uniquely qualified geopolitical thinkers, we at Ethical offer innovative, insightful, cutting-edge analyses of risk assessment to major corporate and national entities. At Ethical we pride ourselves on our integrity, due diligence, and up-to-the-minute cyber skills. Close protection and hostage negotiators available at immediate notice. (*DT*, 10–11)

Toby Bell's immediate reaction to his covert surveillance and its results do not glamorize him, however, as a valiant "traitor." Not only was he prompted by motives unclear to himself to tape-record his supervisor's private conversation, but after listening to the soundtrack Toby is at a loss about how next to proceed. Trained by the Foreign Office in "measured, non-judgemental responses at all times" (*DT*, 117–18) but stunned by what he has learned, Bell converts the analog tape to a digital recording, which he then transfers to a memory stick that he pastes behind a photograph of his maternal grandparents in his Islington flat. Five days later Quinn's private secretary finds himself reassigned to Beirut.

In this context Bell's original mentor, Giles Oakley, begins to play an increasingly important role in shaping his protégé's future course of action. While the Iraq War was looming and fifty-five-year-old Oakley was the British embassy's *éminence grise* in Germany, he sympathetically confided to Toby, then in his early twenties, that "no sovereign nation such as ours should be taken to war under false pretences, least of all by a couple of egomaniac[al] zealots without an ounce of history between them" (*DT*, 51). At the same time, the veteran diplomat prides himself on masking "callow personal opinions" and "doing everything by halves" (*DT*, 51, 52). Oakley, in short, is the consummate careerist who presides over Bell's induction into the Foreign Office's operational mandate for anesthetizing the dictates of individual conscience.

This disjunction reveals itself during Bell's overseas posting in Cairo a few years later. Recalling Oakley's counsel, he diligently "barters intelligence with

his Egyptian opposite numbers" and "under instruction feeds them names of
Egyptian Islamists in London who are plotting against the regime." However,
on weekends

> he enjoys jolly camel rides with debonair military officers and secret police-
> men and lavish parties with the super-rich in their guarded desert condo-
> miniums. And at dawn, after flirting with their glamorous daughters, drives
> home with car windows closed to keep out the stench of burning plastic and
> rotting food as the ragged ghosts of children and their shrouded mothers
> forage for scraps in filthy acres of unsorted rubbish at the city's edge. (*DT*, 54)

Toby's shock seven years later, on accidentally learning that Giles Oakley was
"the closet author of a round-robin letter to the Foreign Secretary about the
insanity of invading Iraq," is therefore understandable (*DT*, 81). The phrase
"closet author" is significant. Implying not only Oakley's ghosted drafting of
the letter for others' signatures, which enables him to disavow the opinions
expressed therein, it hints also at his homosexuality, revealed only at the end
of *A Delicate Truth*, despite his decades-long marriage to "diplomatic *Ur*-wife,
Hermione" (*DT*, 51). Notwithstanding his mentor's advice to destroy the evidence of what he has learned about Operation Wildlife, Toby conceals it until
such time, presumably, as the information becomes actionable.

From this point onward the novel's focus shifts to the state's criminal suppression of the truth about its counterterrorism venture. That pattern begins
to emerge after an outraged Kit Probyn meets with Jay Crispin and is fobbed
off with the lie that Operation Wildlife resulted in no dead mothers or babies.
Probyn, recently retired as high commissioner in the Caribbean, then tracks
down Bell, the former private secretary of MP Quinn (who left politics shortly
after that debacle to accept a post as defense procurement consultant in the
Middle East), and relentlessly cross-examines Toby about the escapade. Any
formal inquiry that their collaborative testimony might occasion, therefore,
would be aimed not at prosecuting Quinn himself but rather at holding the
monolith of Whitehall accountable for deliberately quashing evidence about
Operation Wildlife's outcome. During their face-to-face colloquies at Probyn's
manor in Cornwall, the two men sort out what may have transpired three
years ago, but their tentative inferences require additional substantiation, in
pursuit of which they go their separate ways.

Conditioned by a lifetime of dutiful civil service, Probyn assumes that the
Foreign Office will be receptive to his on-the-scene revelations supplemented

by Jeb Owens's disclosures before his assassination, yet guided by that assumption Sir Christopher is confronted with recently adopted governmental mechanisms against the threat of whistle-blowers. The scene in which Probyn presents his documentation to the department's current mandarins makes clear le Carré's critique of the "Deep State." After being told that he cannot meet with the executive director, a title change indicative of "the Office's rush towards corporatization" (*DT*, 255), Sir Christopher is ushered into an interview with the man's minions. Having pored over Kit's written documentation for an hour and a half, deputy legal advisor Lionel, twenty years ago Probyn's work associate, and consultant lawyer Frances, the new director in charge of security, cross-examine Probyn about the circumstances of his indictment's composition. Despite Lionel's initial pretense of cordiality, he soon closes ranks with Frances in discrediting the allegations of an official cover-up involving Operation Wildlife. Moderating a harsher response by his accomplice, Lionel explains the following to Sir Christopher:

> A *public* inquiry of the sort you're hankering after . . . is light years away from the sort of hearing that Frances and I envisage. Anything deemed in the *smallest* way to go against national security—secret operations successful or otherwise, extraordinary rendition whether merely planned or actually achieved, robust interrogation methods, ours or more particularly the Americans'—goes straight into the Official Secrets box, I'm afraid, and the witnesses with it. . . .
>
> We have a new set of rules since your day for cases where sensitive issues are involved. Some already in place; others, we trust, imminent. And, very unfortunately, *Wildlife* does tick a lot of these boxes. Which would mean, I'm afraid, that any inquiry would have to take place behind closed doors. (*DT*, 266–67)

The upshot of Probyn's overture to the Foreign Office is that he finds himself muzzled by Whitehall's "new set of rules" that all but ensure the inviolability of its regime of secrecy. Such are the stratagems of expediency, according to Nicolas Freeling, by which the Hobbesian Leviathan invokes the abstraction of a *raison d'état* to "enrobe the basest ignominy."

Toby Bell's initiatives, meanwhile, meet with marginally more success. Having long waited for someone like Christopher Probyn to contact him about the "mystery of the Operation That Never Was" (*DT*, 173), he journeys to the home of Jeb Owens's widow, Brigid, in Wales and persuades her to let him copy into his BlackBerry two concealed photographs of the Muslim mother and child slain during Operation Wildlife. While there Bell also learns that one of Jeb's former comrades in Gibraltar, Shorty Pike, who has succumbed to bribery by Ethical Outcomes, is keenly interested in recovering the damning evidence. Before meeting with Pike under the guise of a Welsh journalist reporting on Owens's military career, "Beirut Man" Toby has reason to believe that his flat has been searched (*DT*, 229), but despite that suspicion he keeps his appointment with Shorty, only to be abducted for a face-to-face interview with Jay Crispin. Having discontinued his former company, Crispin now manages a prosperous subsidiary of Rosethorne Protection Services that boasts, among its six hundred personnel, "Five heads of foreign intelligence services. Four still serving. Five ex-directors of British intelligence, all with contracts in place with the Old Firm" (*DT*, 291). Despite Crispin's attempt to recruit him to this team of freebooters, Toby Bell declines the solicitation, recognizing that "Jeb's death was a bridge too far" and that "You want me off the case because . . . I'm a danger to your comfort and safety" (*DT*, 294). Because of his principled refusal to suppress what he knows about Operation Wildlife, Bell is subsequently subjected to a vicious beating.

Well before *A Delicate Truth*'s climax, however, le Carré reintroduces the subnarrative of Giles Oakley's many ignoble compromises. According to Charlie Wilkins, an "unflappable sixty-something English ex-copper with half a lifetime of diplomatic protection under his belt" (*DT*, 206), Oakley, once a "foe of speculative bankers" (*DT*, 209), allied himself with such "parasites" when he was ousted from government service after a discreditable episode in Hamburg's red-light district (*DT*, 210).[19] Oakley's prompt adaptation to his new role adumbrates the corruptive influence of political dissimulation in a post-9/11 environment. After retreating from his private reservations earlier about the invasion of Iraq, Oakley accepted a sinecure as senior vice president of an illustrious banking firm headquartered in London's international business center of Canary Wharf. When Bell visits his former mentor in this milieu, he enters a zone of mummery, to borrow le Carré's image, reminiscent of the seaside resort known as the Lido at the end of Graham Greene's *The Confidential Agent* (1939).[20] Like that ultramodern and surreal mecca of escapism, Oakley's suite of offices at Atlantis House conjures up a spectral past:

> A chill night air whipped off the Thames, almost clearing away the stink of stale cigarette smoke that lingered in every fake Roman arcade and Nazi-style

doorway. By the sodium glare of Tudor lanterns, joggers in red shirts, secretaries in top-to-toe black livery, striding men with crew cuts and paper-thin black briefcases glided past each other like mummers in a macabre dance. Before every lighted tower and at every street corner, bulked-out security guards in anoraks looked [Toby Bell] over. . . .

He passed under a walkway and entered an all-night shopping mall offering gold watches, caviar, and villas on Lake Como. . . .

A tower block rose before him, all its lights blazing. At its base a pillared cupola. On its floor a Masonic starburst of gold mosaic. And round its blue dome, the word *Atlantis*. And at the back of the cupola, a pair of glass doors with whales engraved on them that sighed and opened at his approach. (*DT*, 273)

The scene, even before Toby Bell ascends to Giles Oakley's firmament in "a starlit amphitheatre of white archways and celestial nymphs in white plaster" (*DT*, 273), suggests the rococo extravagance of a Hollywood film set that indiscriminately jumbles together iconic emblems of past empires ("fake Roman arcade[s]," "Nazi-style doorway[s]," "Tudor lanterns") in order to project the impression of a new Atlantis. Nor is it insignificant that this latter-day imperium of transnational finance and commerce requires vigilant protection by "bulked-out security guards" stationed at key intersections.

The hollowness of this sham Xanadu befits the man that Giles Oakley has become. In his plush, rosewood-lined offices with "no windows, no fresh air, no day or night," Oakley at first tries to convince his former understudy Bell with "false jocularity" that "a certain covert operation" of three years ago was "never executed" (*DT*, 274). In response to such sophistry, Toby retorts that at least two innocent people died as a result of Operation Wildlife. Despite his efforts to extenuate these casualties, Oakley pleads ignorance and declaims, "Press your case now, you'll be a pariah for the rest of your life. *You*, Toby! Of all people! That's what you'll be. An outcast who played his cards too early. It's not what you were put on earth for—I know that better than anyone." Despite his onetime mentor's adulation of him in the same entreaty as one of "the real men of England, unspoiled—all right, dreamers too—but with their feet on the ground" (*DT*, 278), Bell leaves the room when Oakley ends by professing his love for Toby.

Pursuant to Bell's merciless beating by Crispin's thugs, Oakley redeems himself to some extent when he provides the protagonist with a photocopied Foreign Office file on the epilogue to Operation Wildlife dubbed "Aftermath and Recommendations" before "*award[ing him]self*," as an attached note explains, "*a lengthy posting to distant parts*" (*DT*, 303, 305). Now equipped with all the evidence he needs to expose Whitehall's cover-up, Bell makes his way to a nearby Internet café, assisted by Kit Probyn's daughter, Emily, where drawing on his memory sticks and BlackBerry he dispatches his cache of information to various news media. Just as he does so, though, Toby realizes too late that he has activated an electronically traceable signal. Le Carré's concluding paragraph pulls out all the stops in a dystopian ending:

> The sirens multiplied and acquired a more emphatic, bullying tone. At first, they seemed to be approaching from one direction only. But as the chorus grew to a howl, and the car brakes screamed in the street outside, Toby couldn't be certain any more—nobody could be certain, even Emily—which direction they were coming from. (*DT*, 310)

Aurally this coda is just the opposite of *Our Kind of Traitor*'s, yet its effect is the same. The omnidirectional "howl" of sirens clearly suggests the well-coordinated punitiveness of the post-9/11 state when one of its own dares to defy newly imposed strictures concerning governmental secrecy. Utterly lost in the scramble for plausible deniability is any concern for how its institutionalized sanctions write off moral issues in the name of expediency.

At issue, then, in *A Delicate Truth* is the oppressive regime of secrecy as it operates to muffle and quell dissent in the public sphere. Le Carré gets at this self-reinforcing dimension of a post-9/11 culture when, before Kit Probyn's ill-fated interview with Lionel and Frances at the Foreign Office, former colleague Molly Cranmore asks him how the file of testimonial evidence he is ready to present should be encoded. Sir Christopher, we are told, "debated the question with himself. A cover name, after all, was what it said it was. It was there to cover things up. Ah, but was a cover name *of itself* something to be covered up? If so, then there would have to be cover names for cover names, ad infinitum" (*DT*, 257). Such, proposes le Carré, is the algorithmic replication of secrecy's dynamic as it affects both insiders and outsiders.

Leading up to his twenty-third novel's ending, in a departure from his usual narrational practice, le Carré pauses to have Toby Bell reflect on Hannah Arendt's famous concept of the banality of evil. Was Jay Crispin, wonders Bell, "merely one of society's faithful servants, obeying market pressures," or was he "your normal, rootless, amoral, plausible, half-educated, nicely spoken frozen adolescent in a bespoke suit, with an unappeasable craving for money, power, and respect, regardless of where he got them from"? (*DT*, 295). What the work's narrator decides, modifying philosopher Leszek Kolakowski's formulations, is that "What the gods and all reasonable humans fought in vain wasn't stupidity at all. It was sheer, wanton, bloody indifference to anybody's interests but their own" (*DT*, 296). The outlook indicates le Carré's conviction toward the end of a distinguished career as a writer that our collective foe is a seemingly inveterate and ineradicable deficiency in concern for others' welfare.[21]

This assessment on le Carré's part is entirely congruent with his assertion in 1966, during the Cold War's most paranoid phase, that "The enemy is not outside us but within."[22] In a parallel vein Fintan O'Toole observes that the fascination of *A Delicate Truth* lies "less in its innate qualities as a thriller than in its bleak and angry reflection on the fate of patriotism in a culture where the only respectable motive is monetary profit."[23] Even in so perceptive a commentary, however, there arises again the preconception of le Carré's typical literary *métier* as being that of the widely discredited "thriller." Without deploying that descriptor, preferring instead the term "spy fiction," reviewer Mark Lawson noted that "*A Delicate Truth* often feels like a formal summation of the concerns that have occupied [le Carré's] fiction for five decades," extending the novelist's critique of the "partisan or tactical interpretation of data" during the Bush-Blair era first broached in *Absolute Friends* and *A Most Wanted Man*.[24]

In the "Acknowledgements" appended to his most recent novel, le Carré thanks Carne Ross, "who by his example demonstrated the perils of speaking a delicate truth to power." Born in 1966, Ross faithfully served the British Foreign Service until 2002 as its delegated expert to the United Nations on the Middle East before he openly criticized England's complicity with the United States in the invasion of Iraq on trumped-up pretenses. Clearly a prototype for le Carré's depiction of Toby Bell, Ross subsequently published a book titled *Independent Diplomat: Dispatches from an Unaccountable Elite* in 2007 that lauds the emergence of a new cadre of similarly minded conscientious objectors to Britain's foreign policies. Le Carré's drawing on the example of such few and far between models of "the real men of England" indicates how steeped *A Delicate Truth* is in contemporary events. Beyond that generalization, however, its author boldly chooses to risk his previous reputation by investigating where the new War on Terror might lead. Somewhat less than surprising, then, is le Carré's suggestion that those in Western democracies are back at the point where they always were both during the Cold War and ever since its end.

CONCLUSION

John le Carré and the Cultural Imaginary

At the outset of this study I related Andrew Pepper's point about "the transnationalization of crime, terrorism, and policing" in much post-9/11 fiction to Lee Horsley's judgment that the twenty-first-century novels of John le Carré, among other writers, are taxonomic hybrids that bring "the [espionage] genre closer to the *noir* existentialism of transgressor-centered crime fiction."[1] The previous two chapters have implicitly argued that, as he moves from *The Mission Song* to *A Most Wanted Man* to *Our Kind of Traitor* to *A Delicate Truth*, le Carré increasingly identifies the secrecy-addicted and surveillant state as the corporate transgressor to be resisted by individuals responsive to the promptings of conscience. Largely for that reason, I would propose, it no longer makes sense to pigeonhole this author in terms of his Cold War preeminence in the literary categories of "spy novels" and "thrillers" unless those problematic rubrics are understood to be under erasure.

How, then, are we to construe le Carré's achievement as an analyst of transnationalism's consequences in an ongoing, apparently interminable, struggle against terrorism? By way of addressing that question, both Timothy Melley's *The Covert Sphere* and Eva Horn's *The Secret War* prove invaluable as critiques of cultural productions pertaining to the legacy of 9/11. Even though I drew on these scholars toward the end of chapter 4 and more briefly at the beginning of chapter 5, conjointly they indicate why le Carré no longer should be considered a niche or narrowly defined genre author.

Melley's main contribution in this regard is his recognition of a "*covert sphere*" that figures as "a cultural imaginary shaped by both institutional secrecy and public fascination with the secret work of the state."[2] The innumerable works of fiction about this kind of secrecy in the form of "spy thrillers," postmodern historiographies, TV melodramas (e.g., *24*), and conspiracy films, he posits, have conditioned their audiences to the hyperrreality, in theorist Jean Baudrillard's terminology, of governmental deception while simultaneously making these popular representations dismissible as "mere entertainment" or "non-serious discourse."[3] The net result, Melley maintains, is a blurring of "fact" and "fiction" that induces a widespread climate of cognitive amnesia. He also observes, in a point to which I will return shortly, that at the heart of the covert sphere lies a "dialectic of spectacle and secrecy" that the National Security State must effectively promote in order to "break down the distinction between politics and theater."[4]

Horn, whose book originally was published in 2007, substantiates Melley's thesis by documenting how heuristic novels such as le Carré's illuminate the regime of state secrecy and "imperial panopticism" through a reconstruction of its logic.[5] Framing her conclusion around a preliminary tribute to Graham Greene's *Our Man in Havana*, le Carré's metatextual foundation for *The Tailor of Panama*, she offers the following trenchant assertions:

> This recursion of fiction into reality and reality into fiction highlights the epistemological structure of the secret. The secret produces reality as a fiction, yet it also requires fiction to track down reality. For it is fiction rather than investigative journalism and historical research that discloses the operative structure of the secret, and it does so precisely because it does not claim to uncover any "ultimate truth." . . .

> Exempt from secrecy clauses or libel suits, fictions are able to shed light on the basic paradox of the political secret in the modern age: the conflict between the political idea of transparency and democratic control on the one hand and the necessary, or at least inevitable, use of covert actions and secret intelligence on the other. It is in modern democracies, more than in any other political system, that the *arcana imperii* come to embody the inherent self-contradiction of politics by opening up a shadowy, uncontrollable domain of illegality marked by lies, deception, cover-ups, theft, disinformation, blackmail, and, in the worst case, murder.[6]

Horn's second paragraph above goes a long way toward explaining why many writers besides le Carré who at one time in their careers were engaged in the world's second oldest profession went on to become "spy novelists." Examples are Ted Allbeury, John Buchan, William F. Buckley, Jr., Anthony Burgess,

Erskine Childers, Manning Coles, Graham Greene, W. Somerset Maugham, Charles McCarry, and Stella Rimington. With the exception of Greene, however, none of these authors rivals le Carré in narratological subtlety.[7] Whereas their plots can generally be compared to a "black box," a speculative Cold War gaming simulation, the structure of le Carré's most recent novels resembles a parabolic Möbius strip whose recursive design exposes secrecy's alternating dimensions of semidisclosure and concealment. Given their sophisticated architectonics, his post–Cold War narratives amply warrant the kind of critical attention that this book has accorded them.

In the end, though, it is probably unrealistic, and perhaps even a waste of time, to invent a new descriptive label for le Carré's fiction of the past two decades. "Spy novels," for better or worse, may be what we are stuck with, but if so that designation should not automatically lessen our sense of what they represent. Maintaining that such tales are "an essential literary genre" of our time, Philip Hensher begins his review of *Absolute Friends* with this statement:

> Spy novels continue their obsessive grip on our imagination, even after the end of the Cold War, because they demonstrate, like a formal dance, some of the most haunting philosophies of indeterminacy and mutually shifting positions. They are dramas of . . . game theory and of chaos theory, schools of thought which focus on the idea that observation changes the thing observed, that behaviour and motivation are not pure things but driven by second-guessing, and second-guessing the second-guessing of other factors.[8]

Certainly a leading indicator of le Carré's attunement to twenty-first-century manifestations of epistemological indeterminacy is his exploration of the "dialectic of spectacle and secrecy" supported by the National Security State. Michel Foucault, then, may have proposed a misleading exclusion when in 1977 he declared that "Our society is one not of spectacle, but of surveillance."[9] At least two other theorists would refute that generalization.

Marxist critic Guy Debord's *Society of the Spectacle*, first published in 1967, begins with this axiom: "In societies where modern conditions of production prevail, all of life presents itself as an immense accumulation of *spectacles*. Everything that was directly lived has moved away into a representation." It follows for Debord that "In all its specific forms, as information or propaganda, as advertisement or direct entertainment consumption, the spectacle is the present *model* of socially dominant life." Only the spectacular, then, becomes fraudulently "real," thereby distorting citizens' grasp of contemporaneous

political events and fulfilling Napoleon's monarchical dream of paralyzing historical memory. Such an induced "cleavage" in human consciousness, Debord
maintains, "is inseparable from the modern *State*," the hidden surveillance
apparatus of which is regulated by a systematic effort to monitor its subjects'
actions and, ultimately, to control their way of thinking.[10]

In his 2002 essay "The Spirit of Terrorism," Baudrillard offers a second
qualification of Foucault's comment. Maintaining that globally disseminat-
ed images of the Twin Towers' collapse made manifest the notion of Western apocalypse, he posits that such "brutal retaliation" was the more or less
inevitable "blowback of a proportionate violence" in "reinventing the real
as the ultimate and most redoubtable fiction."[11] Baudrillard then goes on to
say:

> We try retrospectively to impose some kind of meaning on it, to find some
> kind of interpretation. But there is none. And it is the radicality of the specta-
> cle, the brutality of the spectacle, which alone is original and irreducible. The
> spectacle of terrorism forces the terrorism of spectacle upon us.[12]

Without dismissing the National Security State's surveillance of citizens at
home and enemies abroad, Baudrillard, in his final sentence of rhetorical chi-
asmus, insists on the primacy of spectacularity as an instrument of the modern state's hegemony. At the core of that ascendancy, moreover, is secrecy or
the controlled flow of information. In a parallel vein, as noted earlier, critic
Stewart Crehan observes that le Carré's fiction leverages through indirect narration "a political economy of information based on the principle of *scarcity*
and *ownership*."[13]

When evidence of the state's intentional deception inundates the media, the
immediate effect is usually one of shock offset by a sense that "we knew it all
along." For example, Julian Assange's and Edward Snowden's leaking torrents
of confidential documents related to the invasion of Iraq in 2003 reinforced,
for the most part, existing impressions of Big Government's "collaborative secrecy."[14] Similarly, on December 9, 2014, the *Washington Post* reported that
the US Senate Intelligence Committee had just released a 528-page summary
of its 6,500-page report on the Central Intelligence Agency's detention and
interrogation program launched shortly after 9/11.[15] The study was the product of more than five years of research devoted to reviewing 6.2 million pages of declassified documents from the CIA and the Department of Defense.
Eight years after the US secret overseas prisons were shut down, the public
learned about extrajudicial practices that it may have suspected were part of

the Bush-Blair War on Terror but that at the time of their occurrence was hesitant to criticize. Such empirical proof that substantiates the insights of le Carré's fictional narratives contributes to a cultural imaginary with which his novels are themselves inextricably interwoven. Partly for that reason, I suspect, he makes them depend heavily on a gamut of ventriloquized voices and, more often than not, end inconclusively.

In light of le Carré's indictment of the imperial state's sway in his post-9/11 corpus, it may come as a surprise that such concerns are aired in his début novel of 1961, *Call for the Dead*, in which Elsa Fennan tries to discourage George Smiley's investigation of her husband Samuel's murder by admonishing Smiley as follows:

> Go back to Whitehall and look for more spies on your drawing boards. . . .
> It's an old illness you suffer from, . . . and I have seen many victims of it. The
> mind becomes separated from the body; it thinks without reality, rules a pa-
> per kingdom and devises without emotion the ruin of its paper victims. . . .
>
> It's like the State and the People. The State is a dream too, a symbol of nothing
> at all, an emptiness, a mind without a body, a game played with clouds in
> the sky. But States make war, don't they, and imprison people? To dream in
> doctrines—how tidy! (*CD*, 20–21)

Only a few months after the Cold War's official end, in an introduction dated March 1992 for Penguin's reissued edition of *Call for the Dead*, le Carré reflected on how he came to be a novelist three decades earlier while employed by MI5 after briefly teaching at Eton. The British Security Service at the time, he posits, was excellent preparation for a literary career because "the secret world is exactly the same as the real world, but . . . more so" (*CD*, xi). Extrapolating from this comment, which constitutes an incisive definition of hyperreality, we can assume that he realized even then that the state is an abstract nullity—a "symbol of nothing at all," in Fennan's words—given to gambling with people's lives as token counters in its larger geopolitical campaigns.

Notwithstanding this indication of le Carré's lifelong creed of liberal humanism, which during the 1960s was molded by a repudiation of the Communist bloc's manifest totalitarianism, his post–Cold War fiction scouts new territory as le Carré grapples with what succeeded that epoch-defining framework. After George Smiley and protagonist Ned's sad retrospectives in *The Secret Pilgrim* on the legacy of their involvement in Cold War espionage, *The Night Manager* and *Our Game* seek to identify the default forces at work in a world

suddenly stripped of an all-consuming contest between two ideological superpowers. *The Tailor of Panama* attests to a retrenchment on its author's part
as he reworks Greene's *Our Man in Havana* in order to excavate espionage's
enduring appeal while also distancing himself from the reductive label of "spy
novelist." *Single & Single* extends this trajectory as le Carré wrestles with issues
pertaining to the emergence of a market-oriented New Russia as mirrored by
that development's effect on a generationally divided father and son. Further
extending his critique of transnationalism's outcome, *The Constant Gardener*
documents the novelist's reaction to reports of Big Pharma's profits in Third
World nations from the marketing of drugs such as Dypraxa, another sign
of unbridled capitalism's impulse toward exploitation when unchecked by an
antithetical economic system.

After the pivotal event of 9/11, however, le Carré's fiction makes a decisive
turn. The Western powers' 2003 invasion of Iraq, as he fulminated in op-ed
pieces at the time, abrogated fundamental principles of the democratic process
in giving rise to such heinous practices as extraordinary rendition. *Absolute
Friends* first gives expression to these views, much to the chagrin of conservative reviewers who preferred le Carré's "classic" Cold War tales of moral ambiguity. What those arbiters of opinion tended to overlook, however, was the
author's continuing fidelity to his early and often repeated conviction that "The
enemy is not outside us but within." Broadening the scope of that premise, his
next four novels—*The Mission Song, A Most Wanted Man, Our Kind of Traitor*,
and *A Delicate Truth*—brilliantly examine how it applies to state-sponsored
surveillance and secrecy amid the energetically pursued War on Terror. Conscientious objectors such as Perry Makepiece in *Our Kind of Traitor* and "solitary decider" Toby Bell in *A Delicate Truth* are always rarities in le Carré's
universe, but in tracing their individual struggles le Carré figures as arguably
the most significant ethicist among contemporary writers of fiction.

In the *Boston Globe* on July 31, 2014, Alex Beam asked, "Is John le Carré
the Greatest Living Writer?" Although such literary sweepstakes are always
suspect, he hazarded this assertion: "Long after the likes of [John] Updike and
[Saul] Bellow are . . . forgotten, people will still look to le Carré to discover
a world that now seems to us almost unthinkable." Beam's primary frame of
reference for that assessment is le Carré's Cold War oeuvre, but it is telling
nonetheless that one of the American novelists he mentions recorded a far
different verdict nearly twenty years earlier. In a review of *Our Game* for the
New Yorker, John Updike equated le Carré with Robert Ludlum, Frederick
Forsyth, and Tom Clancy as an author of fundamentally escapist literature.
"Le Carré's prose," he opined with characteristic hauteur, "has an overheated

expertise about it, as if it wished to be doing something other than spinning a thriller."[16] Updike's denigration recalls Bruce Merry's rather strange comment that le Carré is an anomaly because he "operates self-consciously on the highbrow side" in aspiring to the "'Great Novel.'"[17]

As early as 1974, however, the already famous author understood how contrived such academic distinctions are. "There is this endless debate about the difference between a thriller and a novel," he stated to an interviewer, "and it really is a very feeble one."[18] Five years earlier Ralph Harper made exactly the same point in the first scholarly study of the "thriller," which he viewed as a typically twentieth-century permutation of the adventure tale and hard-boiled detective story. The subgenre, Harper maintained, defies conventional lines of demarcation between "popular" and "serious" literature because it explores the existential theme of "crisis situations" in which an antihero comes face-to-face with the sudden intrusion of radical contingency in his or her previously well-ordered life.[19] This critic's argument validates what we consistently encounter in le Carré's post–Cold War novels.

Where, then, does this overview leave us? The literary subgenre known as the "spy thriller" begets, and some would say invites, supplementary narratives. Dan Fesperman's *The Double Game*, published in 2012, is an interesting example of such supplementarity as well as of metafictional homage. After serving as a foreign correspondent in three war zones for the *Baltimore Sun* and other newspapers, Fesperman turned to writing fiction in 1999. His eighth novel bears the title of an imaginary production by the equally fictitious Edwin Lemaster, "the world's premier espionage novelist" and obviously an American version of John le Carré.[20]

Fesperman proceeds to generate a new "thriller" based on fifty-three-year-old protagonist Bill Cage's tracking down textual "clues" encoded within excerpts from the pages of Lemaster/le Carré. Along the way *The Double Game*'s author mentions that bibliophile Cage abandons a lucrative but soul-withering career as a "lonely PR man with a big paycheck" to become a "spy novelist."[21] Fesperman's story, in other words, enacts what transpires when a reader steeped in the literary tradition extending from John Buchan through Eric Ambler and Graham Greene to John le Carré discovers the thinness or hyperreality of everyday life.

Fesperman's prologue titled "A Precaution" explains this advance in his protagonist's grasp of the contemporary situation. "*I no longer believe what I read in books*," Cage begins,

> Unless, of course, the text states clearly that every word is made up, a product of the author's imagination. I especially take notice when a novelist deploys

that oft-used legal disclaimer . . . that says, "Any resemblance to actual persons, living or dead, events, or locales is entirely coincidental."

Sure it is. That statement . . . means truth is about to appear in some elegant and artful disguise.

As for all those dusty "facts" piled in the vast remaindered bin known as nonfiction, well, I've exhumed quite a few such items . . . , and so many have proven to be false that I've lost faith in their authenticity. Along the dim corridors of the secret world I've come to know best, only the so-called inventions of fiction have ever shed any light of revelation.[22]

The artful credibility of fiction for this narrator exposes the inauthenticity of unassimilated facts. We thus have returned to a point with which this study began—namely, le Carré's career-long insistence on the difference between fictional "credibility" and veridical "authenticity"—but perhaps only attentive readers like Cage who are aware of fictionality's pervasive role in their lives can fully appreciate the insight.

In the final paragraph of his 2013 interview, published shortly before the release of *A Delicate Truth*, Dwight Garner reported that le Carré had begun another novel, "though all he would say about it is that it's loosely based on one of Joseph Conrad's stories, one he'd like to translate into espionage terms."[23] My guess is that le Carré's anchoring text will be "The Secret Sharer" (1910), given allusions to that work in his post–Cold War fiction, but I am prepared to be surprised. In the event that this versatile author publishes a twenty-fourth novel, I am willing to reevaluate my conclusions about his achievement over the last few decades, yet whatever proves to be the capstone to his career I doubt that I will be disappointed.

NOTES

INTRODUCTION
JOHN LE CARRÉ'S POST-COLD WAR JOURNEY

1. Robert Giddings, "The Writing on the Igloo Walls: Narrative Technique in *The Spy Who Came In from the Cold*," in *The Quest for le Carré*, ed. Alan Bold (New York: St. Martin's Press, 1988), 208; "All-Time 100 Novels," *Time*, October 16, 2005, http://www.time.com/2005/10/16/all-time-100-novels.

2. John le Carré, "Afterword," *Harper's*, April 2013. In framing this "same old question" for *Harper's*, le Carré was reprising a passage from his open letter to Moscow's *Literaturnaya Gazeta*; see John le Carré, "To Russia, with Greetings: An Open Letter to the Moscow 'Literary Gazette,'" *Encounter* 26 (May 1966): 3–6. Referring there to a Russian critic's review of *The Spy Who Came In from the Cold* in the *Gazeta* of October 14, 1965—ironically, while the novel was banned in the Soviet Union—le Carré wrote, "I tried to tickle the public conscience with the issue of *raison d'état*. I have posed this question: for how long can we defend ourselves— you and we—by methods of this kind, and still remain the kind of society that is worth defending?" (5).

3. Véra Volmane, "John le Carré: The Writer, Like the Spy, Is an Illusionist," interview with John le Carré, September 23, 1965, in *Conversations with John le Carré*, ed. Matthew J. Bruccoli and Judith S. Baughman (Jackson: University Press of Mississippi, 2004), 3 (emphasis added). More than two decades later le Carré made the distinction part of his stock responses to questions about his practice as a writer. See, e.g., several other interviews with John le Carré, all reprinted in Bruccoli and Baughman's *Conversations*: Paul Vaughan, "Le Carré's Circus: Lamplighters, Moles, and Others of That Ilk" (September 13, 1979), 56; Stephen Schiff, "The Secret Life of John le Carré" (June 1989), 100; Alvin P. Sanoff, "The Thawing of the Old Spymaster" (June 19, 1989), 108; Andrew Ross, "Master of the Secret World: John le Carré on Deception, Storytelling, and American Hubris" (October 21, 1996), 140; and George Plimpton, "John le Carré: The Art of Fiction" (Summer

1997), 150. Le Carré's official website echoes the point: "Nothing that I write is authentic[, . . . y]et I am treated by the media as though I wrote espionage handbooks." John le Carre, "About John le Carré," Author's website, May 15, 2013, http://www.johnlecarre.com/author.; see also John le Carré, "Remarks to the Knopf Sales Force," August 12, 1996, in *Conversations*, ed. Bruccoli and Baughman, 134. He reiterated the distinction by saying that "the whole art of writing is to be credible, not to be authentic." Jake Kerridge, "Hay Festival 2013: John le Carré on His New Novel, *A Delicate Truth*," *Telegraph* (London), May 25, 2013.

    4. Robert Lance Snyder: *The Art of Indirection in British Espionage Fiction: A Critical Study of Six Novelists* (Jefferson, NC: McFarland, 2011), 4–5.

    5. Jacques Barzun, "Meditations on the Literature of Spying," *American Scholar* 34, no. 2 (Spring 1965): 167.

    6. Leigh Crutchley, "The Fictional World of Espionage," interview with John le Carré, April 14, 1966, in *Conversations*, ed. Bruccoli and Baughman, 7. See also le Carré, "To Russia," 6; Alan Watson, "Violent Image," interview with John le Carré, March 30, 1969, in *Conversations*, ed. Bruccoli and Baughman, 13; and Sanoff, "Thawing," 108.

    7. For two examples of the fascination with le Carré's tradecraft jargon, especially prominent in *Tinker, Tailor, Soldier, Spy* (1974), see the opening questions of Melvyn Bragg, "The Things a Spy Can Do: John le Carré Talking," interview with John le Carré, January 22, 1976, in *Conversations*, ed. Bruccoli and Baughman, 33–34; and Vaughan, "Le Carré's Circus," 56.

    8. Plimpton, "John le Carré," 152, 153.

    9. Watson, "Violent Image," 13. Eleven years later le Carré told another interviewer the same thing: "If I knew exactly where I stood, I wouldn't write." Miriam Gross, "The Secret World of John le Carré," interview with John le Carré, February 5, 1980, in *Conversations*, ed. Bruccoli and Baughman, 60.

    10. Pierre Assouline, "Spying on a Spymaker," interview with John le Carré, August 1986, in *Conversations*, ed. Bruccoli and Baughman, 89.

    11. Tony Barley, *Taking Sides: The Fiction of John le Carré* (Milton Keynes, UK: Open University Press, 1986), 23.

    12. Clive Bloom suggests that the genre is inescapably political because it revolves around "an obsession with violation by *outside* agencies" and "violation of individual autonomy by *internal* agencies." Clive Bloom, "The Spy Thriller: A Genre under Cover?" in *Spy Thrillers: From Buchan to le Carré*, ed. Clive Bloom (New York: St. Martin's Press, 1990), 2.

    13. Stewart Crehan, "Information, Power[,] and the Reader: Textual Strategies in le Carré," in *The Quest for le Carré*, ed. Alan Bold (New York: St. Martin's Press, 1988), 110, 106.

    14. Wolfgang Iser, *The Act of Reading: A Theory of Aesthetic Response* (Baltimore, MD: Johns Hopkins University Press, 1978); Tzvetan Todorov, *The Poetics of Prose*, trans. Richard Howard (Ithaca, NY: Cornell University Press, 1977); Gérard

Genette, *Narrative Discourse: An Essay in Method*, trans. Jane E. Lewin (Ithaca, NY: Cornell University Press, 1980); Barley, *Taking Sides*, 22.

15. David Seed observes that the structures of le Carré's early fiction hew closely to those of the detective story. "Le Carré repeatedly strikes a balance," he writes, "between search-narratives directed towards the uncovering of information and the adoption of limited perspectives which will retard this process." David Seed, "The Well-Wrought Structures of John le Carré's Early Fiction," in *Spy Thrillers: From Buchan to le Carré*, ed. Clive Bloom (New York: St. Martin's Press, 1990), 158. See also Glenn W. Most, "The Hippocratic Smile: John le Carré and the Traditions of the Detective Novel," in *The Poetics of Murder: Detective Fiction and Literary Theory*, ed. Glenn W. Most and William W. Stowe (San Diego: Harcourt, 1983), 348, 350. Maintaining that le Carré's first two books, *Call for the Dead* (1961) and *A Murder of Quality* (1962), are essentially whodunits in the mold established by Dashiell Hammett and Raymond Chandler, he points out that the literary detective is a "figure for the reader within the text" who, in the words of *Hamlet*, "only by indirections . . . finds directions out." Le Carré's labyrinthine spy mysteries consequently enact "the uncertainties of the activity of interpretation itself."

16. Harold Bloom, ed., *John le Carré* (New York: Chelsea, 1987), viii.

17. James M. Buzard, "Faces, Photos, Mirrors: Image and Ideology in the Novels of John le Carré," in *Image and Ideology in Modern/Postmodern Discourse*, ed. David B. Downing and Susan Bazargan (Albany: State University of New York Press, 1991), 158.

18. Brian E. Crim, "(Im)Perfect Spies: Identity and the Pathology of the Cold War in John le Carré's *A Perfect Spy* and *The Secret Pilgrim*," in *Espionage Fiction: The Seduction of Clandestinity*, ed. Robert Lance Snyder, special issue of *Paradoxa* 24 (2012): 92.

19. Andrew Pepper, "Policing the Globe: State Sovereignty and the International in the Post-9/11 Crime Novel," *Modern Fiction Studies* 57 (Fall 2011): 404–5.

20. David Seed, "Spy Fiction," in *The Cambridge Companion to Crime Fiction*, ed. Martin Priestman (Cambridge, UK: Cambridge University Press, 2003), 115.

21. Lee Horsley, "A Life Spent Lying: The Identity Crises of Post-9/11 Spy Fiction," in *Espionage Fiction: The Seduction of Clandestinity*, ed. Robert Lance Snyder, special issue of *Paradoxa* 24 (2012): 161. In their agreement on this point, Pepper and Horsley substantiate it by an analysis of *A Most Wanted Man*.

22. Pepper, "Policing the Globe," 403.

23. Bruce Merry, *Anatomy of the Spy Thriller* (Montreal: McGill-Queens University Press, 1977), 1, 158, 214.

24. John Atkins, *The British Spy Novel: Styles in Treachery* (New York: Riverrun, 1984), 170.

25. Michael Dean, "John le Carré: The Writer Who Came In from the Cold," interview with John le Carré, September 5, 1974, in *Conversations*, ed. Bruccoli and Baughman, 31.

26. Apropos of this statistic, Peter Lewis commented in 1985, "Le Carré has gathered armfuls of reviews, but examinations of his fiction as a whole or even of individual novels in depth are virtually nonexistent. Without wishing to inflict flocks of predatory graduate students on le Carré, one might question some of the assumptions buried in the collective unconscious of an academic literary establishment that ignores le Carré so assiduously but that has turned another very successful English novelist of his generation, John Fowles, into a major research industry, especially in the USA." Peter Lewis, *John le Carré* (New York: Ungar, 1985), 12. In his review of *The Little Drummer Girl* (1983), William F. Buckley, Jr. compared le Carré favorably to Lawrence Durrell and John Fowles as a "very powerful writer." William F. Buckley, Jr., "Terror and a Woman," *New York Times*, March 13, 1983, reprinted in *Spy Thrillers: From Buchan to le Carré*, ed. Clive Bloom (New York: St. Martin's Press, 1990).

27. Tod Hoffman, "The Constant Writer: Le Carré Spies a New Villain," *Queen's Quarterly* 108 (Spring 2001): 99–107; Vittorio Hösle, "Berufsethik der Geheimdienste und Krise der Hohen Politik: Philosophische Betractungen zum Literarischen Universum von John le Carré's Spionageromanen im Allgemeinen und zu *Absolute Friends* im Besonderen," *Deutsche Vierteljahrsschrift für Literaturwissenschaft und Geistesgeschichte* 79 (March 2005): 131–59; Robert Lance Snyder, "Secrecy's Genesis: John le Carré's *Our Kind of Traitor*," *South Carolina Review* 45, no. 2 (Spring 2013): 113–19; Phyllis Lassner, "Paradoxical Polemics: John le Carré's Responses to 9/11," in *Transatlantic Literature and Culture after 9/11: The Wrong Side of Paradise*, ed. Kristine A. Miller (New York: Palgrave, 2014), 17–33.

28. The surveys that ignore le Carré altogether are Dominic Head, *The Cambridge Introduction to Modern British Fiction, 1950–2000* (Cambridge, UK: Cambridge University Press, 2002); Richard J. Lane, Rod Mengham, and Philip Tew, eds., *Contemporary British Fiction* (Cambridge, UK: Polity, 2003); Nick Rennison, *Contemporary British Novelists* (London: Routledge, 2005); and Philip Tew, *The Contemporary British Novel* (London: Continuum, 2004). Those that mention le Carré in passing are Nick Bentley, *Contemporary British Fiction* (Edinburgh, UK: Edinburgh University Press, 2008); and James F. English, ed., *A Concise Companion to Contemporary British Fiction* (Malden, MA: Blackwell, 2006). Three cursory pages are devoted to le Carré in Richard Bradford, *The Novel Now: Contemporary British Fiction* (Malden, MA: Blackwell, 2007), 110–12.

29. Barley, *Taking Sides*, 167, 169.

30. Eric Homberger, *John le Carré* (New York: Methuen, 1986), 104.

31. David Seed, "Crime and the Spy Genre," in *A Companion to Crime Fiction*, ed. Charles J. Rzepka and Lee Horsley (Chichester, NH: Wiley-Blackwell, 2010), 244.

32. Myron J. Aronoff, *The Spy Novels of John le Carré: Balancing Ethics and Power* (New York: Palgrave, 2001), 37.

33. The *MLA International Bibliography* currently lists 335 scholarly items on McEwan and 590 on Fowles, compared to 136 on le Carré. The differential can only be explained, I think, by le Carré's still being regarded as a "spy novelist," with all of that tag's usually negative connotations.

34. Qtd. in Jon Stock, "Ian McEwan: John le Carré Deserves Booker," *Telegraph* (London), May 3, 2013.

35. A profile of le Carré indicates that when he was nominated in 2011 for the fourth biennial Man Booker International Prize, given for a writer's entire body of work, he requested the withdrawal of his name from further consideration. Dwight Garner, "'I Have Pretended to Be a Gentleman for So Long,'" *New York Times*, April 21, 2013; Kerridge, "Hay Festival."

36. Laura Briggs, Gladys McCormick, and J. T. Way, "Transnationalism: A Category of Analysis," *American Quarterly* 60, no. 3 (September 2008): 625–28.

37. Jost Hindersmann, "'The Right Side Lost, but the Wrong Side Won': John le Carré's Spy Novels before and after the End of the Cold War," *Clues* 23, no. 4 (Summer 2005): 32–33.

38. Paul Gray, "Ice Cubes," *Time*, January 14, 1991.

39. Jonathan Goodwin, "John le Carré's *The Secret Pilgrim* and the End of the Cold War," *Clues* 28, no. 1 (Spring 2010): 104.

40. John Gray's *Black Mass: Apocalyptic Religion and the Death of Utopia* (New York: Farrar, Straus & Giroux, 2007) argues that millenarian beliefs inform nearly all modern political movements. Although his focus is primarily the War on Terror precipitated by 9/11, Gray construes the Cold War struggle between Marxism and Western liberalism, or democratic capitalism, as yet another episode in the post-Enlightenment mythos of utopianism.

41. John Cobbs parses le Carré's oxymoronic title as follows: "A 'pilgrim' on the one hand is an openly dedicated person, committed to a cause with at least quasi-religious overtones. A 'secret' pilgrim, however, is . . . one who hides that commitment in veils of deceit, who pretends somehow not to be a pilgrim at all, shunning and disguising his or her cause. Such, of course, is practically the definition of a spy." John L. Cobbs, *Understanding John le Carré* (Columbia: University of South Carolina Press, 1998), 204. Cobbs ignores what I consider the more likely implication that Ned throughout his career as a Cambridge Circus agent has been an undeclared pilgrim in search of relational openness. Goodwin's linkage of le Carré's title to a phrase in Rupert Brooke's poem "Dust" allows for that possibility. See Goodwin, "John le Carré's *The Secret Pilgrim*," 102.

42. In a passage that clearly echoes the excerpts just quoted from *The Secret Pilgrim*, le Carré's newspaper article states: "But don't imagine for one second that just because the Cold War's over, the spooks aren't having a ball. In times of such uncertainty as this, the world's intelligence industries will be beavering away like never before. For decades to come, the spy world will continue to be the collective couch where the subconscious of each nation is confessed." John le Carré, "Will Spy Novels Come In from the Cold?" *Washington Post*, November 19, 1989.

43. Note here yet another insertion of the parenthetical qualifier "if I am honest," which suggests that while writing his memoirs Ned is making a concerted effort to record the full truth about himself.

44. Stephen Hunter, "Le Carré's Latest Has Aura of Post–Cold War Exhaustion," *Baltimore Sun*, December 30, 1990.

45. Gail Caldwell, "Spycraft's Detritus: Damaged Souls," *Boston Globe*, January 6, 1991.

46. William Boyd, "Oh, What a Lovely Cold War," *New York Times*, January 6, 1991.

47. A key phrase in Ned's comment recalls Graham Greene's declared interest in exploring "the dangerous edge of things," a phrase borrowed from Robert Browning's "Bishop Blougram's Apology" (line 395), which according to Greene could serve as an epigraph for all his novels. Graham Greene, *A Sort of Life* (1971; repr., London: Vintage-Random, 1999), 85. The phrase's likely resonance for le Carré in this context can be inferred from how Greene glossed it in a conversation with Marie-Françoise Allain: "'The dangerous edge of things' remains what it always has been—the narrow boundary between loyalty and disloyalty, between fidelity and infidelity, the mind's contradictions, the paradox one carries within oneself." Marie-Françoise Allain, *The Other Man: Conversations with Graham Greene*, trans. Guido Waldman (New York: Simon & Schuster, 1983), 21.

48. Crim, "(Im)Perfect Spies," 92.

49. See the "dossier" (*SP*, 381–82) that le Carré appended to *The Secret Pilgrim* in 2001. For Bizot's autobiographical account of his experience, see François Bizot, *The Gate*, trans. Euan Cameron (New York: Vintage-Random, 2004), for which le Carré wrote the foreword.

50. Crutchley, "Fictional World," 6.

51. Ibid., 7. Le Carré made this comment to interviewer Leigh Crutchley on April 14, 1966. One month later, when the West's fascination with "the gilded dream of James Bond" was in full cry, le Carré described Ian Fleming's "super-spy" as "the hyena who stalks the capitalist deserts . . . of a materialist[ic] society." He added, "Bond on his magic carpet takes us away from moral doubt, banishes perplexity with action, morality with duty. Above all, he has the one piece of equipment without which not even his formula would work: an entirely evil enemy." Le Carre, "To Russia," 4, 6.

52. Ibid., 7, 8.

53. Jean-Paul Sartre, *What Is Literature?*, trans. Bernard Frechtman (1948; repr., London: Routledge, 2001), 33, 47.

54. Aronoff, *Spy Novels*, 2.

55. Fredric Jameson, *The Political Unconscious: Narrative as a Socially Symbolic Act* (Ithaca, NY: Cornell University Press, 1981), 20.

56. Terry Eagleton, *Literary Theory: An Introduction* (Minneapolis: University of Minnesota Press, 1983), viii.

57. Ibid., 15.

58. Jameson, *The Political Unconscious*, 13–14.

1 *THE NIGHT MANAGER* AND *OUR GAME*
"WE HAVE MET THE ENEMY AND HE IS US"

1. Qtd. in Tim Weiner, "Le Carré on the Most Immoral Premise of All," *New York Times*, July 8, 1993. The subtitle of this chapter is a quotation from cartoonist Walt Kelly that first appeared in his foreword to *The Pogo Papers* (1953), published during the Cold War paranoia of McCarthyism, and subsequently used as a poster slogan for Earth Day in 1970.

2. John le Carré, "The Shame of the West," *New York Times*, December 14, 1994. The novelist ended his op-ed piece by writing, "Perhaps what offends the Western nations most about their victory over Communism is that in cutting a path to the future, they have unleashed the sleeping demons of their accusing past."

3. Jonathan Franzen, "Anger Is My Business," *Los Angeles Times*, June 27, 1993.

4. A. S. Ross, "A Spy's Perspective through the Eyes of John le Carré," *Sun Sentinel* (Fort Lauderdale), July 18, 1993.

5. Polly Toynbee, "On the Trail of the Lonesome Pine," *Guardian*, June 26, 1993.

6. The articulation of this Cold War doctrine is usually credited to Robert Strange McNamara, who served as the secretary of defense under Presidents John F. Kennedy and Lyndon B. Johnson from 1961 to 1968. In a speech on the subject delivered in San Francisco on September 18, 1967, McNamara yoked the doctrine to its more commonly known corollary, "mutually assured destruction," or MAD, coined by mathematician and game theorist John von Neumann (1903–1957). One is reminded of the classic 1964 film satire titled *Dr. Strangelove*.

7. Charles Cumming, "Journey into the Shadows in the Hearts of Men," *Daily Telegraph*, September 20, 2008.

8. Valerie Takahama, "Le Carré Comes In from the Cold Books," *Orange County Register* (Santa Ana, CA), July 9, 1993.

9. Philip Marchand, "Le Carré's Voyeur Takes on the 'Worst Man in the World,'" *Toronto Star*, June 26, 1993.

10. This truism of espionage fiction and cinema surfaces in the James Bond movie *Skyfall* (2012) when MI6's "M" (Judi Dench) comments to Agent 007 (Daniel Craig), as they approach his childhood home in Scotland, that "Orphans always make the best recruits."

11. Toynbee, "On the Trail."

12. Allan Hepburn, *Intrigue: Espionage and Culture* (New Haven, CT: Yale University Press, 2005), xv, xvi.

13. The fictional Joint Steering Committee's charter, according to the text, is based on the "*Lex Goodhew*" developed in Goodhew's paper "Covert Agencies in the New Era," which posited that in the Cold War's aftermath Britain— "more secretly governed . . . than any other Western democracy"—should share

operational intelligence collaterally with the US "Cousins" in a "like-to-like deal: enforcers play with enforcers, spies with spies, no cross-fertilization" (*NM*, 56, 226–27, 410).

14. Michael Holquist, "Introduction," in *The Dialogic Imagination: Four Essays*, by M. M. Bakhtin, ed. Michael Holquist, trans. Caryl Emerson and Michael Holquist (Austin: University of Texas Press, 1981), xxi.

15. M. M. Bakhtin, *The Dialogic Imagination: Four Essays*, ed. Michael Holquist, trans. Caryl Emerson and Michael Holquist (Austin: University of Texas Press, 1981), 263, 261, 265.

16. Ibid., 315 (emphasis added).

17. John le Carré, "In Place of Nations," *Nation*, April 9, 2001.

18. Steven M. Neuse, "Bureaucratic Malaise in the Modern Spy Novel: Deighton, Greene, and le Carré," *Public Administration* 60 (Autumn 1982): 301.

19. Cobbs, *Understanding*, 219.

20. The growing affinity between Roper and Pine during the latter's recuperation at Crystal, the Caribbean retreat of "the worst man in the world," is underscored when le Carré writes, "The friendship between Jonathan and Roper that, as Jonathan now realized, had been budding throughout the weeks at Crystal burst into flower the moment the Roper jet cleared Nassau International Airport. You might have thought the two men had agreed to wait for this shared moment of release before they acknowledged their good feelings for each other" (*NM*, 321). The passage suggests an unanticipated bonding that causes even Leonard Burr to wonder whether he has lost operational control of his agent. And Pine himself reflects that under Roper's influence "he was conniving in the manipulation of his character" (*NM*, 324). This pattern of doubling between protagonist and adversary appears often in espionage fiction. See Laura Tracy, "Forbidden Fantasy: The Villain as Cultural Double in the British Espionage Novel," *Clues* 9, no. 1 (Spring-Summer 1988): 11–37.

21. There may be a bit of whimsy as well in the epilogue's setting atop Penwith Peninsula's headlands, since this is where le Carré has resided for more than forty years in St. Buryan, Cornwall, and where he reportedly owns a mile of cliffs close to Land's End.

22. Plimpton, "John le Carré," 159.

23. Herbert Mitgang, "New Evil. New Empire. Same Fun," *New York Times*, June 23, 1993.

24. David Remnick, "Le Carré's New War," *New York Review of Books*, August 12, 1993.

25. Aronoff, *Spy Novels*, 130, 84.

26. Vaughan, "Le Carré's Circus," 58.

27. Godfrey Hodgson, "The Secret Life of John le Carré," interview with John le Carré, October 9, 1977, in *Conversations*, ed. Bruccoli and Baughman, 42.

28. Cobbs, *Understanding*, 224.

29. The phrase "Hopeless Causes" first appears in this context: "I am Larry's friend as well as his inventor. And as his friend, I know that the so-called Hopeless Causes with which he beats the fetid air of Bath—Stop the Outrage in Rwanda, Don't Let Bosnia Bleed to Death, Action for Molucca Now—are the only means he has left to fill the void the Office left behind when it dumped him and continued on its way" (*OG*, 42). The passage intimates the hunger for socially responsible activism and morally accountable involvement that decades of service in the secret world inspire in a few former agents such as Pettifer.

30. Cobbs, *Understanding*, 227.

31. Ibid., 235.

32. Le Carré's reference to the "England that had made me" may allude to Graham Greene's novel *England Made Me* (1935). Like Timothy Cranmer, Greene's antihero, Anthony Farrant, wrestles with his conscience while grappling with self-threatening moral dilemmas.

33. The ethnic slur "blackarse," *Our Game* informs us, refers to "Russians from the old [Central Asian] Muslim minorities [who] didn't make the foreign side of the KGB as a rule" (*OG*, 55). An Ingush *gorets*, or "mountain man," who managed to become a Soviet case officer during the Cold War, Checheyev was obviously an official embarrassment after he conspired with Pettifer to embezzle 37 million pounds from Russia in order to support his native people's struggle against the Russian campaign of oppression under President Boris Yeltsin.

34. Daniel Richler, "Le Carré's Details Save the Game," *Toronto Star*, May 25, 1995.

35. Charles Gordon, "Le Carré Changes the Rules in *Our Game*," *Ottawa Citizen*, April 9, 1995.

36. Tom Carson, "Le Carré Goes Native Hunting for a Romantic on the Grand Scale," *Los Angeles Times*, March 26, 1995.

37. The parallels between "'Childe Roland to the Dark Tower Came'" and the final fifty pages of *Our Game* are striking. Like Browning's first-person narrator, who thinks that he is being misdirected by a "hoary cripple" en route to "that ominous tract which, all agree, / Hides the Dark Tower" (lines 2, 14–15), le Carré's protagonist questions whether a comparably incapacitated Zorin, now awaiting trial for treason, may not be trying to ensnare him in seeking out Pettifer's whereabouts (*OG*, 285). Both, moreover, are put through a series of nightmarish trials in the course of their journeys through what le Carré calls "enemy territory" (*OG*, 280). Finally, at the end of their quests Childe Roland and Timothy Cranmer suddenly find themselves standing at the foot of a monolithic tower amid surrounding mountain peaks. Browning describes it as a "round squat turret, blind as the fool's heart" (line 182); for le Carré it is an ancient "watchtower" in a village that the Russians have all but obliterated (*OG*, 326). A Jungian explanation of these textual correspondences, of course, would suggest that they are intrinsic to mythological archetypes on which both authors are unconsciously drawing.

38. I invoke this terminology because I know of no better way to conceptualize le Carré's emphasis on how our existential *Geworfenheit* ("thrownness") or *Entfremdung* ("estrangement") from an established order of things governs our responses to the world(s) we inhabit.

39. Reinforcing Checheyev's scathing indictment of post–Cold War geopolitics, *Our Game* includes a similar assessment by Simon Dugdale, a Foreign Office analyst and former NATO Moscow watcher. When Cranmer asks him about the US stance on the North Caucasus, Dugdale replies: "If America *has* a post-Sov[iet] policy down there, it's not to have a policy. . . . Planned apathy is the kindest description I can think of: act natural and look the other way while the ethnic cleansers do their hoovering and restore what politicians call normality. Which means that whatever Moscow does is okay by Washington, provided nobody frightens the horses" (*OG*, 229).

40. Le Carré's familiarity with the antecedents of this Romantic aesthetic is evident from his academic training in German language and literature, first developed when he studied at the University of Bern in 1948–1949, as well as from his fifth novel, *The Naive and Sentimental Lover* (1971), which draws on Friedrich Schiller's reflections on two modes of historical consciousness.

41. Cobbs, *Understanding*, 231.

42. Wesley Wark, "Le Carré Comes In from the Cold," *Globe and Mail* (Toronto), April 22, 1995.

2 THE TAILOR OF PANAMA AND SINGLE & SINGLE
LUDIC FABRICATION, SELF-BEGOTTEN SONS,
AND A NEW WORLD ORDER

1. The neologism *artifactuality* is from G. Thomas Couser, *Memoir: An Introduction* (New York: Oxford University Press, 2012), 15. He coins it to signify the inevitable mixing of artifice, or invention, in the writing of memoir as a form of autobiographical recollection.

2. Assouline, "Spying," 87.

3. John le Carré, "Quel Panama!" *New York Times*, October 13, 1996.

4. Ross, "Master," 137.

5. Ibid., 144.

6. John le Carré, "Remarks to the Knopf Sales Force," August 12, 1996, in *Conversations*, ed. Bruccoli and Baughman, 134.

7. This also is the opinion of John Cobbs, who concludes that "The idea of le Carré seeing himself as Harry may provide the ultimate key to *The Tailor of Panama*'s unique position in his canon." Somewhat prematurely he then adds, "Coming as it does near the end of le Carré's spectacularly successful career, the novel may stand as a kind of personal authorial commentary on his own narrative persona." Cobbs, *Understanding*, 254.

8. Regarding his protagonist's domestic devotion, le Carré writes that "Harry Pendel loved his wife and children with an obedience that can only be understood by people who have never belonged to a family themselves, never known what it is to respect a decent father, love a happy mother, or accept them as the natural reward for being born into the world" (*TP*, 70). Although commitment to family is usually recognized as a self-evident absolute, there is something chilling about le Carré's use of the word "obedience" in this context. Even such devotion, he suggests, may be a conditioned response to the history of one's origins.

9. Norman Rush, "Spying and Lying," *New York Times*, October 20, 1996.

10. Ibid.

11. John le Carré, Letter, *New York Times*, November 3, 1996; Norman Rush, Reply to letter of John le Carré, *New York Times*, November 3, 1996.

12. Dan Collins, "The Secret Worlds of John le Carré," *Los Angeles Times*, November 12, 1996.

13. Douglas Davis, "Spy Novelist le Carré—Not Quite Conventional," *Jewish News* (Whippany, NJ), December 4, 1997.

14. Ibid. Bearing out my suggestion that "alienation" in this context signifies something like "uprootedness," Davis reports that le Carré "skips lightly over a childhood that must have been bewildering, if not deeply painful. His mother, he says, disappeared—'no doubt wisely'—when he was very young. The boy was left to the mercy of a father who chose to occupy the outer fringes of society and was rewarded with several terms in jail." Le Carré then recounts being "safely confined in one or another gloomy English boarding school, learning to become a bogus gentleman."

15. Ibid.

16. Geoffrey Winthrop-Young, "Preface," in *The Secret War: Treason, Espionage, and Modern Fiction*, by Eva Horn, trans. Geoffrey Winthrop-Young (Evanston, IL: Northwestern University Press, 2013), 22–23.

17. "Twentieth-century identities," observes James Clifford, "no longer presuppose continuous cultures or traditions. Everywhere individuals and groups improvise local performances from (re)collected pasts, drawing on foreign media, symbols, and languages." James Clifford, *The Predicament of Culture: Twentieth-Century Ethnography, Literature, and Art* (Cambridge, MA: Harvard University Press, 1988), 14. Indigenousness thus constitutes a passé criterion for positing identity in a transnational world.

18. Alan Cowell, "Learning to Write of a New World Order," *National Post* (Don Mills, ON), April 10, 1999.

19. Further strengthening the latent bond between Yevgeny Orlov and Oliver Single in this scene is a displaced "gratitude" that the protagonist cannot feel for his biological father. While the ever-glib Tiger is trying to assuage his

son's cautiously expressed reservations about the deal for Russian resources, Oliver "finds himself being tugged almost by gravity in an unexpected direction." Le Carré continues:

> Everybody is peering at Oliver, but Yevgeny's wily old gaze is fixed to him like a ship's line, pulling at him, feeling his weight, guessing him—and guessing him, Oliver is convinced of it, correctly. Out of nothing, Yevgeny's goodwill is evident to him. Stranger still, Oliver feels he is taking part in a resumption of an old and natural friendship. He sees a small boy in Georgia in love with everything around him[,] and the child is himself. He feels an unguarded gratitude for favors he has never consciously received. (SS, 122–23)

The last two sentences of this passage suggest that in Yevgeny Orlov the young British lawyer identifies both a surrogate father figure and the child he might have been if not subjected by Tiger to the "buffetings of a privileged English education" at more than one boarding school (SS, 108).

20. Michiko Kakutani, "Hero, Style, and Subject Are Familiar, for a While," *New York Times*, March 2, 1999. The only novel of le Carré's after *Single & Single* that Kakutani acclaims without qualification is *Our Kind of Traitor*, and even then primarily because this "new thriller" is "part vintage John le Carré and part Alfred Hitchcock" ("Innocents Caught in a Web of Intrigue," *New York Times*, October 12, 2010). As indicated by her reviews of le Carré's other post–Cold War fiction, Kakutani obviously regards his earlier work as a benchmark for the recent novels.

21. As an example of an apparently gratuitous element, when Oliver first enters the Orlov farmhouse he makes out among the shadows the seated figure of Tinatin with "an icon of the Christ child above her, suckling . . . at the covered bosom of his mother" (SS, 334). Like such other elements as Oliver's finding his father half naked in a stable, this detail seems meant primarily to hint at the scene's general import.

22. Graham Greene, *Our Man in Havana* (1958; repr., London: Penguin, 1962), 27, 31.

23. Ibid., 10.

24. Ibid., 89.

25. Ibid., 196.

26. Ibid., 213.

27. Ibid., 220.

28. Ibid., 31–32.

29. Brian Morton, "Cold War Thaw," *Sunday Herald* (Glasgow), February 14, 1999.

3 *THE CONSTANT* GARDENER AND *ABSOLUTE FRIENDS*
"WHOEVER OWNS THE TRUTH OWNS THE GAME"

1. Le Carré, "In Place of Nations."

2. Ibid.

3. Heidegger, *Being and Time*, 211–14.

4. See Nels Pearson and Marc Singer, "Open Cases: Detection, (Post)Modernity, and the State," in *Detective Fiction in a Postcolonial and Transnational World*, ed. Nels Pearson and Marc Singer (Farnham, UK: Ashgate, 2009), 1–14.

5. Todd McGowan, "The Temporality of the Real: The Path to Politics in *The Constant Gardener*," *Film-Philosophy* 11, no. 3 (October 2007): 53.

6. Heidegger, *Being and Time*, 279–311.

7. Sartre elaborates his concept of *mauvaise foi* in what originally was a lengthy chapter of *Being and Nothingness* (1943) that translator Hazel E. Barnes included ten years later in *Existential Psychoanalysis*. Associating the phenomenon with self-deception and falsehood, Sartre posits that "in bad faith human reality is constituted as a being which is what it is not and which is not what it is" (191–192).

8. Martin Heidegger, *Discourse on Thinking*, trans. John M. Anderson and E. Hans Freund (New York: Harper, 1966), 46, 48–49, 53, 55.

9. Barbara Dalle Pezze, "Heidegger on *Gelassenheit*," *Minerva* 10 (2006), http://www.ul.ie/~philos/vol10/Heidegger.html. In light of this observation it is significant that le Carré, beginning with Justin's sleuthing of his wife's files on Elba, depicts him as increasingly engaged in an imagined dialogue with Tessa as he tries to determine why she was murdered. The unfolding of that mental "conversation" brings him ever closer to the climactic scene of identification with her at Marsabit on Allia Bay, the site of Tessa's death as well as his own realization of *Gelassenheit*.

10. Heidegger, *Discourse*, 59, 61.

11. Diana Adesola Mafe, "(Mis)Imagining Africa in the New Millennium: *The Constant Gardener* and *Blood Diamond*," *Camera Obscura* 25, no. 3 (2011): 70, 74, 81.

12. Two interviews with le Carré in early 2004 shed light on the compositional history of *Absolute Friends*. In a face-to-face meeting with Mel Gussow of the Paris-based *International Herald Tribune*, the novelist disclosed that sometime before 9/11 he "started to write a story about a young Englishman who by accident and through his background and because of his natural naïveté had drifted into anarchism." After Al Qaeda's attack on the World Trade Center in New York City and the Pentagon in Washington, however, le Carré sensed that "nothing would ever be the same again. . . . I knew my book was just dead in the water." The ensuing invasion of Saddam Hussein's Iraq then persuaded him that his work in progress had "a renewed vitality." Adds Gussow, "He wrote the book swiftly, finishing it in June [2003], then making changes in three sets of galleys." Mel Gussow, "John

le Carré in the Great Game of Politics," *International Herald Tribune*, January 13, 2004.

Shortly after the US release of *Absolute Friends* and a telephone conversation with le Carré, Bob Minzesheimer confirmed this background. The novelist, he reports, began writing the book late in 2000 when, "imagining a new wave of Euro-terrorism," le Carré was "inspired by the violent anti-globalization protests in Seattle and Genoa. But after 9/11, he thought the novel was 'sunk,' torpedoed by reality." Bob Minzesheimer, "Le Carré Was Spooked by Specter of War," *USA Today*, January 8, 2004. The lead-up to the invasion of Iraq in March 2003 then motivated him to resume work on the manuscript and complete it in a few months. The last point can be inferred from two textual details: the narrator of *Absolute Friends* mentions early that "the Iraqi war officially ended little more than a month ago" (*AF*, 5), and on the final page le Carré formally dates the project's completion as June 9, 2003 (*AF*, 453).

13. Jeanne A. LeBlanc, "'Friends' Is Vintage le Carré, without the Subtlety," *Hartford Courant*, January 25, 2004.

14. Michiko Kakutani, "Adding Reality's Worries to a Thriller," *New York Times*, January 7, 2004.

15. Steven Poole, "Spies and Lies," *Guardian*, December 20, 2003.

16. George Walden, "Tinker Tailor Soldier Propagandist John le Carré's Latest Novel Falls Victim to His Clumsy Politicking," *Telegraph* (London), December 14, 2003.

17. Robert McCrum, "A Master's Voice: He Nods to Maugham and Greene, but John le Carré Is Still Unequalled," *Observer*, December 7, 2003.

18. Philip Hensher, "After the War Was Over . . . ," *Spectator* (London), December 27, 2003.

19. Gussow, "John le Carré."

20. Melissa Block and Robert Siegel, "David Cornwell Discusses His Novel *Absolute Friends*, Which Was Written under His Pen Name, John le Carré," *All Things Considered*, NPR, February 4, 2004, in *Conversations*, ed. Bruccoli and Baughman, 173–74.

21. I take my cue for describing Dimitri as an ogre from the novel itself, which recounts Mundy's impression of his first and only face-to-face meeting with this figure as follows: "I'm in a movie . . . : James Bond visits the ogre's castle" (*AF*, 318). That le Carré borrows from John Buchan in depicting Dimitri can be gauged from his elusiveness as a villain. "I'd sooner trail Lucifer," Mundy is told. "He doesn't use telephones. . . . Computers, e-mails, electronic typewriters, the humble post, forget it. . . . He'll travel five thousand miles to whisper into a man's ear in the middle of the Sahara desert" (*AF*, 379). Le Carré later mentions Buchan by name in writing that "Mundy is never certain that he hasn't lifted the scenario from the pages of John Buchan" (*AF*, 417).

22. Michael Denning, *Cover Stories: Narrative and Ideology in the British Spy Thriller* (London: Routledge, 1987), 151.

23. In context the phrase *hall of mirrors* refers to Mundy's scanning images in reflective surfaces of Sasha's unexpected materialization after many years of separation, suggesting the former double agent's ingrained wariness of being caught off guard. "A hall of mirrors," writes le Carré, "is a deliberate bastion against reality. Multiplied images of reality lose their impact as they recede into infinity. A figure who face to face might instill stark fear or perfect pleasure becomes, in his numberless reflections, a mere premise, a putative form" (*AF*, 19).

24. Christian Caryl, "Le Carré's War on Terror," *New York Review of Books*, August 12, 2004.

25. Jost Hindersmann, "Irak-Krieg und Anti-Terror-Kampf der Bush-Regierung: John le Carré's *Absolute Freunde* und Richard A. Clarke's *The Scorpion's Gate*," in *Krimijahrbuch 2006*, ed. Dieter Paul Rudolph (Wuppertal, Germany: NordPark, 2006), 142.

26. Hösle, "Berufsethik der Geheimdienste."

27. Anne McClintock, "Imperial Ghosting and National Tragedy: Revenants from Hiroshima and Indian Country in the War on Terror," *PMLA* 129 (October 2014): 819.

28. Ibid., 820, 826, 821.

29. Lassner, "Paradoxical Polemics," 18.

30. Ibid., 20.

31. Ibid., 21.

32. In support of her argument about the parodic histrionics of Bakhtinian heteroglossia in *Absolute Friends*, Lassner quotes the following passage from one of Sasha's tirades at a Free University of Berlin protest rally in 1970:

> He has poured scorn and hatred on America for the carpet-bombing of Vietnam's cities . . . and napalming of her jungles. He has called for the Nuremberg Tribunal to be reconvened, and the fascist-imperialist American leadership arraigned before it on charges of genocide and crimes against humanity. He has accused the morally degenerate American lackeys of the so-called government in Bonn of sanitizing Germany's Nazi past with consumerism, and turning the Auschwitz generation into a flock of fat sheep. . . . He has listed America's wars of aggression, from Hiroshima through Korea by way of . . . South America and Africa to Vietnam. (*AF*, 104)

"Despite similar targets," comments Lassner, "the cumulative effect of this list distinguishes it from le Carré's modulated voice in his earlier novels and from his current vituperative essays" (26). Mimicry mocks, paradoxically, soapbox polemics.

4 *THE MISSION SONG* AND *A MOST WANTED MAN*
COVERT SURVEILLANCE, DENIABLE SYNDICATES,
AND EXTRAORDINARY RENDITION

1. Michel Foucault, *Discipline and Punish: The Birth of the Prison*, trans. Alan Sheridan (New York: Vintage, 1977), 217.

2. There have been numerous scholarly books and articles on surveillance over the past twenty-five years, but it is noteworthy that in 2007 an organization called the Surveillance Studies Network (http://www.surveillance-studies.net), which sponsors the quarterly journal *Surveillance & Society*, was established in the United Kingdom.

3. Kevin D. Haggerty, "Tear Down the Walls: On Demolishing the Panopticon," in *Theorizing Surveillance: The Panopticon and Beyond*, ed. David Lyon (Cullompton, UK: Willan, 2006), 23. "The panopticon is oppressive," this iconoclastic essay begins. Expanding on this observation, Haggerty continues:

> Since Foucault's famous reinterpretation of Bentham's utopian project of prison architecture, the panopticon has stood for sinister manifestations of power/knowledge. Today, however, the panopticon is oppressive in an entirely different sense. That is because the panopticon is now considerably more than a brick and mortar edifice[;] . . . it is also easily the leading scholarly model or metaphor for analysing surveillance. In this latter role the panopticon has . . . become oppressive. The sheer number of works that invoke the panopticon is overwhelming. More problematically, the panoptic model has become reified, directing scholarly attention to a select subset of attributes of surveillance.

For two other scholars who agree with Haggerty, see Greg Elmer and Andy Opel, "Pre-empting Panoptic Surveillance: Surviving the Inevitable War on Terror," in *Theorizing Surveillance: The Panopticon and Beyond*, ed. David Lyon (Cullompton, UK: Willan, 2006), 140–41.

4. "Britain Is 'Surveillance Society,'" BBC News, November 2, 2006, http://news.bbc.co.uk/2/hi/uk_news/6108496.stm.

5. David Murakami Wood, "Globalization and Surveillance," in *Routledge Handbook of Surveillance Studies*, ed. Kirstie Bell, Kevin D. Haggerty, and David Lyon (London: Routledge, 2012), 341.

6. My conflation of *translator* and *interpreter* scants a distinction between the two designations regarding which le Carré's protagonist in *The Mission Song* is quite insistent. "Never mistake, please, your mere translator for your top interpreter," he declares. "An interpreter is a translator, true, but not the other way round. . . . [T]he simultaneous interpreter . . . has to think as fast as a numbers boy in a coloured jacket buying financial futures. Better sometimes if he doesn't think

at all, but orders the spinning cogs on both sides of his head to mesh together, then sits back and waits to see what pours out of his mouth" (*MS*, 14).

7. "This is the first time le Carré has completely surrendered narrative omniscience, and, at one level, it's a roll of the dice that benefits the reader with a bravura performance." Robert McCrum, "Back into the Heart of Darkness," *Observer*, September 24, 2006.

8. Foucault, *Discipline and Punish*, 221.

9. Christopher Hope suggests that *The Mission Song*'s plot may seem preposterous "until you remember how coups in Africa often look like *opéra bouffe*, but with real blood." He adds, "Le Carré seems to have another putsch in mind. In 2004, a group of Old Etonians, former SAS [Special Air Service] soldiers and muscular South African mercenaries, with supporters ranging from Mark Thatcher to other political figures abroad, and with the connivance of the British and Spanish secret services, planned an assault on Equatorial Guinea, a country even more unhappy, if that is possible, than the Congo. The idea was to overthrow a man-eating tyrant named Obiang Nguema and install a puppet president, who would then turn over a large slice of the country's considerable oil revenues to what was known as 'the Syndicate.'" Christopher Hope, "Candide in Africa," *Guardian*, September 23, 2006.

10. Neil Gordon, "The Constant Translator," *New York Times*, September 17, 2006.

11. "She had known from the start," asserts the narrator-protagonist, "that Brinkley was no good. She had no need of One-Day Courses in security to tell her that in Salvo she was dealing with the remnants of a misguided loyalty that was lodged like a virus in my system and needed to work itself out with time. . . . She had gone her own way as I had gone mine. We had both veered from the same path, each in our separate directions, she to her people, I to mine. She had done nothing that required my forgiveness" (*MS*, 311).

12. John le Carré, "Reality Check for My Warlords, " *Globe and Mail* (Toronto), September 16, 2006.

13. Michiko Kakutani, "A Translator Searching for Words of His Own," *New York Times*, September 26, 2006.

14. In this respect the film adaptation of the book, though technically accomplished in conveying a post-9/11 atmosphere of transatlantic suspicion, is disappointing. By focusing from beginning to end on the sole perspective of Günther Bachmann, played by Philip Seymour Hoffman in his last screen role, Anton Corbijn's 2014 movie ignores the layered narrational complexity of le Carré's novel.

15. Annabel Richter's connecting a "Mr. *Lipizzaner*" with Tommy Brue is one of the extremely rare plotting oversights in le Carré's fiction. As mentioned in my next paragraph, the son of Edward Amadeus Brue has kept the existence of Lipizzaner accounts a closely guarded secret, supposedly known only to him and his

secretary, Frau Ellenberger. Although seven years ago Ellenberger "made a voluntary sworn statement" to the German authorities about "certain concerns [she] had regarding the activities of [her] employer at that time" (*MW*, 200), are we to speculate that knowledge of Brue Frères PLC's harboring such money-laundering accounts somehow filtered back to Richter in her activities as a Sanctuary North advocate? Perhaps this otherwise unexplained anomaly in the plot is a minor example of secrecy's inevitable leakage, a fairly common motif in le Carré's corpus.

16. Albeit a minor point, "majestic Martha" reprises *The Night Manager*'s "Darling Katie," officially "Mrs. Katherine Handyside Dulling, Economic Counselor of the British Embassy in Washington." When it comes to his depiction of female CIA agents, le Carré tends toward stereotypes.

17. Luc Boltanski, *Mysteries and Conspiracies: Detective Stories, Spy Novels, and the Making of Modern Societies*, trans. Catherine Porter (Cambridge, UK: Polity, 2014), xiv, xv.

18. Ibid., 14, 22.

19. The occasion is a second meeting of the Joint Steering Committee to which Dr. Keller invites "swiftly risen managers of the post-9/11 boom market in intelligence and allied trades." Regarding this cohort le Carré writes, "Only a tiny handful . . . had ever heard a bomb explode in anger, but in the long, silent war for the leadership of their Service, they were case-hardened veterans." Those in attendance, in other words, are ladder-climbing espiocrats. Günther Bachmann, who is preparing to address this largely US-led group, would like to warn them that

> . . . however many of the latest spies' wonder toys they had in their cupboards, however many magic codes they broke and hot-signals chatter they listened to, and brilliant deductions they pulled out of the ether regarding the enemy's organizational structures, or lack of them, and internecine fights they had, and however many tame journalists were vying to trade their questionable gems of knowledge for slanted tip-offs and something for the back pocket, in the end it was the spurned imam, the love-crossed secret courier, the venal Pakistani defense scientist, the middle-ranking Iranian military officer who's been passed over for promotion, the lonely sleeper who can sleep alone no longer, who among them provide the hard base of knowledge without which all the rest is fodder for the truth benders, ideologues[,] and politopaths who ruin the earth. (*MW*, 236)

Few of le Carré's "longueurs," in Charles Cumming's phrase, capture as trenchantly as this passage his disdain for post-9/11 bureaucrats "managing" the War on Terror and his recognition that truly useful "intelligence" derives ultimately from human sources.

20. Timothy Melley, *The Covert Sphere: Secrecy, Fiction, and the National*

Security State (Ithaca, NY: Cornell University Press, 2012).

21. Ibid., 3.

22. One striking measure of this expansion, points out Melley, is that in 1964 two critics chastised the United States for harboring an "Invisible Government" (CIA) that secretly employed approximately 200,000 people. "Fifty years later," continues Melley,

> the United States has sixteen intelligence agencies employing untold civilian and military personnel at a public cost of $75 billion per year—a figure that, while only recently disclosed and almost certainly understated, is still more than any other nonmilitary discretionary budget item and more than the total spent on intelligence by all other world governments combined. A total of forty-five U.S. agencies, 1,271 government organizations, and 1,391 private corporations now do intelligence and counterterrorism work. Over 850,000 U.S. citizens—one in every 181 U.S. workers—hold a "top secret" clearance. . . . Yet the proliferation of such agencies cannot be understood simply as a response to the events of 9/11. It is a structural legacy of Cold War counterespionage tactics, which require extraordinary compartmentalization of knowledge. (Ibid., 4–5)

What Melley terms the expansionary "covert sector," then, has increasingly invaded a putative "private sphere" and made it vulnerable to "a cultural imaginary shaped by both institutional secrecy and public fascination with the secret work of the state" (5). My conclusion addresses this formation of a "cultural imaginary" in relation to le Carré's post–Cold War canon.

23. Here we might note that Günther Bachmann, unlike Annabel Richter and Tommy Brue, is never depicted in terms of normative domiciliary arrangements. With Erna Frey, "his long-standing workmate" and unconventional partner (*MW*, 46), he occasionally, when staying late at his operational headquarters, bunks down in "the cramped emergency bedroom at the end of the corridor" (*MW*, 52), but otherwise this agent of the National Security State is not associated with a private sphere.

24. Boltanski, *Mysteries*, 160, 167. The immediate context of Boltanski's observations is his analysis of le Carré's *The Spy Who Came In from the Cold*, although he regards his comments as also applicable to *A Most Wanted Man* (see 292n13).

25. Melley, *Covert Sphere*, 3.

26. Ibid., 124. This epistemic conflict, Melley points out a few pages later, "is reflected in the very structure of the CIA, which is divided into a Directorate of Intelligence, charged with understanding the world, and a Directorate of Operations, charged with secretly changing it" (128).

27. Ibid., 30.

28. Ibid., 8, 2, 10.

29. Jürgen Habermas, "The Public Sphere: An Encyclopedia Article," *New*

German Critique 3 (1974): 49–55; *The Structural Transformation of the Public Sphere: An Inquiry into a Category of Bourgeois Society*, trans. Thomas Burger with Frederick Lawrence (Cambridge, MA: MIT Press, 1989).

30. Melley, *Covert Sphere*, 5.

31. Michael Rogin, "'Make My Day!': Spectacle as Amnesia in Imperial Politics," *Representations* 29 (Winter 1990): 102, 103, 105.

32. Jean Baudrillard, *Simulacra and Simulation*, trans. Sheila Faria Glaser (Ann Arbor: University of Michigan Press, 1994).

33. Eva Horn, *The Secret War: Treason, Espionage, and Modern Fiction*, trans. Geoffrey Winthrop-Young (Evanston, IL: Northwestern University Press, 2013), 25.

34. Frederick P. Hitz, *The Great Game: The Myth and Reality of Espionage* (New York: Alfred A. Knopf, 2004).

35. Horn, *Secret War*, 38.

36. Ibid., 96, 99, 111.

5 *OUR KIND OF TRAITOR* AND *A DELICATE TRUTH*
"WHO WERE WE DOING ALL THIS SECRECY STUFF FOR?"

1. Nicolas Freeling, *Criminal Convictions: Errant Essays on Perpetrators of Literary License* (Boston: David R. Godine, 1994), 22.

2. The intertwining of "friends" and "enemies" in le Carré's fiction harks back to *The Spy Who Came In from the Cold*, in which Alec Leamas's despised ex-Nazi rival, Hans-Dieter Mundt, turns out to be a double agent employed by Cambridge Circus (MI6) who orchestrates the escape of Leamas and Liz Gold from prison in East Germany. Meanwhile, the upright Fiedler, a Jew tortured during the Third Reich and the East German Secret Service's counterintelligence prosecutor of Mundt as a suspected collaborator, is sentenced to death.

3. James Naughtie, "*Our Kind of Traitor* by John le Carré: Review," *Telegraph* (London), September 12, 2010; Yvonne Klein, Reviewing the Evidence, December 2010, ttp://www.reviewingtheevidence.com/review.html. Although I support Klein's insight about *Our Kind of Traitor*'s "fluid" point of view, I question her claim that it "represent[s] something of a departure from anything [le Carré]'s done before," as indicated by my earlier discussions of *The Tailor of Panama*, *The Constant Gardener*, and *A Most Wanted Man*.

4. Peter Millar, "Return of the Master," *Times* (London), September 11, 2010.

5. Frank Kermode, *The Genesis of Secrecy: On the Interpretation of Narrative* (Cambridge, MA: Harvard University Press, 1979), 14, 47, 4.

6. Christopher J. Knight, *Omissions Are Not Accidents: Modern Apophaticism from Henry James to Jacques Derrida* (Toronto: University of Toronto Press, 2010), 185–91.

7. Ibid., 8.

8. Hector Meredith's loathing of this "two-faced, devious, backsliding, dishonest[,] and well-connected" former colleague transcends personal antipathy.

"Aubrey Longrigg," writes le Carré, "was not mere *enemy* in Hector's eyes—that would have been too easy altogether—he was an archetype; a classic symptom of the canker that was devouring not just the City, but our most precious institutions of government" (*OK*, 165).

9. As I noted in chapter 4, Anderson declares to Salvador in *The Mission Song*: "And has it never occurred to you that it might be God's will that the world's resources, which are dwindling even as we speak, do better in the hands of civilised Christian souls with a cultured way of life than some of the most backward heathens on the planet?" (*MS*, 297).

10. Even though as an espiocrat Matlock is thought to be an implacable foe of his predecessor Longrigg, both men are allied with the same political party in England, and le Carré records of "Billy Boy" that "his Midlands accent . . . had become more noticeable under New Labour, but was receding with the prospect of electoral defeat" (*OK*, 145). The differences between "friends" and "enemies" obviously become obscured given the vagaries of politics.

11. These cover identities, significantly, deprive Perry and Gail of "the power of natural speech," and they find themselves "talking to each other like an ideal couple in a television commercial" (*OK*, 187). This development reinforces the novel's theme of secrecy's falsifying influence on its subjects.

12. *Our Kind of Traitor* anticipates this development when MI6's "Queen of Human Resources," something of a fixture in le Carré's post–Cold War fiction, icily advises Luke Weaver that after Iraq he might consider outsourced placement because "the terror thing, *and* the threat of civil unrest, were doing *wonders* for the private-security sector" (*OK*, 122, 123).

13. Fintan O'Toole, "The Real Men of England," *New York Review of Books*, June 6, 2013. Raw intelligence, this now commercialized "product," according to one of Toby Bell's friends in Her Majesty's Treasury Department, is "straight from the shelf, direct to *buyer*, no stops between. *Un*spun, *un*tested, *un*pasteurized[,] and above all untouched by bureaucratic hands" (*DT*, 66). Crispin, in other words, is in the business of selling unverified information to the highest bidder—a lucrative business given Western anxieties in the "Global War on Terror," to which Whitehall officials in *A Delicate Truth* refer as "*G-WOT*" (*DT*, 56).

14. O'Toole, "Real Men."

15. Indicative of this inclination in le Carré's novel is Roy Stormont-Taylor, "Queen's Counsel" and "the silkiest silk in the business," who on television is seen expounding on "the essential differences between law and justice" (*DT*, 120). He also advises Member of Parliament Fergus Quinn on the technical legality of Operation Wildlife.

16. Reviewers of *A Delicate Truth* besides Fintan O'Toole take note of the novel's moral polarity. See Declan Burke, "Spymaster Back with Bracing Tale of Dirty Tricks," *Irish Times*, May 11, 2013; Sarah Churchwell, "Secrets and Lies" *New Statesman* (London), April 26, 2013.

17. Le Carré inscribes this difference in both novels as arising from their

yeoman stock. Like Perry's full first name of Peregrine, "traditionally the property of the English upper classes" (*MW*, 1), "*Toby*, which might by the sound of it set him higher on the English social ladder than his provenance deserved, . . . derived from nothing more elevated than his father's pride in the holy man Tobias, whose wondrous filial virtues are set down in the ancient scripts" (*DT*, 48). As such, both characters attest to le Carré's faith in the underlying integrity of Britons untainted by the emergence of a "Deep State" and its willful blindness to moral trespasses.

18. Quinn's response to the tactical counsel relayed by Probyn is a stellar example of bureaucratic disavowal and doublespeak: "Kindly note I am *not* the field commander in this situation. Military decisions are the sole province of the senior soldier on the ground, as you are aware. However, I may *recommend*. You will therefore inform Jeb that, on the basis of the operational intelligence before me, I *recommend* but do not *command* that he would be well advised to put Operation Wildlife into immediate effect. The decision to do so is of course his own'" (*DT*, 43).

19. The incident involved Oakley's arrest for drunk and disorderly behavior after being "flagellated in the normal manner" (*DT*, 211), according to a police superintendent, at one of the Reeperbahn's notorious establishments for indulging sadomasochistic fetishes. On short notice Toby Bell drives from Berlin to Hamburg at three o'clock in the morning to take his secretly gay mentor into custody. News of the episode somehow reaches Whitehall and makes Oakley no longer "bankable" (*DT*, 210). That pun on le Carré's part (since Oakley then becomes a banker) seems intentional.

20. For a further discussion of the Lido and its symbolism, including features of the panopticon, see Robert Lance Snyder, "'Shadow of Abandonment': Graham Greene's *The Confidential Agent*," *Texas Studies in Literature and Language* 52 (Summer 2010): 218–19.

21. One reviewer notes, "The enemy in le Carré's universe, both fictional and not, isn't America. It's the virus of shortsightedness, hypocrisy, lies and unfettered greed that plagues the 'post-imperial, post–Cold War world' Toby Bell so wants to help shape." Olen Steinhauer, "Le Carré's Latest," *New York Times*, May 5, 2013.

22. Le Carré, "To Russia," 6.

23. O'Toole, "Real Men."

24. Mark Lawson, "The Privatisation of Spying," *Guardian*, April 20, 2013. Lawson's seeming avoidance of the deprecatory tag "thriller," however, did not register with the *Guardian*'s editors, who provided the article with the subhead "Mark Lawson Applauds a Thriller That Resonates with Whitehall Secrecy during the Bush-Blair Era."

CONCLUSION
JOHN LE CARRÉ AND THE CULTURAL IMAGINARY

1. Pepper, "Policing the Globe," 404–5; Horsley, "Life Spent Lying," 161.

2. Melley, *Covert Sphere*, 5.

3. Melley discusses at length numerous examples of such simulacral "fictions"

and includes occasionally condensed lists of the same. Ibid., 27–28, 172, 214. See also Matt Bai, "The '24' Effect," Yahoo News, December 11, 2014, http://news .yahoo.com/the—24—effect-002709277.html. This article insightfully bears out Melley's argument in terms of the popular Fox television series that premiered just a few days after 9/11.

4. Melley, *Covert Sphere*, 43, 81.

5. Horn, *Secret War*, 138.

6. Ibid., 353–54.

7. "The art of examining . . . information that shapes le Carré's narrative poetics," writes Horn, "does not aim for a coherent story but for anything that disrupts narrative and causal connections: omissions, ellipses, vagueness, lies, self-serving declarations, or downright refusals to speak." Le Carré's cultivation of such aporias, she alleges, makes his *"retrospective narratives"* comparable to Jorge Luis Borges's self-reflexive fiction. Ibid., 273, 274.

8. Hensher, "After the War."

9. Foucault, *Discipline and Punish*, 217.

10. Guy Debord, *Society of the Spectacle* (1967; repr., Detroit: Black & Red, 1983), paras. 1, 6, 24. This edition does not provide page numbers but only paragraph numbers.

11. Jean Baudrillard, *The Spirit of Terrorism and Other Essays*, trans. Chris Turner (London: Verso, 2012), 7, 11, 22.

12. Ibid., 23.

13. Crehan, "Information, Power[,] and the Reader," 110.

14. Julian Assange, "Conspiracy as Governance," Cryptome, December 3, 2006, http://cryptome.org/0002/ja-conspiracies.pdf

15. Greg Miller, Adam Goldberg, and Julie Tate, "Senate Report on CIA Program Details Brutality, Dishonesty," *Washington Post*, December 9, 2014.

16. John Updike, "Le Carré's Game: British Spies Soldier On in a Thawed World," *New Yorker*, March 20, 1995.

17. Merry, *Anatomy of the Spy Thriller*, 214.

18. Dean, "John le Carré," 31.

19. Ralph Harper, *The World of the Thriller* (Cleveland, OH: Case Western Reserve University Press, 1969), 46.

20. Dan Fesperman, *The Double Game* (New York: Alfred A. Knopf, 2012), 6.

21. Ibid., 22.

22. Ibid., n.p.

23. Garner, "'I Have Pretended.'"

BIBLIOGRAPHY

Abrams, M. H. *Natural Supernaturalism: Tradition and Revolution in Romantic Literature*. New York: W. W. Norton, 1971.

Achebe, Chinua. "An Image of Africa." *Massachusetts Review* 18, no. 4 (1977): 782–94.

Allain, Marie-Françoise. *The Other Man: Conversations with Graham Greene*. Translated by Guido Waldman. New York: Simon & Schuster, 1983.

"All-Time 100 Novels." *Time*, October 16, 2005. http://www.time.com/2005/10/16/all-time-100-novels.

Arendt, Hannah. *The Human Condition*. Chicago: University of Chicago Press, 1958.

Aronoff, Myron J. *The Spy Novels of John le Carré: Balancing Ethics and Power*. New York: Palgrave, 2001.

Assange, Julian. "Conspiracy as Governance." Cryptome, December 3, 2006. http://cryptome.org/0002/ja-conspiracies.pdf.

Assouline, Pierre. "Spying on a Spymaker." Interview with John le Carré, August 1986. In *Conversations with John le Carré*, edited by Matthew J. Bruccoli and Judith S. Baughman, 86–89. Jackson: University Press of Mississippi, 2004.

Atkins, John. *The British Spy Novel: Styles in Treachery*. New York: Riverrun, 1984.

Babette's Feast. Directed by Gabriel Axel. Panorama, 1987.

Bai, Matt. "The '24' Effect." Yahoo News, December 11, 2014. http://news.yahoo.com/the—24—effect-002709277.html.

Bakhtin, M. M. *The Dialogic Imagination: Four Essays*. Edited by Michael Holquist. Translated by Caryl Emerson and Michael Holquist. Austin: University of Texas Press, 1981.

Barley, Tony. *Taking Sides: The Fiction of John le Carré*. Milton Keynes, UK: Open University Press, 1986.

Barzun, Jacques. "Meditations on the Literature of Spying." *American Scholar* 34, no. 2 (Spring 1965): 167–78.

Baudrillard, Jean. *Simulacra and Simulation*. Translated by Sheila Faria Glaser. Ann Arbor: University of Michigan Press, 1994.

———. *The Spirit of Terrorism and Other Essays*. Translated by Chris Turner. London: Verso, 2012.

Beam, Alex. "Is John le Carré the Greatest Living Writer?" *Boston Globe*, July 31, 2014.

Beene, LynnDianne. *John le Carré*. New York: Twayne, 1992.

Bentley, Nick. *Contemporary British Fiction*. Edinburgh, UK: Edinburgh University Press, 2008.

Bizot, François. *The Gate*. Translated by Euan Cameron. New York: Vintage-Random, 2004.

Block, Melissa, and Robert Siegel. "David Cornwell Discusses His Novel *Absolute Friends*, Which Was Written under His Pen Name, John le Carré." *All Things Considered*, NPR, February 4, 2004. In *Conversations with John le Carré*, edited by Matthew J. Bruccoli and Judith S. Baughman, 171–74. Jackson: University Press of Mississippi, 2004.

Bloom, Clive. "The Spy Thriller: A Genre under Cover?" In *Spy Thrillers: From Buchan to le Carré*, edited by Clive Bloom, 1–11. New York: St. Martin's Press, 1990.

Bloom, Harold, ed. *John le Carré*. New York: Chelsea, 1987.

Bold, Alan, ed. *The Quest for le Carré*. New York: St. Martin's Press, 1988.

Boltanski, Luc. *Mysteries and Conspiracies: Detective Stories, Spy Novels, and the Making of Modern Societies*. Translated by Catherine Porter. Cambridge, UK: Polity, 2014.

Boyd, William. "Oh, What a Lovely Cold War." Review of *The Secret Pilgrim*, by John le Carré. *New York Times*, January 6, 1991.

Bradford, Richard. *The Novel Now: Contemporary British Fiction*. Malden, MA: Blackwell, 2007.

Bragg, Melvyn. "The Things a Spy Can Do: John le Carré Talking." Interview with John le Carré, January 22, 1976. In *Conversations with John le Carré*, edited by Matthew J. Bruccoli and Judith S. Baughman, 33–37. Jackson: University Press of Mississippi, 2004.

Briggs, Laura, Gladys McCormick, and J. T. Way. "Transnationalism: A Category of Analysis." *American Quarterly* 60, no. 3 (September 2008): 625–48.

"Britain Is 'Surveillance Society.'" BBC News, November 2, 2006. http://news.bbc.co.uk/2/hi/uk_news/6108496.stm.

Browning, Robert. *The Complete Poetical Works of Browning*. Edited by Horace E. Scudder. Boston: Houghton Mifflin, 1895.

Bruccoli, Matthew J., and Judith S. Baughman, eds. *Conversations with John le Carré*. Jackson: University Press of Mississippi, 2004.

Buchan, John. *The Thirty-Nine Steps*. Edited by Christopher Harvie. 1915. Reprint, New York: Oxford University Press, 1993.

Buckley, William F., Jr. "Terror and a Woman." Review of *The Little Drummer Girl*, by John le Carré. *New York Times*, March 13, 1983. Reprinted in *Spy Thrillers: From Buchan to le Carré*, edited by Clive Bloom, 113–16. New York: St. Martin's Press, 1990.

Burke, Declan. "Spymaster Back with Bracing Tale of Dirty Tricks." Review of *A Delicate Truth*, by John le Carré. *Irish Times*, May 11, 2013.

Bush, George H. W. "Address before a Joint Session of the Congress on the Persian Gulf Crisis and the Federal Budget Deficit." September 11, 1990. Washington, DC. http://bushlibrary.tamu.edu/research/public_papers.php?id=2217&year=1990&month=9.

Buzard, James M. "Faces, Photos, Mirrors: Image and Ideology in the Novels of John le Carré." In *Image and Ideology in Modern/Postmodern Discourse*, edited by David B. Downing and Susan Bazargan, 153–79. Albany: State University of New York Press, 1991.

Caldwell, Gail. "Spycraft's Detritus: Damaged Souls." Review of *The Secret Pilgrim*, by John le Carré. *Boston Globe*, January 6, 1991.

Carson, Tom. "Le Carré Goes Native Hunting for a Romantic on the Grand Scale." Review of *Our Game*, by John le Carré. *Los Angeles Times*, March 26, 1995.

Caryl, Christian. "Le Carré's War on Terror." *New York Review of Books*, August 12, 2004.

Cawelti, John G., and Bruce A. Rosenberg. *The Spy Story*. Chicago: University of Chicago Press, 1987.

Churchwell, Sarah. "Secrets and Lies." Review of *A Delicate Truth*, by John le Carré. *New Statesman* (London), April 26, 2013.

Clifford, James. *The Predicament of Culture: Twentieth-Century Ethnography, Literature, and Art*. Cambridge, MA: Harvard University Press, 1988.

Cobbs, John L. *Understanding John le Carré*. Columbia: University of South Carolina Press, 1998.

Collins, Dan. "The Secret Worlds of John le Carré." *Los Angeles Times*, November 12, 1996.

Conrad, Joseph. *Heart of Darkness*. Edited by Paul O'Prey. 1902. Reprint, New York: Penguin, 1985.

———. *The Secret Agent: A Simple Tale*. Edited by John Lyon. 1907. Reprint, Oxford, UK: Oxford University Press, 2004.

———. *The Secret Sharer and Other Stories*. Edited by John G. Peters. New York: W. W. Norton, 2015.

The Constant Gardener. Directed by Fernando Meirelles. Focus Features, 2005.

The Conversation. Directed by Francis Ford Coppola. Paramount, 1974.

Couser, G. Thomas. *Memoir: An Introduction*. New York: Oxford University Press, 2012.

Cowell, Alan. "Learning to Write of a New World Order." Review of *Single & Single*, by John le Carré. *National Post* (Don Mills, ON), April 10, 1999.

Crehan, Stewart. "Information, Power[,] and the Reader: Textual Strategies in le Carré." In *The Quest for le Carré*, edited by Alan Bold, 103–28. New York: St. Martin's Press, 1988.

Crim, Brian E. "(Im)Perfect Spies: Identity and the Pathology of the Cold War in John le Carré's *A Perfect Spy* and *The Secret Pilgrim*." In *Espionage Fiction: The Seduction of Clandestinity*, edited by Robert Lance Snyder, 91–106. Special issue of *Paradoxa* 24 (2012).

Crutchley, Leigh. "The Fictional World of Espionage." Interview with John le Carré, April 14, 1966. In *Conversations with John le Carré*, edited by Matthew J. Bruccoli and Judith S. Baughman, 6–9. Jackson: University Press of Mississippi, 2004.

Cumming, Charles. "Journey into the Shadows in the Hearts of Men." Review of *A Most Wanted Man*, by John le Carré. *Daily Telegraph*, September 20, 2008.

Davis, Douglas. "Spy Novelist le Carré—Not Quite Conventional." *Jewish News* (Whippany, NJ), December 4, 1997.

Dean, Michael. "John le Carré: The Writer Who Came In from the Cold." Interview with John le Carré, September 5, 1974. In *Conversations with John le Carré*, edited by Matthew J. Bruccoli and Judith S. Baughman, 27–32. Jackson: University Press of Mississippi, 2004.

Debord, Guy. *Society of the Spectacle*. 1967. Reprint, Detroit: Black & Red, 1983.

Deighton, Len. *The Ipcress File*. 1962. Reprint, London: HarperCollins, 2009.

Denning, Michael. *Cover Stories: Narrative and Ideology in the British Spy Thriller*. London: Routledge, 1987.

Dr. Strangelove. Directed by Stanley Kubrick. Columbia, 1964.

Eagleton, Terry. *Literary Theory: An Introduction*. Minneapolis: University of Minnesota Press, 1983.

Elmer, Greg, and Andy Opel. "Preempting Panoptic Surveillance: Surviving the Inevitable War on Terror." In *Theorizing Surveillance: The Panopticon and Beyond*, edited by David Lyon, 139–59. Cullompton, UK: Willan, 2006.

English, James F., ed. *A Concise Companion to Contemporary British Fiction*. Malden, MA: Blackwell, 2006.

Fesperman, Dan. *The Double Game*. New York: Alfred A. Knopf, 2012.

Foucault, Michel. *Discipline and Punish: The Birth of the Prison*. Translated by Alan Sheridan. New York: Vintage, 1977.

Franzen, Jonathan. "Anger Is My Business." Review of *The Night Manager*, by John le Carré. *Los Angeles Times*, June 27, 1993.

Freeling, Nicolas. *Criminal Convictions: Errant Essays on Perpetrators of Literary License*. Boston: David R. Godine, 1994.

Garner, Dwight. "'I Have Pretended to Be a Gentleman for So Long.'" *New York Times*, April 21, 2013.

Genette, Gérard. *Narrative Discourse: An Essay in Method*. Translated by Jane E. Lewin. Ithaca, NY: Cornell University Press, 1980.

Giddings, Robert. "The Writing on the Igloo Walls: Narrative Technique in *The Spy Who Came In from the Cold.*" In *The Quest for le Carré*, edited by Alan Bold, 188–210. New York: St. Martin's Press, 1988.

Goodwin, Jonathan. "John le Carré's *The Secret Pilgrim* and the End of the Cold War." *Clues* 28, no. 1 (Spring 2010): 102–9.

Gordon, Charles. "Le Carré Changes the Rules in *Our Game.*" Review of *Our Game*, by John le Carré. *Ottawa Citizen*, April 9, 1995.

Gordon, Neil. "The Constant Translator." Review of *The Mission Song*, by John le Carré. *New York Times*, September 17, 2006.

Gray, John. *Black Mass: Apocalyptic Religion and the Death of Utopia*. New York: Farrar, Straus & Giroux, 2007.

Gray, Paul. "Ice Cubes." Review of *The Secret Pilgrim*, by John le Carré. *Time*, January 14, 1991.

Greene, Graham. *The Confidential Agent*. 1939. Reprint, London: Heinemann and Bodley Head, 1971.

———. *England Made Me*. 1935. Reprint, London: Penguin, 1992.

———. *Our Man in Havana*. 1958. Reprint, London: Penguin, 1962.

———. *A Sort of Life*. 1971. Reprint, London: Vintage-Random, 1999.

Gross, Miriam. "The Secret World of John le Carré." Interview with John le Carré, February 3, 1980. In *Conversations with John le Carré*, edited by Matthew J. Bruccoli and Judith S. Baughman, 60–71. Jackson: University Press of Mississippi, 2004.

Gussow, Mel. "John le Carré in the Great Game of Politics." *International Herald Tribune*, January 13, 2004.

Habermas, Jürgen. "The Public Sphere: An Encyclopedia Article." *New German Critique* 3 (1974): 49–55.

———. *The Structural Transformation of the Public Sphere: An Inquiry into a Category of Bourgeois Society*. Translated by Thomas Burger, with Frederick Lawrence. Cambridge, MA: MIT Press, 1989.

Haggerty, Kevin D. "Tear Down the Walls: On Demolishing the Panopticon." In *Theorizing Surveillance: The Panopticon and Beyond*, edited by David Lyon, 23–45. Cullompton, UK: Willan, 2006.

Harper, Ralph. *The World of the Thriller*. Cleveland, OH: Case Western Reserve University Press, 1969.

Head, Dominic. *The Cambridge Introduction to Modern British Fiction, 1950–2000*. Cambridge, UK: Cambridge University Press, 2002.

Heidegger, Martin. *Being and Time*. Translated by John Macquarrie and Edward Robinson. 1962. Reprint, New York: HarperCollins, 2008.

———. *Discourse on Thinking*. Translated by John M. Anderson and E. Hans Freund. New York: Harper, 1966.

Hensher, Philip. "After the War Was Over . . . " Review of *Absolute Friends*, by John le Carré. *Spectator* (London), December 27, 2003.

Hepburn, Allan. *Intrigue: Espionage and Culture*. New Haven, CT: Yale University Press, 2005.

Hindersmann, Jost. "Irak-Krieg und Anti-Terror-Kampf der Bush-Regierung: John le Carré's *Absolute Freunde* und Richard A. Clarke's *The Scorpion's Gate*." In *Krimijahrbuch 2006*, edited by Dieter Paul Rudolph, 142–48. Wuppertal, Germany: NordPark, 2006.

———. "'The Right Side Lost, but the Wrong Side Won': John le Carré's Spy Novels before and after the End of the Cold War." *Clues* 23, no. 4 (Summer 2005): 25–37.

Hitz, Frederick P. *The Great Game: The Myth and Reality of Espionage*. New York: Alfred A. Knopf, 2004.

Hodgson, Godfrey. "The Secret Life of John le Carré." Interview with John le Carré, October 9, 1977. In *Conversations with John le Carré*, edited by Matthew J. Bruccoli and Judith S. Baughman, 41–46. Jackson: University Press of Mississippi, 2004.

Hoffman, Tod. "The Constant Writer: Le Carré Spies a New Villain." *Queen's Quarterly* 108 (Spring 2001): 99–107.

Holquist, Michael. "Introduction." In *The Dialogic Imagination: Four Essays*, by M. M. Bakhtin. Edited by Michael Holquist. Translated by Caryl Emerson and Michael Holquist. Austin: University of Texas Press, 1981.

Homberger, Eric. *John le Carré*. New York: Methuen, 1986.

Hope, Christopher. "Candide in Africa." Review of *The Mission Song*, by John le Carré. *Guardian*, September 23, 2006.

Horn, Eva. *The Secret War: Treason, Espionage, and Modern Fiction*. Translated by Geoffrey Winthrop-Young. Evanston, IL: Northwestern University Press, 2013.

Horsley, Lee. "A Life Spent Lying: The Identity Crises of Post–9/11 Spy Fiction." In *Espionage Fiction: The Seduction of Clandestinity*, edited by Robert Lance Snyder, 161–76. Special issue of *Paradoxa* 24 (2012).

Hösle, Vittorio. "Berufsethik der Geheimdienste und Krise der Hohen Politik: Philosophische Betractungen zum Literarischen Universum von John le Carré's Spionageromanen im Allgemeinen und zu *Absolute Friends* im Besonderen." *Deutsche Vierteljahrsschrift für Literaturwissenschaft und Geistesgeschichte* 79 (March 2005): 131–59.

Hunter, Stephen. "Le Carré's Latest Has Aura of Post–Cold War Exhaustion." Review of *The Secret Pilgrim*, by John le Carré. *Baltimore Sun*, December 30, 1990.

The Interpreter. Directed by Sydney Pollack. Universal, 2005.

Iser, Wolfgang. *The Act of Reading: A Theory of Aesthetic Response*. Baltimore, MD: Johns Hopkins University Press, 1978.

Jameson, Fredric. *The Political Unconscious: Narrative as a Socially Symbolic Act*. Ithaca, NY: Cornell University Press, 1981.

Kakutani, Michiko. "Adding Reality's Worries to a Thriller." Review of *Absolute Friends*, by John le Carré. *New York Times*, January 7, 2004.

———. "Hero, Style, and Subject Are Familiar, for a While." Review of *Single & Single*, by John le Carré. *New York Times*, March 2, 1999.

———. "Innocents Caught in a Web of Intrigue." Review of *Our Kind of Traitor*, by John le Carré. *New York Times*, October 12, 2010.

———. "A Translator Searching for Words of His Own." Review of *The Mission Song*, by John le Carré. *New York Times*, September 26, 2006.

Kelly, Walt. *The Pogo Papers*. New York: Simon & Schuster, 1953.

Keniston, Ann, and Jeanne Follansbee Quinn, eds. *Literature after 9/11*. New York: Routledge, 2008.

Kermode, Frank. *The Genesis of Secrecy: On the Interpretation of Narrative*. Cambridge, MA: Harvard University Press, 1979.

Kerridge, Jake. "Hay Festival 2013: John le Carré on His New Novel, *A Delicate Truth*." *Telegraph* (London), May 25, 2013.

Klein, Yvonne. Review of *Our Kind of Traitor*, by John le Carré. Reviewing the Evidence, December 2010. http://www.reviewingtheevidence.com/review.html.

Knight, Christopher J. *Omissions Are Not Accidents: Modern Apophaticism from Henry James to Jacques Derrida*. Toronto: University of Toronto Press, 2010.

Laing, R. D. *The Divided Self: An Existential Study in Sanity and Madness*. London: Tavistock, 1960.

———. *The Politics of Experience*. New York: Ballantine, 1971.

———. *The Self and Others*. London: Tavistock, 1961.

Lane, Richard J., Rod Mengham, and Philip Tew, eds. *Contemporary British Fiction*. Cambridge, UK: Polity, 2003.

Lassner, Phyllis. "Paradoxical Polemics: John le Carré's Responses to 9/11." In *Transatlantic Literature and Culture after 9/11: The Wrong Side of Paradise*, edited by Kristine A. Miller, 17–33. New York: Palgrave, 2014.

Lawson, Mark. "The Privatisation of Spying." Review of *A Delicate Truth*, by John le Carré. *Guardian*, April 20, 2013.

LeBlanc, Jeanne A. "'Friends' Is Vintage le Carré, without the Subtlety." Review of *Absolute Friends*, by John le Carré. *Hartford Courant*, January 25, 2004.

le Carré, John. "About John le Carré." Author's website, May 15, 2013. http://www.johnlecarre.com/author.

———. *Absolute Friends*. 2003. Reprint, New York: Back Bay–Little, 2004.

———. "Afterword." *Harper's*, April 2013.

———. *Call for the Dead*. 1961. Reprint, New York: Penguin, 2012.

———. *The Constant Gardener*. 2001. Reprint, New York: Charles Scribner's Sons, 2004.

———. *A Delicate Truth*. New York: Viking, 2013.

———. "In Place of Nations." *Nation*, April 9, 2001.

————. Letter. *New York Times*, November 3, 1996.

————. *The Little Drummer Girl*. New York: Alfred A. Knopf, 1983.

————. *The Mission Song*. London: Hodder & Stoughton, 2006.

————. *A Most Wanted Man*. New York: Charles Scribner's Sons, 2008.

————. *A Murder of Quality*. 1962. Reprint, New York: Penguin, 2012.

————. *The Naive and Sentimental Lover*. 1971. Reprint, New York: Penguin, 2011.

————. *The Night Manager*. New York: Ballantine-Random, 1993.

————. *Our Game*. 1995. New York: Ballantine-Random, 1996.

————. *Our Kind of Traitor*. New York: Viking, 2010.

————. *A Perfect Spy*. 1986. London: Penguin, 2011.

————. "Quel Panama!" *New York Times*, October 13, 1996.

————. "Reality Check for My Warlords." *Globe and Mail* (Toronto), September 16, 2006.

————. "Remarks to the Knopf Sales Force." August 12, 1996. In *Conversations with John le Carré*, edited by Matthew J. Bruccoli and Judith S. Baughman, 133–35. Jackson: University Press of Mississippi, 2004.

————. *The Russia House*. New York: Viking, 1989.

————. *The Secret Pilgrim*. 1990. Reprint, New York: Ballantine-Random, 2008.

————. "The Shame of the West." *New York Times*, December 14, 1994.

————. *Single & Single*. New York: Charles Scribner's Sons, 1999.

————. *The Spy Who Came In from the Cold*. 1963. Reprint, New York: Pocket-Simon, 2001.

————. *The Tailor of Panama*. New York: Alfred A. Knopf, 1996.

————. *Tinker, Tailor, Soldier, Spy*. New York: Alfred A. Knopf, 1974.

————. "To Russia, with Greetings: An Open Letter to the Moscow 'Literary Gazette.'" *Encounter* 26 (May 1966): 3–6.

————. "The United States Has Gone Mad." *Times* (London), January 15, 2003.

————. "We Have Already Lost." *Globe and Mail* (Toronto), October 13, 2001.

————. "Will Spy Novels Come In from the Cold?" *Washington Post*, November 19, 1989.

Lewis, Peter. *John le Carré*. New York: Ungar, 1985.

Lyon, David, ed. *Theorizing Surveillance: The Panopticon and Beyond*. Cullompton, UK: Willan, 2006.

Mafe, Diana Adesola. "(Mis)Imagining Africa in the New Millennium: *The Constant Gardener* and *Blood Diamond*." *Camera Obscura* 25, no. 3 (2011): 69–99.

Marchand, Philip. "Le Carré's Voyeur Takes on the 'Worst Man in the World.'" Review of *The Night Manager*, by John le Carré. *Toronto Star*, June 26, 1993.

McClintock, Anne. *Imperial Ghosting: Perpetual War in the Twilight of U.S. Power*. Durham, NC: Duke University Press, 2015.

———. "Imperial Ghosting and National Tragedy: Revenants from Hiroshima and Indian Country in the War on Terror." *PMLA* 129 (October 2014): 819–29.

McCrum, Robert. "Back into the Heart of Darkness." Review of *The Mission Song*, by John le Carré. *Observer*, September 24, 2006.

———. "A Master's Voice: He Nods to Maugham and Greene, but John le Carré Is Still Unequalled." *Observer*, December 7, 2003.

McEwan, Ian. *The Innocent*. New York: Anchor-Random, 1999.

———. *Sweet Tooth*. New York: Doubleday-Random, 2012.

McGowan, Todd. "The Temporality of the Real: The Path to Politics in *The Constant Gardener*." *Film-Philosophy* 11, no. 3 (October 2007): 52–73.

Melley, Timothy. *The Covert Sphere: Secrecy, Fiction, and the National Security State*. Ithaca, NY: Cornell University Press, 2012.

Merry, Bruce. *Anatomy of the Spy Thriller*. Montreal: McGill-Queen's University Press, 1977.

Millar, Peter. "Return of the Master." Review of *Our Kind of Traitor*, by John le Carré. *Times* (London), September 11, 2010.

Miller, Greg, Adam Goldberg, and Julie Tate. "Senate Report on CIA Program Details Brutality, Dishonesty." *Washington Post*, December 9, 2014. http://www.washingtonpost.com/world/national-security/senate-report-on-cia-program-details-brutality-dishonesty/2014/12/09/1075c726-7f0e-11e4-9f38-95a187e4c1f7_story.html?hpid+z1.

Minzesheimer, Bob. "Le Carré Was Spooked by Specter of War." *USA Today*, January 8, 2004.

Mitgang, Herbert. "New Evil. New Empire. Same Fun." Review of *The Night Manager*, by John le Carré. *New York Times*, June 23, 1993.

Monaghan, David. *The Novels of John le Carré: The Art of Survival*. Oxford, UK: Basil Blackwell, 1985.

———. *Smiley's Circus: A Guide to the Secret World of John le Carré*. New York: St. Martin's Press, 1986.

Morton, Brian. "Cold War Thaw." Review of *Single & Single*, by John le Carré. *Sunday Herald* (Glasgow), February 14, 1999.

Most, Glenn W. "The Hippocratic Smile: John le Carré and the Traditions of the Detective Novel." In *The Poetics of Murder: Detective Fiction and Literary Theory*, edited by Glenn W. Most and William W. Stowe, 341–65. San Diego: Harcourt, 1983.

A Most Wanted Man. Directed by Anton Corbijn. Lionsgate, 2014.

Naughtie, James. "*Our Kind of Traitor* by John le Carré: Review." *Telegraph* (London), September 12, 2010.

Neuse, Steven M. "Bureaucratic Malaise in the Modern Spy Novel: Deighton, Greene, and le Carré." *Public Administration* 60 (Autumn 1982): 293–306.

O'Toole, Fintan. "The Real Men of England." Review of *A Delicate Truth*, by John le Carré. *New York Review of Books*, June 6, 2013.

Panek, LeRoy L. *The Special Branch: The British Spy Novel, 1890–1980*. Bowling Green, OH: Bowling Green University Popular Press, 1981.

Pearson, Nels, and Marc Singer. "Open Cases: Detection, (Post)Modernity, and the State." In *Detective Fiction in a Postcolonial and Transnational World*, edited by Nels Pearson and Marc Singer, 1–14. Farnham, UK: Ashgate, 2009.

Pepper, Andrew. "Policing the Globe: State Sovereignty and the International in the Post-9/11 Crime Novel." *Modern Fiction Studies* 57 (Fall 2011): 403–24.

Pezze, Barbara Dalle. "Heidegger on *Gelassenheit*." *Minerva* 10 (2006). http://www.ul.ie/~philos/vol10/Heidegger.html.

Plimpton, George. "John le Carré: The Art of Fiction." Interview with John le Carré, Summer 1997. In *Conversations with John le Carré*, edited by Matthew J. Bruccoli and Judith S. Baughman, 145–61. Jackson: University Press of Mississippi, 2004.

Poole, Steven. "Spies and Lies." Review of *Absolute Friends*, by John le Carré. *Guardian*, December 20, 2003.

Remnick, David. "Le Carré's New War." Review of *The Night Manager*, by John le Carré. *New York Review of Books*, August 12, 1993.

Rennison, Nick. *Contemporary British Novelists*. London: Routledge, 2005.

Richler, Daniel. "Le Carré's Details Save the Game." Review of *Our Game*, by John le Carré. *Toronto Star*, May 25, 1995.

Rogin, Michael. "'Make My Day!': Spectacle as Amnesia in Imperial Politics." *Representations* 29 (Winter 1990): 99–123.

Ross, Andrew. "Master of the Secret World: John le Carré on Deception, Storytelling, and American Hubris." Interview with John le Carré, October 21, 1996. In *Conversations with John le Carré*, edited by Matthew J. Bruccoli and Judith S. Baughman, 136–44. Jackson: University Press of Mississippi, 2004.

Ross, A. S. "A Spy's Perspective through the Eyes of John le Carré." Review of *The Night Manager*, by John le Carré. *Sun Sentinel* (Fort Lauderdale), July 18, 1993.

Ross, Carne. *Independent Diplomat: Dispatches from an Unaccountable Elite*. Ithaca, NY: Cornell University Press, 2007.

Rush, Norman. Reply to letter of John le Carré. *New York Times*, November 3, 1996.

——— . "Spying and Lying." Review of *The Tailor of Panama*, by John le Carré. *New York Times*, October 20, 1996.

Sanoff, Alvin P. "The Thawing of the Old Spymaster." Interview with John le Carré, June 19, 1989. In *Conversations with John le Carré*, edited by Matthew J. Bruccoli and Judith S. Baughman, 107–11. Jackson: University Press of Mississippi, 2004.

Sartre, Jean-Paul. *Existential Psychoanalysis*. Translated by Hazel E. Barnes. Chicago: Henry Regnery, 1962.

——— . *What Is Literature?* Translated by Bernard Frechtman. 1948. Reprint, London: Routledge, 2001.

Sauerberg, Lars Ole. *Secret Agents in Fiction: Ian Fleming, John le Carré, and Len Deighton*. New York: St. Martin's Press, 1984.

Schiff, Stephen. "The Secret Life of John le Carré." Interview with John le Carré, June 1989. In *Conversations with John le Carré*, edited by Matthew J. Bruccoli and Judith S. Baughman, 93–106. Jackson: University Press of Mississippi, 2004.

Seed, David. "Crime and the Spy Genre." In *A Companion to Crime Fiction*, edited by Charles J. Rzepka and Lee Horsley, 233–44. Chichester, NH: Wiley-Blackwell, 2010.

———. "Spy Fiction." In *The Cambridge Companion to Crime Fiction*, edited by Martin Priestman, 115–34. Cambridge, UK: Cambridge University Press, 2003.

———. "The Well-Wrought Structures of John le Carré's Early Fiction." In *Spy Thrillers: From Buchan to le Carré*, edited by Clive Bloom, 140–59. New York: St. Martin's Press, 1990.

Sisman, Adam. *John le Carré: The Biography*. New York: Harper, 2015.

Snyder, Robert Lance. *The Art of Indirection in British Espionage Fiction: A Critical Study of Six Novelists*. Jefferson, NC: McFarland, 2011.

———, ed. *Espionage Fiction: The Seduction of Clandestinity*. Special issue of *Paradoxa* 24 (2012): 1–289.

———. "Secrecy's Genesis: John le Carré's *Our Kind of Traitor*." *South Carolina Review* 45, no. 2 (Spring 2013): 113–19.

———. "'Shadow of Abandonment': Graham Greene's *The Confidential Agent*." *Texas Studies in Literature and Language* 52 (Summer 2010): 203–26.

Skyfall. Directed by Sam Mendes. Twentieth Century Fox, 2012.

Steinhauer, Olen. "Le Carré's Latest." Review of *A Delicate Truth*, by John le Carré. *New York Times*, May 5, 2013.

Stock, Jon. "Ian McEwan: John le Carré Deserves Booker." *Telegraph* (London), May 3, 2013.

Takahama, Valerie. "Le Carré Comes In from the Cold Books." Review of *The Night Manager*, by John le Carré. *Orange County Register* (Santa Ana, CA), July 9, 1993.

Tew, Philip. *The Contemporary British Novel*. London: Continuum, 2004.

Todorov, Tzvetan. *The Poetics of Prose*. Translated by Richard Howard. Ithaca, NY: Cornell University Press, 1977.

Toynbee, Polly. "On the Trail of the Lonesome Pine." Review of *The Night Manager*, by John le Carré. *Guardian*, June 26, 1993.

Tracy, Laura. "Forbidden Fantasy: The Villain as Cultural Double in the British Espionage Novel." *Clues* 9, no. 1 (Spring-Summer 1988): 11–37.

Updike, John. "Le Carré's Game: British Spies Soldier On in a Thawed World." Review of *Our Game*, by John le Carré. *New Yorker*, March 20, 1995.

Vaughan, Paul. "Le Carré's Circus: Lamplighters, Moles, and Others of That Ilk." Interview with John le Carré, September 13, 1979. In *Conversations with*

John le Carré, edited by Matthew J. Bruccoli and Judith S. Baughman, 53–59. Jackson: University Press of Mississippi, 2004.

Versluys, Kristiaan. *Out of the Blue: September 11 and the Novel.* New York: Columbia University Press, 2009.

Volmane, Véra. "John le Carré: The Writer, Like the Spy, Is an Illusionist." Interview with John le Carré, September 23, 1965. In *Conversations with John le Carré*, edited by Matthew J. Bruccoli and Judith S. Baughman, 3–5. Jackson: University Press of Mississippi, 2004.

Walden, George. "Tinker Tailor Soldier Propagandist John le Carré's Latest Novel Falls Victim to His Clumsy Politicking." Review of *Absolute Friends*, by John le Carré. *Telegraph* (London), December 14, 2003.

Wark, Wesley. "Le Carré Comes In from the Cold." Review of *Our Game*, by John le Carré. *Globe and Mail* (Toronto), April 22, 1995.

Watson, Alan. "Violent Image." Interview with John le Carré, March 30, 1969. In *Conversations with John le Carré*, edited by Matthew J. Bruccoli and Judith S. Baughman, 10–14. Jackson: University Press of Mississippi, 2004.

Weiner, Tim. "Le Carré on the Most Immoral Premise of All." *New York Times*, July 8, 1993.

Winthrop-Young, Geoffrey. "Preface." In *The Secret War: Treason, Espionage, and Modern Fiction*, by Eva Horn. Translated by Geoffrey Winthrop-Young. Evanston, IL: Northwestern University Press, 2013.

The Wizard of Oz. Directed by Victor Fleming. Metro-Goldwyn-Mayer, 1939.

Wolfe, Peter. *Corridors of Deceit: The World of John le Carré.* Bowling Green, OH: Bowling Green State University Popular Press, 1987.

Wood, David Murakami. "Globalization and Surveillance." In *Routledge Handbook of Surveillance Studies*, edited by Kirstie Bell, Kevin D. Haggerty, and David Lyon, 333–42. London: Routledge, 2012.

Wrong, Michela. *In the Footsteps of Mr. Kurtz: Living on the Brink of Disaster in Mobutu's Congo.* New York: HarperCollins, 2001.

Yeats, William Butler. "The Second Coming." In *The Norton Anthology of English Literature.* 8th ed. Vol. 2. Edited by Stephen Greenblatt et al. New York: W. W. Norton, 2006.

INDEX